D0811725

STUDIES IN AMERICAN LITERATURE

Volume XXXI

ORPHEUS IN BROOKLYN:

ORPHISM, RIMBAUD, and HENRY MILLER

by

Bertrand Mathieu

University of New Haven

Preface by

Wallace Fowlie

1976

MOUTON

THE HAGUE - PARIS

ISBN 90 279 3036 8

Cover Illustration by

Valerie J. Neale

Printed in the Netherlands

Dedicated
to
Eleni, Rusty, Rachel –
naturally!

Vous serez une part
de la saveur du fruit.

(René Char)

ACKNOWLEDGEMENTS

I would like to express my gratitude to the many friends and colleagues who provided encouragement and assistance in the completion of this book. First of all, to Douglas Robillard, Srilekha Bell, Camille Jordan, Beth Moffitt, Paul Marx, Ralf Carriuolo, Phillip and Vivian Kaplan, Edna Paul, John Collinson, Marylou Oslander, Asa Pieratt, Tom and Arlene Violante, Helen and Nathaniel Kaplan – who always stood by me in the sometimes murky groves of Academe. To my brothers, Don, Joe, and Matt – whose kindnesses to me are too numerous to count, whose lives and outlooks are Orphic through and through. To Lawrence Ferlinghetti, Stephen Berg, Anna Balakian, Wallace Fowlie, Allen Ginsberg, Gina Lee Abeles, Erica Jong, Sigmund Abeles, Anna Jaffee, Viktoria Dietrich, Sally Wallian, Al Poulin, Lili Bita, Robert Zaller, Mike Parker, John Perry, Yánnis Rítsos, Katerína Angheláki-Rooke, Anaís Nin, and Henry Miller – whose rich imaginative presences and sheer humanity have been indispensable to me all along the way. To Elke and Robi Geiger – my oldest and best European friends. To Lyn Root – whose favorite food out in California is the oranges of Hieronymous Bosch. To Judy Rosenthal – who is an ineffaceable feature in the landscape of my life. To Nancy Ann Watanabe and Heidi Atkins, my summer Eurydices of '76 – and for years to come, I hope. To my father and mother, Armand and Loretta Mathieu – whom mere words cannot do hommage to. And finally, to "the Colossus of Maroussi" himself, George Katsimbalis of Athens, Greece – whose answers to my many questions, in the Spring and Summer of 1974, have made this a much more illuminating book and whose hospitality made yet another trip to Greece more radiant, more "colossal." May you all live forever!

TABLE OF CONTENTS

PREFACE

by
Wallace Fowlie

The title and the subtitle of this book on Henry Miller represent a condensation in very few words of Bertrand Mathieu's illuminating theory and analysis. The mythical Greek poet from Thrace and the young French poet from the Ardennes are the true ancestors of the American writer from a borough of New York City, who inherited from them the will to break with the world in order to recreate it.

As I was reading this book, I had the feeling that all the previous critics of Miller stopped in their interpretations at the point where Mathieu begins. I believe he has found, more accurately than others, the clue to the magnetism in Miller's writings. He is the first critic to see and analyze the importance of *The Colossus of Maroussi*, which relates Henry Miller's five-month visit to Greece in 1939. Bertrand Mathieu, in a most convincing manner, treats the book as an Orphic text, as one best understood in terms of Illuminist doctrine.

In his close reading of this book, Mathieu discovers it to be not only Orphic but also *Symboliste* in its design. The Orpheus myth – or, we might say, the Orphic paradigm – plays a significant role in French Symbolism and especially in Rimbaud. In *Colossus* and in other works by Henry Miller, especially *The Time of the Assassins*, Mathieu studies Miller's self-identification with Rimbaud. But he never discusses Rimbaud as a mere literary influence on Miller. The encounter was much more than that. Justifiably, Mathieu sees Miller as an avatar of Rimbaud.

It is foolhardy to attempt any brief synthesis of such a book as *Orpheus in Brooklyn*. Centrally, it concerns the role of the writer in the world. What Rimbaud and Henry Miller have said on this subject *must*, according to Bertrand Mathieu's thesis, resemble the role of the priest-poet in those ancient Orphic rites about which we know nothing for certain. The poet's descent into hell (or into the subconscious or into the waste land of his own day) represents the indispensable mortifications he must undergo in order to rise above them into some kind of reunion with what is transcendent and luminous. The writer's role, when he is close to the role of the *vates*, is to reintegrate into the world something that was missing in his own time, whether he be in Charleville or Brooklyn or Delphi. Baudelaire brought back Satan, and Nerval brought back the ancient gods of Greece and Egypt. Rimbaud brought back the angel, after he had incarnated the *éternal maudit* in the events of his own life, the experiences that he calls his *encrapulement* (dissoluteness).

To be the *maudit*, as Rimbaud and Miller deliberately chose to be, each in his own way, is to undergo the necessary askesis, the discipline of a season in hell at the end of which one has the chance to reach the unknown, *l'inconnu*. If I am reading accurately these pages of Bertrand Mathieu, "the unknown" in Rimbaud's letter to Demeny is the authentic state of being a poet, of being one chosen by the gods in keeping with the beliefs of Greece, one who possesses all knowledge and all wisdom, who bears the awesome burden of the past in him and announces the future.

This alliance of Rimbaud and Henry Miller is fascinating in the textual study that Mathieu provides, and it is *staggering* in the implications which deal with the Orpheus figure standing behind both writers. Thanks to his extensive knowledge of Greece, both ancient and modern, thanks to his study of Gnosticism and his familiarity with the French *Symbolistes*, Bertrand Mathieu persuasively leads his readers to a realization that Rimbaud and Henry Miller are two of those rare visionaries and prophets who manage to communicate with God without passing through the temple. *Orpheus in Brooklyn* should make this plain to all its readers.

WALLACE FOWLIE
Duke University
Summer '76

CHAPTER ONE

PRÓLOGOS

Writers' ancestries are obscure. The ascertainment of an author's final genealogical position in relation to the literary forebears who have had a seminal influence on his work is, at best, an inexact science. It often requires decades, even generations, for a writer's lineage to be established with absolute precision. Quite often, the most popular works of a writer during his own lifetime – one could cite Herman Melville's *Typee* and *Omoo* and Henry James' "Daisy Miller" or *The American* as examples – don't prove, with the passage of time, to have been the most enduring or the most artistically important in the canon that will be left for posterity to work out. And at times, an author's less significant work becomes so popular that it prevents the truly crucial work from being promptly identified and appreciated.

Henry Miller's reputation as a writer, for example, rests primarily on such early books as *Tropic of Cancer* (1934), *Black Spring* (1936), and *Tropic of Capricorn* (1939), as well as on the more sensationally erotic passages in the later trilogy, *The Rosy Crucifixion*, consisting of *Sexus* (1949), *Plexus* (1956), and *Nexus* (1960). These books have enjoyed an exaggerated notoriety largely because of their author's reputation for nihilistic excesses and for the widely celebrated lubricity of his descriptive talents, so it's not entirely surprising that the most sustained and most penetrating critical efforts of Miller scholars to date should have tended to focus on them.

So much attention has been paid to these highly publicized works, in fact, that Miller's remarkable book on Greece, *The Colossus of Maroussi* (1941) – which its author[1] and a handful of his critics esteem more highly than Miller's better-known books – has been almost entirely ignored. Many critics have spoken well of the book. But the majority have dealt summarily with it, making appreciative but casual allusions to the lucidity of its fine prose, the brilliance of the author's descriptions of the Greek landscape, and the memorable gallery of characters Miller parades before his readers' eyes. Not one of the numerous books and articles devoted to Miller so far even attempts to analyze the technical and structural devices that account for the compelling power of *The Colossus of Maroussi*. Even its most sympathetic critics, William A. Gordon in *The Mind and Art of Henry*

1 See, for example, Georges Belmont, *Entretiens de Paris avec Georges Belmont* (Paris: Editions Stock, 1970), p. 36, and F. -J. Temple, *Henry Miller* (Paris: Editions Universitaires, 1965), p. 71.

Miller (1965) and Ihab Hassan in *The Literature of Silence: Henry Miller and Samuel Beckett* (1967), give *Colossus* short shrift after commending its creator for the radiance of the book's contents and the special magic of its style.

Yet a careful reading of *Colossus* provides ample evidence that this outwardly simple and charming "travel book" has a great deal of the inner complexity and coherence of a collection of *Symboliste* prose poems. It has particularly obvious affinities, both in its deployment of "illuminist" doctrine and in its artistic methods, with the French poet Arthur Rimbaud's masterpiece, *Illuminations* (1886). But what strikes me as equally deserving of close analytical study and clearer critical "definition" is that Miller's insufficiently appreciated book on Greece, with its deftly discursive parallels and occasional sly parodyings of the Ancient Greek myth of Orpheus, seems to constitute an implicit re-enactment of that myth as well as one of the most strikingly original "Orphic" texts in modern literature!

The Colossus of Maroussi is ostensibly a more or less sequential account of Henry Miller's journey through various parts of Greece at the close of his decade-long residence in Europe in the 1930's. In reality, the book is not a straight narrative but a series of loosely connected "illuminations" – some written in plain style, some in rather self-consciously composed poetic prose – which reveal, "mysteriously" but with a sure artistic touch, the manner in which Miller finally comes to accept himself and his destiny as a result of his exposure to the "miraculous" *tópos* of Greece and to the extraordinary human beings who serve him as guides during a five-month "vacation" from ordinary reality. The topographical map with which Miller's narrative equips the reader is merely a master-chart of indexes to experiences which take place largely *within* the writer.

Miller's *Colossus* is divided into three sections. Each section represents a different stage in Miller's attempt – through the use of alternating devices such as anecdotes, pertinent conversations, descriptions of the Greek scene, musings and occasional sermons, and sheer intensity of *desire* – to resacralize the lot of common humanity and to restore the dimension of the "magical" to everyday life. Part One deals with Miller's arrival in Greece and his initial encounters with the title-character, George Katsimbalis, the prototype of a host of larger-than-life cicerones whose function will be to help Miller find his way around the outer and inner terrain he must now explore. In this section, Miller has a number of significant "initiatory" experiences which take him from Athens and Corfu to Nauplia and Epidaurus. On the whole, these are rather somber experiences (further darkened by the threat of World War Two which was hanging over Europe in the summer of 1939), but no experience in Part One is more somber – or, a typically Millerian paradox, more *luminous* – than the culminating episode of this section which takes place at Agamemnon's tomb in Mycenae. In his description of this descent which is really an ascent, Henry Miller fashions a powerful and sustaining metaphor which is both an appropriate conclusion to this paradox-filled section and one of the artistic triumphs of the book.

The highlights of Part Two of *Colossus* are the revelation of Knossos in Crete and the pure visionary rapture of the visit to Phaestos (which Miller hyperbolically refers to as "the perpetual dawn of man's awakening"[2]), but this section does not open with such materials. Instead Miller begins with three preliminary anecdotes which seem, superficially, to have no bearing on the climactic illuminations which occur later. The first anecdote deals with a viewing of the American film *Juarez* in an Athens movie-theater, the second with a visit to an astronomical observatory with Lawrence Durrell, and the third with an encounter Miller has with the sister of the Greek poet Seferis which leads Miller to a disquisition on the qualities in women which attract and repel, which sustain the drama of sexual love and hate.

Although these anecdotes seem totally unrelated, in their *negative* way they are highly effective symbolic preludes which foreshadow the affirmative visions of community and pure light which Miller will be vouchsafed later on in this section at Knossos and Phaestos. In Miller's mind (as subsequent quotations from *Colossus* will make evident), light can only come after darkness; the ascent can only follow the descent. The plight of Mexico under Maximillian's dictatorship depicted in the film *Juarez* foreshadows the free experience of community which Miller achieves with Kyrios Alexandros at Phaestos. The "false" cerebral knowledge of the scientists which Miller and Durrell ridicule at the astronomical observatory is obviated, later on in Part Two, by the alphabet of Knossos (which still possessed magic) and the radiant beauty of Phaestos (which contained "all the elements of the heart"). As for the anecdote concerning the New World's

2 Henry Miller, *The Colossus of Maroussi* (New York: New Directions, 1941), p. 159.

alleged capacity to make women positively *ugly*, Miller intuitively perceives in a decisive illumination later on in Part Two that in the world of Knossos women played an important and equal role in the affairs of men and that Phaestos was nothing less than the abode of the queens.

Part Three is the most loosely constructed and most miscellaneous section of *Colossus*. It is devoted largely to Miller's last weeks in Greece and is full of light-hearted descriptions of brief, random excursions to Delphi, Mycenae, Eleusis, and Sparta. Humor and an almost facile sense of blissfulness are its most conspicuous characteristics. These qualities accord entirely with the mood of euphoria produced in Miller by the extravagant predictions of an Armenian soothsayer, fairly early in Part Three, to the effect that Miller is fated literally to live forever and to be the bringer of great joy to the world. If this section of *The Colossus of Maroussi* is regarded as a fitting *mise-en-scène* for the Armenian's prognostications as well as a point of validation for a book which sets out to restore "magic" to human life, then it becomes clear that Henry Miller has energetically assumed the responsibilities of the thaumaturgic role forecast for him at very *least*. Part Three is replate with such "magical procedures"[3] as comic stories illustrating the need to give away one's money gratuitously, nostalgic recollections of friends and enemies from whom the author has been fortuitously separated, and eulogistic incantations in praise of the "messengers" who bring glad tidings to the human race from the spheres of the "miraculous." And with a memorably poetic finale, the book is brought to a close with Miller's own ecstatic canticle of praise and gratitude to all creation.

The failure of literary criticism to recognize the centrality of *The Colossus of Maroussi* in Miller's total *oeuvre* and to come to grips with a number of Miller's crucial literary "ancestors" (whose influence is clear in some of the earlier and later books but most discernible in *Colossus*) has, in my opinion, deprived Miller of the rightful reputation he deserves for controlled artistic achievement of a very specific kind. The aim of this book will be to analyze in detail the "Orphic/

3 C. G. Jung's term for ritual devices used to bring about transformational experiences. Cf. C. G. Jung, *Archetypes and the Collective Unconscious* in *The Collected Works of C. G. Jung* (New York: Bollingen Series XX, 1959), pp. 128 ff.

Symboliste" design Miller has constructed in *The Colossus of Maroussi* out of the rhythms, the colors, and the personalities he encountered during his Greek *Wanderjahr* – a design that transparently owes a great deal to lessons Miller had learned from his acquaintance with the salient features of the myth of Orpheus and Eurydice, his understanding of the major strategies of French *Symbolisme*, and his knowledge of Rimbaud. But I don't intend to limit my critical discussion of Miller's achievement to the *Colossus*. There are many passages in Miller's writings, both earlier and later than *Colossus*, which reinforce the notion that Miller can most usefully be approached as a writer in light of his adherence to a basically *Symboliste* aesthetic and a lifelong interest in the manifold varieties of "Orphic" thinking, including theosophy, Eastern mysticism, Swedenborgian illuminism, and Rosicrucianism. These other Miller works will be cited frequently to support my contention that, by and large, Miller's *entire* output as a writer can be regarded as "Orphic/*Symboliste*" rather than merely Dadaist or pornographic.

Miller's indebtedness to some of the writers who influenced his development has been fairly competently explored by his chief critics. Certain of these exemplars Miller himself had acknowledged with an almost pedantic thoroughness (in *The Books in My Life*, 1952) – among others, D. H. Lawrence and James Joyce, Dostoevsky and Knut Hamsun, Marcel Proust and Blaise Cendrars. It seems surprising, therefore, that his patiently reiterated acknowledgement of an early infatuation with and discipleship to Arthur Rimbaud's works should have been ignored. To be sure, the rebellious stance and scatalogical – at times blasphemous – verve of the *Tropics* have several times been identified with the Rimbaldian tradition of revolt by such writers as Georges Villa, Karl Shapiro, and Ihab Hassan. But these identifications deal, for the most part, with matters of ideology and attitude in Miller's work. They are, in any case, merely glancing at best. In *The Colossus of Maroussi*, Miller's devotion to Rimbaud the craftsman is much more evident than anyone has yet cared to point out. And I think it can be proved beyond a serious doubt that it is Miller's quiet but brilliantly varied appropriation of the French poet's *Symboliste* tricks of metaphor and rhetoric that accounts for much of the "magic" which many have sensed while reading what could be thought of as Miller's Americanized transcription of Rimbaud's *Illuminations*.

This should come as no surprise. Miller himself has, after all, written a revealing book on Rimbaud (*The Time of the Assassins*, 1956) which the eminent Rimbaud scholar, Wallace Fowlie – who dedicated his own magisterial study of Rimbaud to Henry Miller – has acclaimed as one of the most perceptive ever written about the enigmatic boy-poet, although Karl Shapiro was surely right in insisting that *The Time of the Assassins* tells us as much about Miller as about Rimbaud. Miller's self-identification with Rimbaud is that complete. In fact, Miller's Rimbaud study is seriously offered as a catalogue of "parallels," "affinities," and "correspondences" which Miller has observed between the French poet and himself! Miller even seems to intimate – with typically Rimbaldian megalomania – that he is an avatar of Rimbaud (Miller was born in 1891, the year of Rimbaud's death.) But Miller makes some remarkably pertinent observations on Rimbaud's literary methods which reveal how thoroughly he understood his mentor's *aims*. These observations will serve as points of departure in the case I intend to make for the spiritual and artistic consanguinity which exists between the Orphic/visionary "illuminism" of Rimbaud and the *Symboliste* tactics in Henry Miller's writings – particularly *The Colossus of Maroussi.*

CHAPTER TWO

THE LINEAMENTS OF “FATHER ORPHEUS”

1. "*The Image's Truth*"

"Here *are hopes. But what will you see and hear of them, if you have not experienced glance and glow and dawn of day in your own souls? I can only suggest – I cannot do more! To move the stones, to make animals men – would you have me do* that? *Alas, if you are yet stones and animals, you must seek your Orpheus!*"

Friedrich Nietzsche in *The Joyful Wisdom*

It may seem startling to suggest, in this opening chapter, that Henry Miller's characteristic major works were consciously structured with a view to up-dating and re-telling the myth of Orpheus in a systematic and consecutive fashion – the way James Joyce's *Ulysses* re-tells the myth of Odysseus or Eugene O'Neill's *Mourning Becomes Electra* the myth of Agamcmnon and Clytemnestra. An artist as pugnaciously slapdash, as "anarchic," as Henry Miller prides himself on being could scarcely have aspired to anything of the kind.

Nevertheless, the image of Orpheus is clearly the mythopoeic backbone and *support* of Miller's entire output as a writer. The lineaments of "famous Orpheus" and of Orphic ways of seeing and experiencing things – almost invariably implicit, but very persuasive and uncannily consistent with the outlines of the ancient myth – are recurrent presences in all of Miller's well-known works, particularly in his masterpiece, *The Colossus of Maroussi*. In fact, I intend to argue in the course of a close analytical study of Miller's book on Greece that this extraordinary book belongs among the important examples of twentieth-century mythic writing in the genuineness of its mythic content and the beauty of its execution.

What *is* the Orphic myth? What role has it played in modern literature? Walter A. Strauss goes so far as to identify Orpheus with *poetry itself* in times of disaster like our own:

> Orpheus is not only poetry; he has become, in modern times, the agony of poetry – a sort of ambassador without portfolio of poetry. He is the figure, the myth, entrusted with the burden of poetry and myth. His metamorphosis is the change in poetic climate itself, placed against an ever-darkening sky in which poetry recedes more and more toward secret and unexplored spaces, spaces that are obscure and must be illuminated by constellations of the mind ever threatened by disaster and extinction.[1]

Strauss' book on the Orphic theme in modern literature, *Descent and Return*, deals chiefly with Novalis, Mallarmé, Nerval, and Rilke. But such a study could equally have made room for figures like Rimbaud, Hart Crane, and Henry Miller – writers who taught themselves how to revindicate the role of poet in the face of modern horrors by tactically combining the stance of Prometheus and Orpheus, the defiant fire-stealer and the resourceful singer. In fact, Gwendolyn Bays' illuminating book, *The Orphic Vision* – to which I plan to return in later chapters – takes Rimbaud as the supreme exemplar of the Orphic writer in modern times. Since Miller, like Hart Crane, has again and again acknowledged the influence of Rimbaud on his development, the line of descent from their common progenitor, Orpheus, is made even more explicit.

Before giving a synopsis of the life and achievement of Orpheus, it may be useful to define what I mean by "myth" and "mythic writing." Although Henry Miller writes prose narratives, I intend to place him unhesitatingly among the poets and mythomanes. My reasons for doing so will be obvious by the completion of my study, but Miller – whose first serious writings were prose poems which he sold from door to door the way Whitman had done a century earlier – has repeatedly referred to himself as a poet[2] and is manifestly a writer of profound mythopoeic endowments. What he has achieved in *The Colossus of Maroussi*, as well as in the earlier *Tropic of Cancer* and *Tropic of Capricorn*, amounts to the creation of what Hugh Kenner would call a "homeomorph"[3] of the Orpheus myth. By recognizing the personal traits and outlook of the hero of a myth in his own personality, a writer acquires the power to instruct us in the urgencies

1 Walter A. Strauss, *Descent and Return* (Cambridge: Harvard University Press, 1971), p. 17.

2 Cf. *Colossus* (New York: New Directions, 1941), pp. 61 and 112, and *The Books in My Life* (New York: New Directions, 1952), pp. 147 and 166.

3 Hugh Kenner, *The Pound Era* (Berkeley and Los Angeles: University of California Press, 1971), pp. 33-34.

and triumphs of that myth simply by telling us his own story.

Our word "myth" is derived from a Greek word which merely means "story," but "mythic writing" as I plan to use the term in this book has overtones and vibrancies that go well beyond mere story-telling. It is closer to what Mircea Eliade, the great Roumanian mytho-analyst, has in mind when he writes: "Myths reveal the structure of reality, and the multiple modalities of being in the world. That is why they are the exemplary models for human behaviour; they disclose the *true* stories, concern themselves with the *realities* (Eliade's italics)."[4] Eliade's use of words like "reveal" and "disclose" indicates that the mythic outlook is, in the most precise sense, a way of *seeing* reality and of transcribing, clearly, the results of what one has seen. The modern psyche, like its ancient counterpart, teems with half-remembered myths and hierophantic symbols. The triumph of mechanistic technology has not altered the fact that radiant residues of mythological matter survive for those who have the ability to *see* them.

Henry Miller, like Arthur Rimbaud, is committed to the doctrine that the true poet is a "seer." Neither writer would have found it difficult to agree with the words of Emerson: "What we are, that only can we see... Build therefore your own world. As fast as you conform your life to the pure idea in your own mind, that will unfold its great proportions. A correspondent revolution in things will attend the influx of the spirit."[5] The mythic writer has had to recognize the dynamics of a particular myth (as well as its significance for other people) *within himself* first of all. This is the secret of his "power." Wallace Stevens brilliantly describes the genus in this fashion:

> A mythology reflects its region. Here
> In Connecticut, we never lived in a time
> When mythology was possible – but if we had –
> That raises the question of the image's truth.
> The image must be of the nature of its creator.
> It is the nature of its creator increased,
> Heightened. It is he, anew, in a freshened youth.[6]

4 Mircea Eliade, *Myths, Dreams and Mysteries* (New York: Harper & Row, 1967), p. 15.
5 Ralph Waldo Emerson, *Essays of Ralph Waldo Emerson* (New York: The Book League of America, 1941), p. 363.
6 Wallace Stevens, *Opus Posthumous* (New York: Knopf, 1957), p. 118.

If "the image's truth" has been validated within the experience and art of the mythologist, Stevens suggests, it will prove to be identical with him but "anew, in a freshened youth." Mircea Eliade is completely in accord with the poet in this respect: Man is "contemporary with the cosmogony... because ritual projects him into the mythical epoch of the beginning. A bacchant, through his orgiastic rites, imitates the suffering Dionysos; an Orphic, through his initiation ceremonial, repeats the original gestures of Orpheus."[7] Renewal is as integral a feature of myth as is *repetition*, and this is the source of some of the greatest excitements and the greatest vexations in the study of the mythic temperament in action. There is nothing simple about the way a writer like Henry Miller (or Arthur Rimbaud or Rainer Maria Rilke) consciously, sometimes half-consciously, adopts the attributes of an Orpheus and projects the accents of his own inimitable humanness through the mask of the god.

The observations of the French scholar Eva Kushner on this subject seem to me highly pertinent. Professor Kushner considers myths highly complex realities which have the power to move people mysteriously, often independently of the skills of the author who employs them. Myths, she believes, are never merely stories. Primitive man genuinely *lived* the myths on which his mental universe was based. But modern man, with his hard-won knowledge, distrusts his own imagination and prefers to "stick to the facts." Every now and then, however, a contemporary writer allows himself to be seduced by a myth to the point of discovering in it the form *par excellence* of his own spiritual life or of an aspect of it. Whether this indicates a lack of realism on his part depends entirely on how one defines the term "reality." According to Professor Kushner, any writer who assigns a prominent role to the myth of Orpheus in his work has merely opted for the view that reality is not to be found in material objects alone but rather in the subtler connections that exist between man and his universe, sometimes perceptible, sometimes intelligible, and sometimes wholly elusive to human understanding. But there is no simple, one-to-one connection between the latter view and the intricate modalities of the Orphic myth. The truth, as Professor Kushner puts it,

7 Mircea Eliade, *The Myth of the Eternal Return* (Princeton: Princeton University Press, 1971), p. 22.

est beaucoup plus subtile, et comme le myth lui-même, elle échappe aux abstractions toujours trop approximatives. Le rapport entre le poète et le mythe ne se conforme à aucune loi générale car il est aussi personnel que l'âme de chacun; la critique ne peut que s'en approcher avec respect, sachant que l'analyse la plus scrupuleuse ne saurait en révéler le secret... Le contenue de la mythologie est en mouvement perpétuel et soumis à de perpétuelles transformations, même s'il lui arrive parfois d'être fixé dans le moule de quelque tradition sacrée. Le mythe se donne à lui-même sa propre forme; il se passe d'interprétations et d'explications. Comme la musique, il s'exprime totalement lui-même. Ainsi, le mode d'expression mythologique est irremplaçable, si bien qu'aucun autre moyen d'expression ne saurait en rendre la plénitude. "Comme la musique a un sens intelligible qui, comme toute entité intelligible génératrice de satisfactions, procure un contentement, ainsi en est-il du mythologème. Ce sens, il est difficile de l'exprimer en langage de la science, pour la raison même qu'il ne peut pleinement s'exprimer sur le mode mythologique." Kerényi conclut en disant que la seule manière de comprendre le mythe, c'est de l'écouter simplement: d' "avoir de l'oreille" pour son sens profond, de vibrer à l'unisson avec lui comme avec une oeuvre musicale.[8]

Miller's own thinking on the subject of myth is much the same as that of Mircea Eliade and Eva Kushner. Toward the close of *The Colossus of Maroussi*, after commenting on the intoxication of the Greeks with their own myth, he writes:

We forget, in our enchantment with the myth, that it is born of reality and is fundamentally no different from any other form of creation, except that it has to do with the very quick of life. We too are creating myths, though we are perhaps not aware of it. But in our myths there is no place for the gods. We are building an abstract, dehumanized world out of the ashes of an illusory materialism. We are proving to ourselves that the universe is empty, a task which is justified by our own empty logic. We are determined to conquer and conquer we shall, but the conquest is death.[9]

He concludes by apotheosizing the book's "colossal" hero and its principal avatar of Orpheus, George Katsimbalis – one of the many spellbinding mythomanes in *Colossus* whom Miller, with the self-reflecting eyes of the Orphic, is so quick to identify and celebrate:

There are men who are so rich, so full, who give themselves so completely that each time you take leave of them you feel that it is absolutely of no con-

8 Eva Kushner, *Le mythe d'Orphée dans la littérature française contemporaine* (Paris: A.G. Nizet, 1961), pp. 12 and 13, and p. 15.
9 *Colossus*, pp. 236-237.

sequence whether the parting is for a day or forever. They come to you brimming over and they fill you to overflowing. They ask nothing of you except that you participate in their superabundant joy of living. They never inquire which side of the fence you are on because the world they inhabit has no fences. They make themselves invulnerable by habitually exposing themselves to every danger. They grow more heroic in the measure that they reveal their weaknesses. Certainly in those endless and seemingly fabulous stories which Katsimbalis was in the habit of recounting there must have been a good element of fancy and distortion, yet even if truth was occasionally sacrificed to reality the man behind the story only succeeded thereby in revealing more faithfully and thoroughly his human image... It was also taken for granted by everybody, it seemed to me, that Katsimbalis not only had a right to improvise as he went along but that he was expected to do so. He was regarded as a virtuoso, a virtuoso who played only his own compositions and had therefore the right to alter them as he pleased.[10]

One of the most eminent British historians of the Orphic movement in Ancient Greece, W.K.C. Guthrie, would have found nothing untoward about such a procedure. The Orphics in ancient times, according to Guthrie, also knew a thing or two about improvisation:

The Orphic writers had taken what suited them from popular mythology. They had added something to its matter and much to its significance. It was a crystallization around a new centre, and the centre was the story of the dismemberment of Dionysos, the revenge of Zeus on the Titans and the birth of mankind from their ashes.[11]

In order to provide a clear framework of reference for the case I want to make for Henry Miller as a writer of unquestionably Orphic orientation, I think it will be useful to provide here a detailed synopsis of the principal events of the career of the paradigmatic Orpheus. I will content myself largely with paraphrasing the excellent accounts given by Robert Graves in *The Greek Myths* and the *New Larousse Encyclopaedia of Mythology*, although much more detailed accounts can be found in W.K.C. Guthrie's *Orpheus and Greek Religion* and Ivan M. Linforth's *The Arts of Orpheus* (qq. v.).

According to the original myth, Orpheus was the most famous poet and musician who ever lived. He was born in Thrace, in northeastern

10 *Ibid*., pp. 238-240.
11 W.K.C. Guthrie, *Orpheus and Greek Religion* (New York: W.W. Norton & Co., 1966), p. 153.

Greece, and was very early identified with the cult of Dionysos. Apollo had presented him with a lyre and the Muses had taught him how to play it, so that he not only enchanted wild beasts but made the trees and rocks move from their places to follow the sound of his marvelous music. At Zone, in Thrace, a number of ancient mountain oaks are said to be standing to this day in the pattern of one of Orpheus' dances. Orpheus possessed not only remarkable musical powers, but was also endowed (like a Siberian shaman) with the prophetic gifts of the seer.

After a visit to Egypt, Orpheus the voyager joined the Argonauts and sailed with them to Colchis. During the journey, the magical powers of his music helped the Argonauts overcome many of their difficulties. He even managed to charm the Sirens with his extraordinary singing voice so that the Argo and its crew escaped destruction. When he returned from his journey, Orpheus married Eurydice and settled in Thrace. One day, near Tempe, Eurydice met a young man named Aristaeus, who tried to seduce her against her will. She stepped on a snake while trying to escape and died of its bite. Orpheus, overcome with grief, decided to descend into Hades to try to bring her back among the living. He not only charmed the ferryman Charon, the watch-dog Cerberus, and the three Judges of the Dead with his beautiful plaintive music, but temporarily suspended the tortures of the damned. His music was so irresistible that he managed to soothe the savage heart of Hades and win permission to restore Eurydice to the upper world. Hades made only one condition: that Orpheus could not look behind him until Eurydice had crossed over the edge of the underworld into the light of the sun. Eurydice is said to have followed up through the dark passageway, guided by the sounds of his lyre, but just as they reached the outer limits of Hades, Orpheus turned around to see if Eurydice was still behind him. He thereby lost her forever and had to return to the upper world all alone. Some say that Orpheus thereafter avoided the company of women and introduced homosexuality into Greece.

Later, when Dionysos invaded Thrace, the myth tells us Orpheus neglected to honor the god. Instead, he taught the sacred mysteries and preached the evil of murder to the men of Thrace. Every morning he would rise early to greet the sun on the summit of Mount Pangaeum, preaching that Helios (whom he called Apollo) was the greatest of the gods. Angered by this, Dionysos sent his Maenads after him in Macedonia. First waiting until their husbands had entered Apollo's temple, where Orpheus served as a priest, the Maenads seized the weapons stacked outside, burst in, murdered their husbands, and tore Orpheus apart limb from limb. They threw his head into the Hebros River, but we are told it floated, still singing, down to the sea and was carried to the island of Lesbos. Tearfully, the Muses collected his limbs and buried them at Leibethra, at the foot of Mount Olympus, where the nightingales are now said to sing more sweetly than anywhere else in the world.

Some authorities, according to Robert Graves, hold that Orpheus had condemned the Maenad's promiscuity while he went about preaching homosexual love. This caused Aphrodite to be as angered as Dionysos had been. Her fellow-Olympians, however, could not agree that Orpheus' murder had been justified and Dionysos spared the Maenads' lives by turning them into oak trees, which remained forever rooted to the ground. The Thracian men who had survived the massacre decided, with a colorful flair for the cruelties of justice, to tattoo their wives as a warning against the murder of singers and priests!

As for Orpheus' head, after being attacked by a jealous Lemnian serpent (which Apollo immediately changed into a stone) it was laid to rest in a cave at Antissa, sacred to Dionysos. There it prophesied day and night until Apollo, finding that his oracle at Delphi was becoming deserted, came and stood over the head and said: "Cease from interfering in my affairs. I have stood enough from you and your singing!" Immediately after this, the head of Orpheus became silent. His lyre had also drifted to Lesbos and had been laid up in the temple of Apollo. At the intercession of Apollo and the Muses, the Lyre was placed in the heavens where it has been shining ever since in the form of a constellation called The Lyre, a symbol of the indestructibility of song.[12]

But at this point in the chapter we must ask ourselves how well acquainted Henry Miller was, exactly, with the specifics of the myth of Orpheus and Eurydice. Is it pure coincidence that all of the salient features of this myth form a loose choreographic plan for some of his most artful and most typical work? How *much* of the Orphic mytho-

12 Robert Graves. *The Greek Myths* (Baltimore: Penguin Books. 1948), pp. 111-113 and *passim*, and *New Larousse Encyclopaedia of Mythology* (London: Prometheus Press, 1968), pp. 193-198 and *passim*.

logem did the "unschooled" Henry Miller really know? A great deal. In fact, the evidence I have uncovered points to a rather detailed and obsessive interest in mythic materials such as those embodied in the myth of Orpheus. In *The Books in My Life*, published over ten years after *Colossus*, Miller indicates how far back into his childhood this interest extends:

When I stood amid the ruins of Knossos and of Mycenae did my thoughts turn to school books, to my penal instructors and the enchanting tales they told us? No. I thought of the stories I had read as a child; I saw the illustrations of those books I had thought buried in oblivion; I thought of our discussions in the street and the amazing speculations we had indulged in. I recalled my own private speculation about all these exciting, mysterious themes connected with past and future. Looking out over the plain of Argos from Mycenae, I lived over again – and how vividly! – the tale of the Argonauts [whose adventurings, it will be remembered, Orpheus had safeguarded with his music]. Gazing upon the Cyclopean walls of Tiryns I recalled the tiny illustration of the wall in one of my wonder books – it corresponded exactly with the reality confronting me. Never, in school, had a history professor even attempted to make living for us these glorious epochs of the past which every child enters into naturally as soon as he is able to read. With what childlike faith does the hardy explorer pursue his grim task! We learn nothing from the pedagogues. The true educators are the adventurers and wanderers, the men who plunge into the living plasm of history, legend, myth.[13]

In a special appendix to this book, Miller lists the one hundred books which influenced him most. The list not only conspicuously includes "Greek Myths and Legends," but at least a dozen other books that could have served him as sources of Orphic materials.[14]

The itch to emulate Orpheus is amply attested in essays Miller wrote before *Colossus*,[15] but there can be no doubt that it even antedates the publication of his first book. In a work schedule "drafted and used by H.M. during the Clichy period of 1932-1933," we find Miller reminding himself to "clarify the symbolism still more [in *Tropic of Cancer*] – mother's womb, hero-wanderer, labyrinth-

13 *Books*, pp. 85-86.
14 *Ibid.*, pp. 317-319.
15 Cf. esp., *The Wisdom of the Heart* (New York: New Directions, 1941), pp. 187-191 and *The Cosmological Eye* (New York: New Directions, 1939), p. 325.

throngs..."[16] An agenda prepared at that time lists Jane Harrison's *The Orphic Myths* and Dante as essential reading.[17] And in preparation for a book on D.H. Lawrence which Miller was beginning to write, he asks Anaïs Nin (in a letter dated October, 1933) to provide him with, among other things, the "Orphic myth (*Birth of Tragedy* gives it better than anything)."[18]

But Miller's letters to Anaïs Nin contain even more conclusive proof of his conscious discipleship to the myth of Orpheus and to his determination to put his own Orphic sensibility to formal use in his books. This passage, from a letter of February, 1934, strikingly illustrates both an Emersonian/Orphic tendency to see reality in terms of *himself* and a vivid consciousness of his own Orphic nature:

With the arrival of your note I've thrown everything on the floor. What I once thought was the material of a book lies about me, not in fragments, but in shreds. It would take a wizard to put it together – *and I am that wizard*! I've discovered in myself what I've been shouting about in the theory of annihilation, via Nietzsche, Jung, Father Orpheus, Mother Incest, etc. etc. I've smashed the fucking thing into a million pieces in order that I may ingest it piecemeal and throw it out again in a macrocosmic poem. I am learning method, structure, order – teaching it to myself, the highest kind of order, of form and structure, the poem in itself, as it were. I use this word "poem" in a new sense, please notice. I borrow it from my friend Walter Lowenfels – my friend! Note! Yes, I feel proud of it – as if it were an achievement. It was a creation, if you like. Last night the great conjunction, the breaking down of all asymptotical relations by the creation of new orbits. Is it Lowenfels I see truly now, or myself? Same thing. I see that in him which was blind in me, or vice versa. I went down with him last night into some kind of chthonian underworld of the mind where the supreme point of identification is reached. I come home and order my book: Part 1. – Genetics of Idea; Part 2. – Poem and Exegesis. Important to note is "Poem." New meaning – *for me*. Here I have been complaining all along that I know no one in Paris with whom I can communicate, no man of sufficient stature. And by the most roundabout route I have come to exactly the man I wanted to meet. Did I create him, or did he create me? He is my counterpart, the other half of me which has been wandering through the underworld in search of Eurydice (Miller's italics).[19]

16 Bern Porter (ed.)., *Henry Miller Miscellanea* (Berkeley, California: Bern Porter, 1945), pp. 20-21.
17 *Ibid.*, p. 25.
18 Henry Miller, *Letters to Anaïs Nin* (New York: G.P. Putnam's Sons, 1965), p. 70.
19 *Ibid.*, pp. 127-128.

The reference to "Father Orpheus" is too pointed to require additional comment. The imagery of Miller's letter is saturated with Orphic notions and he is evidently intent on translating his Orphic "theory of annihilation" into more ambitious literary terms, in writings to come, as a result of his catalytic friendship with Lowenfels, which to all appearances has merely caused his own thinking to clarify itself. And I think a careful examination of the mythic elements in Henry Miller's key works will bear out my contention that Miller's literary strategies are those of a faithful follower and avatar of "Father Orpheus." The landscapes they describe – whether inner or outer, real or imaginary, in Brooklyn or in Greece – are quite simply what Wallace Stevens would term "supreme fictions" in the Orphic mode. They are a self-styled and self-taught Orphic writer's attempt to validate, within the limits of his own personal experience, "the image's truth" of a much larger paradigm.

2. Orpheus as Musician: The Spellbinder Motif

"I don't say that God is one grand laugh: I say that you've got to laugh hard before you can get anywhere near God. My whole aim in life is to get near to God, that is, to get nearer to myself. That's why it doesn't matter to me what road I take. But music is very important. Music is a tonic for the pineal gland. Music isn't Bach or Beethoven; music is the can opener of the soul. It makes you terribly quiet inside, makes you aware that there's a roof to your being."

Henry Miller in *Tropic of Capricorn*

It's as a singer and music-maker that Orpheus was famous in ancient times, and it's as a singer and music-maker that Henry Miller projects his author's *persona* upon the awareness of his readers at the very start of his career. *Tropic of Cancer*, his first published book, virtually opens with a gesture of self-identification with the singer Orpheus who must descend into Hades in search of Eurydice:

To sing you must first open your mouth. You must have a pair of lungs, and a little knowledge of music. It is not necessary to have an accordion, or a guitar. The essential thing is to *want* to sing. This then is a song. I am singing... When into the womb of time everything is again withdrawn chaos will be restored and chaos is the score upon which reality is written. You, Tania, are my chaos. It is why I sing. It is not even I, it is the world dying, shedding the skin of time. I am still alive, kicking in your womb, a reality to write upon.[20]

It's entirely in keeping with what we know about Orpheus and his character for a writer like Henry Miller to connect the etiology of

20 Henry Miller, *Tropic of Cancer* (Paris: The Obelisk Press, 1934), p. 12.

his own gift *with woman* and with the sense of desolation and hope evoked by woman. The Orphic theme of re-birth is immediately audible in these strains.

Not only did Miller at one time seriously aspire to become a concert pianist, but his books are saturated with musical terminology. He has referred to some of the characteristically Millerian literary devices which he uses as "cadenzas" and "codas" and he bears witness, in some of his earliest letters, to the crucial role music has played in his life:

Now I really hear! I can relate these themes and motifs and big canvases and little to all things. It isn't music alone – it's all life, all history. And it has a great lulling and provocative effect, *both*. It drives you deep inward and permeates the tone of your feeling, your thought. Music purifies, no doubt of that. Especially, the highly organic, the great formal compositions... When I get to the subject of music I feel I am on the brink of something profound. Are you *sure* you get all that on music which Nietzsche gives (Miller's italics)?[21]

The Orphics, according to all the authorities, were not only greatly devoted to the arts of music but to the purification of the spirit.

Among his major books, *The Colossus of Maroussi* may easily be regarded as the *locus classicus* of Miller's attempt to re-enact the bewitching performances of Orpheus. It contains some of Miller's most dazzling monologues, but it is also a veritable gallery of portraits of great spellbinding "singers" in the Orphic tradition. From the opening paragraphs to Lawrence Durrell's glowing anecdote on the midnight cocks of Attica in the concluding coda, Miller treats his readers to a procession of human types who share his unique gift for casting a spell with words.

Here, to begin at the beginning, is the opening paragraph of *The Colossus of Maroussi:*

I would never have gone to Greece had it not been for a girl named Betty Ryan who lived in the same house with me in Paris. One evening, over a glass of white wine, she began to talk of her experiences in roaming about the world. I always listened to her with great attention, not only because her experiences were strange but because when she talked about her wanderings she seemed to paint them: everything she described remained in my head like finished canvases by a master. It was a peculiar conversation that evening: we began by talking about China and the Chinese language which she had begun to study. Soon we were in

21 *Letters to Anaïs Nin*, pp. 94-95.

> North Africa, in the desert, among peoples I had never heard of before. And then suddenly she was all alone, walking beside a river, and the light was intense and I was following her as best I could in the blinding sun but she got lost and I found myself wandering about in a strange land listening to a language I had never heard before. She is not exactly a story teller, this girl, but she is an artist of some sort because nobody has ever given me the ambiance of a place so thoroughly as she did Greece. Long afterwards I discovered that it was near Olympia that she had gone astray and I with her, but at the time it was just Greece to me, a world of light such as I had never dreamed of and never hoped to see.[22]

Betty Ryan, whose name faintly resembles that of Beatrice, Dante's irresistible guide to a Paradise that can only be reached after descending into the bowels of the Inferno, may be regarded as the prototype of a number of other beguiling Eurydices in the book: Lawrence Durrell's wife Nancy, the resplendant Jeanne Seferiades, the young Greek girl with the reddish-gold hair whose "slow, sustained smile" prompts Miller to liken her to "the dancers of Java and of Bali... the culminating expression of the spiritual achievement of the human race,"[23] and that "strange monster with six toes" who, according to Miller, "had the smile of the insatiable one to whom a thousand burning kisses are only the incentive to renewed assaults. In some strange and inexplicable fashion she has remained in my memory as that symbol of unbounded love which I sensed in a lesser degree in all Greek women."[24] All these women intimate the possibility of the paradisiac to Miller, but it is Beatrice/Betty Ryan's blandishments which actually persuade Miller to abandon Paris and make the "descent" south to Greece by way of the Dordogne region of France with its "black, mysterious river at Dômme."[25]

Although *The Colossus of Maroussi* is merely an implicit re-enactment of the Orphic drama in which the names of Orpheus and Eurydice are not mentioned once, it's interesting that at the very out-

22 *Colossus*, pp. 3-4.
23 *Ibid.*, p. 109.
24 *Ibid.*, p. 112.
25 *Ibid.*, p. 4. Pandelís Prevelákis, a close friend and biographer of the Greek novelist Níkos Kazantzákis, notes the same resemblance between the names of Betty Ryan and Beatrice in a very short article on Henry Miller entitled "Prospéro le jeune" in the Belgian magazine *Synthèses*, February/March 1967, p. 32: "Son Paradis fut la Grèce qu'il connut grâce à la médiation d'une femme nommée Betty (qui rappelle Béatrice)." But Prevelákis pursues this lead no further.

set Miller identifies the "black, mysterious river at Dômme" with the poet Rainer Maria Rilke. The author of *Sonnets to Orpheus* seems a paradigmatic enough figure to Miller to deserve the place of initiatory presence at the outset of Miller's own *katábasis*. That presence presides, implicitly, over much of the book. The journey to Greece is taken under the patronage, so to speak, of Rilke. When Miller describes his first airplane trip in Part Two of *Colossus*, his attitude to the experience is a reminder that Rilke had devoted a good deal of his life to warning his own generation against the mechanization of their lives, and, as his biographer E.M. Butler puts it, to

> imploring them...to turn their thoughts away from the beauty and complexity of aeroplanes, to the spaces they are traversing, that they [might] *become* those far-distant bourns. Determined though he was to glorify all existing things and to worship metamorphosis, Rilke could not affirm with any conviction the changes accomplished by the march of history and the industrial revolution. Our modern methods of haste and luxury, our mechanized lives have separated us from the gods of old; our sacred fires now burn in boilers; our strength has entered automatic hammers, and we are swooning like exhausted swimmers.[26]

Here is the way Miller expresses the same thought a few decades later:

> I had never been in a plane before and I probably will never go up again. I felt foolish sitting in the sky with hands folded; the man beside me was reading a newspaper, apparently oblivious of the clouds that brushed the window-panes. We were probably making a hundred miles an hour, but since we passed nothing but clouds I had the impression of not moving. In short, it was unrelievedly dull and pointless. I was sorry that I had not booked passage on the good ship Acropolis which was to touch at Crete shortly. Man is made to walk the earth and sail the seas; the conquest of the air is reserved for a later stage in his evolution, when he will have sprouted real wings and assumed the form of the angel which he is in essence.[27]

But Rilke is not the only Orphic poet whose music enchants Miller in the *Colossus*. Aside from being dazzled by the light-filled Greek landscapes, Miller is fascinated by the cunning art of contemporary Greek "singers" who, like their "Father Orpheus" before them, can enchant wild beasts and make the rocks and trees move from their places. *Colossus* pays tribute to the poet Seferis with his wonderful talk of poetry and American jazz; to Dr. Theodore Stephanides with his

26 E.M. Butler, *Rainer Maria Rilke* (New York: Macmillan, 1941), p. 352.
27 *Colossus*., pp. 112-113.

inexhaustible knowledge of "plants, flowers, trees, rocks, minerals, ...diseases, planets, comets...and his hallucinating descriptions of his life in the trenches...during the World War;"[28] to Captain Antoniou, the sea-voyager poet, with his feverish obsession with the American writer, Sherwood Anderson, whose loneliness Antoniou shares with the sons of Orpheus in general; to Stavros Tsoussis, the bureaucrat-as-Orpheus, beside whose adroit machinations and dynamic double-talk Miller believes a minor spellbinder like Adolf Hitler would seem a "caricature" and Mussolini "an old-fashioned Ben Greet player."[29]

The most important manifestation of the Orphic genius dealt with by Miller in *Colossus*, however, is George Katsimbalis. This well-known Greek magazine editor and bibliographer, who lived in the Athenian suburb of Maroussi at the time of Miller's journey in 1939, is the "colossus" of the title. Like everything he talks about with such verve, Katsimbalis as Miller describes him is considerably larger than life. From the first encounter with Katsimbalis, Miller is mesmerized by the man's extraordinary gifts as a raconteur. The quality of Katsimbalis' talk, despite his ailing health and "a great element of the tragic in him,"[30] could, according to Miller, "galvanize the dead."[31] One is reminded immediately that Orpheus not only charmed the ferryman Charon, the watch-dog Cerberus, and the three Judges of the Dead with his plaintive music, but temporarily suspended the tortures of the damned.[32]

Miller becomes eloquent himself, in the Orphic manner, when he attempts a portrait of Katsimbalis' self-infatuated technique. For, as he explains, Katsimbalis "talked about himself because he himself was the most interesting person he knew." Miller adds: "I liked that quality very much – I have a little of it myself."[33] Only an extended quotation could do justice to this *self*-entranced Orpheus *describing Orpheus*. And since paraphrases always invites some measure of distortion, I quote Miller's own words in their entirety:

28 *Ibid.*, p. 17.
29 *Ibid.*, p. 169.
30 *Ibid.*, p. 28.
31 *Ibid.*, p. 30.
32 Robert Graves, *Greek Myths*, p. 112.
33 *Colossus*, p. 28.

It wasn't just talk he handed out, but *language* – food and beast language. He always talked against a landscape, like the protagonist of a lost world. The Attic landscape was best of all for his purpose: it contains the necessary ingredients for the dramatic monologue. One has only to see the open air theatres buried in the hillsides to understand the importance of this setting. Even if his talk carried him to Paris, for example, to a place like the Faubourg Montmartre, he spiced and flavored it with his Attic ingredients, with thyme, sage, tufa, asphodel, honey, red clay, blue roofs, acanthus trimmings, violet light, hot rocks, dry winds, *rezina*, arthritis, and the electrical crackle that plays over the low hills like a swift serpent with a broken spine. He was a strange contradiction, even in his talk. With his snake-like tongue which struck like lightning, with fingers moving nervously, as though wandering over an imaginary spinet, with pounding, brutal gestures which somehow never smashed anything but simply raised a din, with all the boom of surf and the roar and sizzle and razzle-dazzle, if you suddenly observed him closely you got the impression that he was sitting there immobile, that only the round falcon's eye was alert, that he was a bird which had been hypnotized, or had hypnotized itself, and that his claws were fastened to the wrist of an invisible giant, a giant like the earth. All this flurry and din, all these kaleidoscopic prestidigitations of his, were only a sort of wizardry which he employed to conceal the fact that he was a prisoner – that was the impression he gave me when I studied him, when I could break the spell for a moment and observe him attentively. But to break the spell required a power and a magic almost equal to his own; it made one feel foolish and impotent, as one always does when one succeeds in destroying the power of illusion. Magic is never destroyed – the most we can do is to cut ourselves off, amputate the mysterious antennae which serve to connect us with forces beyond our power of understanding. Many a time, as Katsimbalis talked, I caught that look on the face of a listener which told me that the invisible wires had been connected, that something was being communicated which was over and above language, over and above personality, something magical which we recognize in dream and which makes the face of the sleeper relax and expand with a bloom such as we rarely see in waking life. Often when meditating on this quality of his I thought of his frequent allusions to the incomparable honey which is stored by the bees on the slopes of his beloved Hymettos. Over and over he would try to explain the reasons why this honey from Mount Hymettos was unique. Nobody can explain it satisfactorily. Nobody can explain anything which is unique. One can describe, worship and adore. And that is all I can do with Katsimbalis' talk.[34]

One needn't feel as helpless as Miller acknowledges himself to be in the face of such accomplished musical performances, however. W.K.C. Guthrie tells us that the proto-Orpheus was first and foremost the musician "with magic in his notes," and surely there is a great deal in the virtuoso monologues of George Katsimbalis *and* Henry Miller that

34 *Ibid.*, pp. 30-32.

can be called "magic," that can legitimately make its hearers sense the "powerlessness" all magic is capable of producing. But it is a magic which, like that of any authentically skilled performance, will sustain a certain amount of analysis. As Richard Poirier has put it:

Performance is an exercise of power, a very curious one. Curious because it is at first so furiously self-consultive, so even narcissistic, and later so eager for publicity, love, and historical dimension. Out of an accumulation of secretive acts emerges at last a form that presumes to compete with reality itself for control of the minds exposed to it. Performance in writing, in painting, or in dance is made up of thousands of tiny movements, each made with a calculation that is also its innocence.[35]

Miller's most sustained solo performance in the *Colossus* is a seven-page monologue which owes its rhythmic style to Negro jazz improvisations and its violent imagery and mood to the example of Rimbaud. It is provoked by the prissy French wife of a Greek whose souvenir shop Miller visits in Crete and, on the face of it, it has the appearance of pure logorrhoea – a sassy and rather long-winded verbal jag. But there is extraordinary artistic control[36] in this outwardly fluid passage; its "thousands of tiny movements" have been carefully chosen and its spell is skillfully created. The monologue is a paean to the freedom-giving openness of music (as opposed to the stiff Frenchwoman's love of "gardens with high walls") and the numerous variations on Miller's theme are improvised with a fitting "music": Miller orchestrates an imagery of angels, golden torques, blue skies, wild flowers, holidays, and open roads with fetching boogie-woogie rhythms. He even resorts to the "innocent calculation" of alliteration. In the following passage, for instance, the f's seem to suggest the fatuous Frenchwoman's windy passivity while the explosive b's (especially at the close) strongly suggest a tone of blunt rejection of what the woman stands for:

Madame, there are always two paths to take: one back towards the com*f*ort and security of death, the other *f*orward to nowhere. You would like to *f*all back amongst your quaint tombstones and *f*amiliar cemetery walls. *F*all back then, *f*all back deep and *f*athomless into the ocean of annihilation. *F*all back into that

35 Richard Poirier, *The Performing Self* (New York: Oxford University Press, 1971), p. 87.
36 *Colossus*, pp. 138-145.

bloody torpor which permits idiots to be crowned as kings. *F*all back and writhe in torment with the evolutionary worms. I am going on, on *p*ast the last *b*lack and white squares. The game is *p*layed out, the *f*igures have melted away, the lines are *f*razzled, the *b*oard is mildewed. Everything has become *b*arbarious again...*B*oogie woogie came *b*ack with *b*lood on his knees.[37]

Earlier in *Colossus*, Miller the poet makes an even more elaborate use of alliteration in a three-page cadenza on the planet Saturn, his lugubrious astrological nemesis. His mock-description of Saturn would have appealed to the *Symboliste* poet Gérard de Nerval, who referred to this planet as "le froid Saturne [qui] aime le plomb" in *Les Illuminés* (p. 376). Miller's insistent string of hissing s's, counterpointed with abundant f's and v's, almost too richly suggests the evil influences Miller associates with this planet:

*S*aturn i*s* male*f*ic through *f*orce of inertia. It*s* ring, which i*s* only paperweight in thickne*ss*, according to the *s*a*v*ant*s*, i*s* the wedding ring which *s*ignifie*s* death or mi*s*f*o*rtunes de*v*oid of all *s*igni*f*icance. *S*aturn, whatever it may be to the a*s*tronomer, i*s* the *s*ign of *s*en*s*ele*ss* *f*atality to the man in the *s*treet. He carrie*s* it in hi*s* heart becau*s*e hi*s* whole li*f*e, de*v*oid of *s*igni*f*icance a*s* it i*s*, i*s* wrapped up in thi*s* ultimate *s*ymbol which, i*f* all el*s*e *f*ail*s* to do him in, thi*s* he can count upon to *f*inish him o*ff*. *S*aturn i*s* li*f*e in *s*u*s*pen*s*e, not dead *s*o much as deathle*ss*, i.e., incapable of dying. *S*aturn is like dead bone in the ear – double ma*s*toid *f*or the soul.[38]

Here the sinister impression created by a mass of sibilants and affricates is obvious to the point of redundancy, but Miller can be much more subtle in his handling of alliteration. There is a fine instance of this in a passage preceding the coda of Part One of *Colossus* in which Miller creates a remarkable extended melody based on the capacity of the phoneme */m/* to suggest pure delight and pleasurable self-awareness. The passage is doubly effective because Miller intimates that a transformation takes place as he enters the tomb of Agamemnon. The "*m*an I a*m*" is metamorphosed before one's eyes and ears, as if through Orphic magic, into the larger onomatic figure of "Aga*mem*non" (upon whose two m's the entire sequence of m's climactically converges). Whether or not Miller is entirely conscious of striving for this effect, the passage has a remarkably uniform insistence:

37 *Ibid.*, pp. 142-143.
38 *Ibid.*, p. 105.

> I a*m* still the *m*an I *m*ight have beco*m*e, assu*m*ing every benefit of civilization to be showered upon *m*e with regal indulgence. I a*m* gathering all of this potential civilized *m*uck into a hard, tiny knot of understanding. I a*m* blown to the *maximum*, like a great bowl of *m*olten glass hanging fro*m* the ste*m* of a glass-blower. *M*ake *m*e into a fantastic shape, use all your art, exhaust your lung-power – still I shall only be a thing fabricated, at the best a beautiful cultured soul. I know this, I despise it. I stand outside full-blown, the *m*ost beautiful, the *m*ost cultured, the *m*ost *m*arvellously fabricated soul on earth. I a*m* going to put *m*y foot over the threshold – now. I do so. I hear nothing. I a*m* not even there to hear *my*self shattering into a billion splintered s*m*ithereens. Only Aga*m*e*m*non is there.[39]

There is, in addition to the effective tonal arrangement of m's in this passage, another interesting trick used by Miller. It concerns the telling use of the personal pronoun "I." Very conspicuously, Miller uses this pronoun fourteen times in rapid succession to direct attention to the over-blown personal ego that comes to the tomb of Agamemnon. But that is clearly done to be able to annihilate it the more effectively when Miller puts his foot over the threshold: "Only Agamemnon is here." When the "I" reappears a little later in the paragraph, it is in the form of a highly chastened "I": "a nomad, a spiritual nobody." This obliteration of the too-assonantal "I" is also part of Miller's music.

Admittedly, there is a margin of subjectivity to all interpretations of alliterative and assonantal patterns, but the *presence* of such patterns on these pages can scarcely be doubted. Miller, in his own fashion, is "singing." And as the poet Rilke has put it,

> ...*this* is Orpheus. His metamorphosis
> in this one and in that. We should not make
>
> searches for other names. Once and for all,
> it's Orpheus when there's song. He comes and goes.[40]

Miller comes closest to explicitly proclaiming his affinity with Orpheus in the description he gives of his trip to Delphi. If it is borne in mind that the Muse (woman/Eurydice/June) had given birth to Orpheus' powers of song and that the waters of the Castellian Spring

39 *Ibid*., pp. 92-93.

40 Rainer Maria Rilke, *Selected Works*, trans. by J.B. Leishman (New York: New Directions, 1960), p. 255.

were said to stimulate one's capacity to remember (thereby putting one more closely in touch with the materials of self-expression), it is possible to recognize, embedded in the matrix of Miller's casual-sounding account of his visit to the Castellian Spring, a genuine awareness of his Orphic mission. In order to facilitate the recognition of similarities between the two, I've placed this passage and a quotation from the great mythographer of Illuminism, Edouard Shuré, in parallel columns. Note that, aside from the difference of context *in time*, it is almost as if the two writers were talking about the same thing:

I. (Shuré)

In the sanctuaries of Apollo which possessed the Orphic tradition, a mysterious festival was celebrated at the vernal equinox. This was the time when the narcissus bloomed again near the fountain of Castalia. The tripods and the lyres of the temple vibrated of their own accord, and the invisible god was said to return to the country of the Hyperboreans in a chariot drawn by swans. Then the great priestess, dressed as a Muse and crowned with laurel, her forehead bound with sacred bands, sang before the initiates *The Birth of Orpheus*, the son of Apollo and of a priestess of god. The Muse called upon the soul of Orpheus, immortal and thrice-crowned, in hell, on earth, and in heaven, a star upon his forehead, walking among the constellations and the gods.[41]

II. (Miller)

We had a drink at the Castellian Spring where I suddenly remembered my old friend Nick of the Orpheum Dance Palace on Broadway because he had come from a little village called Castellia in the valley beyond the mountains. In a way my friend Nick was largely responsible for my being here, I reflected, for it was through his terpsichorean instrumentations that I met my wife June [whom Miller depicts as a sort of Eurydice/Muse type in *Capricorn* and *The Rosy Crucifixion*] and if I hadn't met her I should probably never have become a writer, never have left America [the voyager motif], never have met Betty Ryan, Lawrence Durrell, and finally Stephanides, Katsimbalis and Ghika [whom Miller virtually regards as oracles and gods].[42]

Even the number three, sacred both to the Apollonian cult of Orpheus ("tripod," "thrice-crowned") and to Dante (the Trinity, terza rima), has a special hold on Henry Miller's imagination. Not only is *Colossus*

41 Edouard Shuré, *The Mysteries of Ancient Greece: Orpheus/Plato* (Blauvelt, New York: Rudolf Steiner Publications, 1971), p. 35.
42 *Colossus*, p. 195.

divided into three parts, but things tend to occur in groups of three's with unsurprising regularity in the book (I intend to return to this subject in my chapter on Miller as a *Symboliste*). Certain leitmotifs which occur in all three parts of the book serve Miller the artist as clever ordering devices to hold together a book which, outwardly, seems to delight in the fluidity of its "improvisations." One of these is the sound of the flute. According to one authority, the flute "corresponds to erotic or funereal anguish"[43] in the sound it makes – precisely in accord with the ethos of the Orphic myth and in keeping with the use Miller makes of the symbol in all three parts of the book. It can be heard in distinctly "Orphic" settings in Part One[44] and Part Two.[45] But it is in Part Three that the sound of the flute conjures up one of the grimmest episodes in the Orphic myth: the dismemberment of the singer (*sparagmós*). The "plight of the creative artist" in the face of neglect and outright hostility is a favorite theme throughout Miller's *oeuvre*. Miller knows from experience that the fate of Orpheus is no more felicitous in the modern world than it was in the ancient. Jealous gods and maenads are always eager to tear apart the bringer of song and light. There are numerous illustrations of this in *The Colossus of Maroussi*, including the battered and luckless Katsimbalis himself, but the following episode is given the heightened quality of genuinely mythic treatment by Miller:

> It is Christmas Eve [in Corinth], but there is nothing here to indicate that anyone is aware of it. Approaching a lonely house lit up by a smoky kerosene lamp we are suddenly arrested by the queer strains of a flute. We hasten our steps and stand in the middle of the wide street to take in the performance. The door of the house is open, revealing a room filled with men listening to an uncouth figure playing the flute. The man seems to be exalted by his own music, a music such as I have never heard before and probably never will again. It seems like sheer improvisation and, unless his lungs give out, there promises to be no end to it. It is the music of the hills, the wild notes of the solitary man armed with nothing but his instrument. It is the original music for which no notes have been written and for which none is necessary. It is fierce, sad, obsessive, yearning and defiant. [It is easy to see, here, the analogy with Miller's own "improvisations."] It is not for men's ears but for God's. It is a duet in which the other instrument is silent. In the midst of the performance a man approach-

43 Juan Eduardo Cirlot, *A Dictionary of Symbols* (New York: Philosophical Library, 1962), p. 105.
44 *Colossus*, p. 19.
45 *Ibid.*, p. 126.

es us on a bicycle, dismounts and doffing his hat inquires respectfully if we are strangers, if we had arrived perhaps just to-day. He is a telegraph messenger and he has a message in his hand for an American woman, he says. Durrell laughs and asks to see the message. It is a Christmas greeting to the Countess von Reventlow (Barbara Hutton). We read it – it is in English – and pass it back to him. He goes off, peering like a scout into the darkness, ready no doubt to intercept the next tall woman with golden hair whom he sees dressed like a man. The incident reminded me of my own days in the telegraph service, of a winter's night when I came upon a messenger walking the streets of New York in a daze with a fistful of undelivered messages. Noticing the blank stare in his eyes I led him back to the office he had come from, where I learned that he had been missing for two days and nights. He was blue with cold and chattering like a monkey. When I opened his coat to see if he had any messages in his inside pockets I discovered that under the coarse suit he was naked. In one of his pockets I found a program of musical compositions which he had evidently printed himself since almost the entire list of pieces indicated him as being the composer. The incident came to a close in the observation ward at Bellevue where he was pronounced insane.[46]

There is nothing improvisatory about such effects. Clearly, the departure of the messenger in Corinth ("peering like a scout into the darkness") prepares the reader for the New York messenger/composer's final *sparagmós*. The hard fate of the music-maker is admirably evoked in a single anecdote by means of which Henry Miller apotheosizes the forlorn singer through the medium of music.

Toward the close of *The Colossus of Maroussi*, Miller states prophetically that parting from his Orphic companions in Greece to return to America will leave him often at the mercy of frightening and uncomprehending forces. As soon as he boards the American boat to New York, he feels he is "in another world. I was among the go-getters again, among the restless souls who, not knowing how to live their own lives, wish to change the world for everybody."[47] Maenads are lurking everywhere. An Orpheus with Henry Miller's sense of humour could probably even be prompted to interpret the slashing and merciless attacks on him in such recent works as Kate Millett's *Sexual Politics*[48] as "symbolic" acts of maenadic fury! All that remains now is for the final apotheosis of the Lyre in the heavens to take place.

46 *Ibid.*, pp. 213-214.
47 *Ibid.*, p. 233.
48 Kate Millett, *Sexual Politics* (Boston: Atlantic, Little-Brown, 1971), cf. esp. pp. 302-313.

3. Orpheus as Voyager: the Sense of Quest

"Johnny Appleseed was never a boaster at all. In life he had been John Chapman (1775?-1847), a New England Swedenborgian who had conceived it to be his mission to sow fruit trees through the Middle West, and had spent nearly half a century travelling by canoe and on foot, reading aloud from the Bible and leaving orchards behind him. The Indians thought of him as a great medicine man. After his death from pneumonia following a long hard trip to a distant orchard, he became a frontier saint, almost a god of fertility."

F.O. Matthiesen in *American Renaissance*

The lure of the journey, with its attendant perils and excitements, is a very old theme in literature. In order to succeed on their journeys, quest heroes often have to depend on occult wisdom or some magic object to help them evade dangers along the way. Launcelot relies on a magic ring to protect him from enchantments in his search for Guinevere; Gawain is assisted by a green girdle in his search for the Green Knight. But the most famous voyage in Greek antiquity was the Argonauts' quest for the Golden Fleece. Orpheus himself participated in this voyage and, as the British classicist W.K.C. Guthrie points out, it was the magic power of his music that granted immunity to the heroes from perils such as the Semplegades (Clashing Rocks) and, ultimately, lulled to sleep the dragon that guarded the Golden Fleece.[49]

The sense of quest is a remarkably persistent theme in Henry Miller. In an early essay called "Reflections on Writing," Miller compares both the writers' vocation and life itself to a "voyage of discovery": "The adventure is a metaphysical one: it is a way of approaching life indirectly, or acquiring a total rather than a partial view

49 *Orpheus*, p. 28.

of the universe. The writer lives between the upper and lower worlds: he takes the path in order eventually to *become* that path himself."[50] And in an essay on the diary of Anaïs Nin written at about the same time, Miller says:

The diary is full of voyages; in fact, like life itself it might be regarded as nothing but voyage. The epic quality of it, however, is eclipsed by the metaphysical. The diary is not a journey towards the heart of darkness, in the stern Conradian sense of destiny, not a *voyage au bout de la nuit*, as with Céline, nor even a voyage to the moon in the psychological sense of escape. It is much more like a mythological voyage towards the source and fountainhead of life – I might say an *astrologic* voyage of metamorphosis (Miller's italics).[51]

Years later, the theme of voyaging persists in *The Books in My Life:*

All is voyage, all is quest. We are not even aware of the goal until we have reached it and become one with it. To employ the word reality is to say myth and legend. To speak of creation means to bury oneself in chaos. We know not whence we come nor whither we go, nor even who we are. We set sail for the golden shores, sped on sometimes like "arrows of longing," and we arrive at our destination in the full glory of realization – or else as unrecognizable pulp from which the essence of life has been squashed.[52]

It is no exaggeration to call Henry Miller's whole literary output the log-book of a loquacious latter-day Argonaut in his quest for the "golden fleece" of the Absolute of joy. *Tropic of Cancer* and *Tropic of Capricorn*, with their cartographer's titles derived from the high and low points (parallel to the equator) touched by the sun in the earth's journeyings around it, are both accounts of journeys of self-discovery. *Tropic of Cancer* chronicles, for the most part, Miller's picaresque travels through the *demi-monde* of Paris, whereas *Tropic of Capricorn* records his madcap journey on the "ovarian trolley" of human existence in search of a satisfying vocation. *Capricorn* takes him as far from his native Manhattan as Florida (where he tries, without notable success, to sell encyclopedias) and California (where he works, in absolute desperation, as an orange-picker in the orange groves of Chula Vista).

Not until he takes his Orphic trip to Greece – "that quest for a

50 *Wisdom*, p. 19.
51 *Cosmological Eye*, pp. 269-270.
52 *Books*, p. 98.

dark but 'pure' center," as one critic has called such journeys[53] – does Miller make the decisive "descent" into his own (and Greece's) psychic-subterranean depths which will earn him the privilege to emerge into the paradisiacal light of authentic happiness. *The Colossus of Maroussi* is not only a "travel book" in the classic sense of that phrase, but a luminous account of an Orphic *katábasis* and *palingénesis*. I will deal with the "descent into Hades" and the subsequent "joy of re-birth" later, but at this point I will merely isolate some of the references to voyaging in the *Colossus* which confirm my opinion that Miller was thoroughly aware that his visit to Greece was a genuine *psychomachia* and not mere idle globe-trotting.

Miller's dissatisfaction with outward travels, from place to place, sets in rather early in the book:

> I was doing a great deal of traveling; people came to me at the cafés and poured out their journeys to me; the captain was always returning from a new trajectory; Seferiades was always writing a new poem which went back deep into the past and forward as far as the seventh root race; Katsimbalis would take me on his monologues to Mt. Athos, to Pelion and Ossa, to Leonidion and Monemvasia; Durrell would set my mind whirling with Pythagorean adventures; a little Welshman, just back from Persia, would drag me over the high plateaus and deposit me in Samarkand where I would meet the headless horseman called Death. All the Englishmen I met were always coming back from somewhere, some island, some monastery, some ancient ruin, some place of mystery. I was so bewildered by all the opportunities lying before me that I was paralyzed.[54]

It is precisely the people who talk most eloquently about the traveling they have done, however, who awaken a need for more satisfying voyages in Miller:

> I never cease to marvel how it happens that, with certain individuals whom I know, within a few minutes after greeting them we are embarked on an endless voyage comparable in feeling and trajectory only to the deep middle dream which the practiced dreamer slips into like a bone into its socket. Often, after one of these suprasensible séances, endeavoring to capture the thread which had broken, I would work my way back as far as some trifling detail – but between that bespangled point of repair and the mainland there was always an impassible void, a sort of no man's land which the wizardry of the artist had encumbered with shell holes and quagmires and barbed wire.[55]

53 Walter A. Strauss, *Descent and Return*, p. 10.
54 *Colossus*, pp. 51-52.
55 *Ibid.*, pp. 71-72.

But having learned a great deal about the art of traveling during his six-month exploration of the dark depths and luminous heights of Greece, Miller is finally able to experience the merging of dream and reality. Near the close of the book, he describes a moment in a trip he took, between Thebes and Delphi, with Katsimbalis, the painter Ghika, and the latter's friend Pericles Byzantis:

There was a terrific synchronization of dream and reality, the two worlds merging in a bowl of pure light, and we the voyagers suspended, as it were, over the earthly life. All thought of destination was annihilated; we were purring smoothly over the undulating ground, advancing towards the void of pure sensation, and the dream, which was hallucinating, had suddenly become vivid and unbearably real.... We were in the dead center of that soft silence which absorbs even the breathing of the gods. Man had nothing to do with this, nor even nature. In this realm nothing moves nor stirs nor breathes save the finger of mystery; this is the hush that descends upon the world before the coming of a miraculous event.[56]

On the return trip from the Theban hilltops that prompted this burst of illumination, Miller ponders on the Orphic notion that *palingénesis* must ever be preceded by a *katábasis* into the depths:

[A]s with the sacred places so with the murderous spots – the record of events is written into the earth. The real joy of the historian or the archeologist when confronted with a discovery must lie in the fact of confirmation, corroboration, not in surprise. Nothing that has happened on this earth, however deeply buried, is hidden from man. Certain spots stand out like semaphores, revealing not only the clue but the event – provided, to be sure, they are approached with utter purity of heart. I am convinced that there are many layers of history and that the final reading will be delayed until the gift of seeing past and future as one is restored to us.[57]

The idea is stated again several pages later, but in terms of *inner* (psychic) rather than outer (geographical) reality:

To live creatively, I have discovered, means to live more and more unselfishly, to live more and more *into* the world, identifying onself with it and thus influencing it at the core, so to speak. Art, like religion, it now seems to me, is only a preparation, an initiation into the way of life. The goal is liberation, freedom, which means assuming greater responsibility.[58]

56 *Ibid.*, pp. 188-189.
57 *Ibid.*, p. 198.
58 *Ibid.*, p. 206.

The nature of Miller's quest is clearly religious. It is the voyage of the spirit in search of the "golden fleece" of a more transcendant reality. Richard Sommer contends that when metaphors of travel are used in a "specifically and seriously religious" sense in literature, the writer's impulse toward renewal and regeneration "tends to represent the *personal* expectations of belief, whether Christian or otherwise. The journey toward God is here regarded in terms of the renovation of *self*, life renewed, salvation and immortality granted (Sommer's italics)."[59] When an Armenian soothsayer Miller is taken to by Katsimbalis assures Miller that self-fulfillment and immortality are assured him *despite* his lack of financial wherewithal and unsettled way of life, Miller says: "I...felt exalted. But above all I felt a sense of responsibility such as I have never known before. A sense of responsibility toward myself, let me hasten to add."[60] Miller appears to have arrived intuitively at the conclusion C.G. Jung reached only at the end of a long lifetime devoted to rigorous psychoanalytical research, i.e., when one "follows the path of individuation" and "lives one's own life," one must "take mistakes into the bargain." There can never be any guarantee that one will not "fall into error or stumble into deadly peril," according to Jung. What we consider the "sure road" is the "road of death" on which the "right things" invariably fail to happen: "Anyone who takes the sure road is as good as dead."[61] But the *un*sure road, in the Orphic tradition, leads to eternal life and oneness with God.[62] Miller's most conclusive words on the subject of the search for that particular "golden fleece" occur in *The Colossus of Maroussi* in his account of a trip to the Ancient Greek healing center and religious shrine at Epidaurus:

> Epidaurus is merely a place symbol: the real place is in the heart, in every man's heart, if he will but stop and search it. Every discovery is mysterious in that it reveals what is so unexpectedly immediate, so close, so long and intimately known. The wise man has no need to journey forth; it is the fool who seeks the pot of gold at the rainbow's end. But the two are always fated to meet and

59 Richard Sommer and Georg Roppen, *Strangers and Pilgrims* (New York: Humanities Press, 1964), p. 17.
60 *Colossus*, p. 206.
61 C.G. Jung, *Memories, Dreams, Reflections* (New York: Pantheon Books, 1963), p. 297.
62 W.K.C. Guthrie, *Orpheus*, p. 207.

unite. They meet at the heart of the world, which is the beginning and the end of the path. They meet in realization and unite in transcendence of their roles.[63]

63 *Colossus*, p. 80.

4. Orpheus as Peace-Maker: Abstention from Murder

"It is precisely here that one detects the abysmal gulf which separates a Christ or a Buddha, let us say, from a Hitler or a Mussolini. With the latter it is sheer Will which manifests itself, and which in the end destroys itself. In the case of the former it is a vital emanation from a being at peace with himself and the world, and consequently irresistible. The use of the will is the sign of death; it is only as half-being that the man of will triumphs. What lives on, when he has worked his will, is the death which was in him."

Henry Miller in *The Wisdom of the Heart*

According to W.K.C. Guthrie, "the most striking feature of the Orphic life" to the Greek contemporaries of Orpheus was that Orpheus "taught men to abstain from killing."[64] The influence of Orpheus always tended to oppose bloodshed and encourage "the arts of peace":

His outstanding quality is a gentleness amounting at times to softness... From warlike attributes he is entirely free... The atmosphere of calm which surrounds him differs strangely too from the normal habits of the wild mountain-god whose religion he adopted. Music may excite as well as soothe, but the cymbals and tympana of a Thracian or Phrygian orgy seem at first to have little to do with the sweet tones of Orpheus' lyre. The power of the lyre was to soften the hearts of warriors and turn their thoughts to peace, just as it could tame the wildest of the beasts.[65]

64 *Orpheus*, p. 196.
65 *Ibid.*, p. 40.

The religion of Orpheus is a religion of light (Helios) and brotherhood (Eros), completely opposed to the spirit of war. Walter A. Strauss considers Orpheus "truly a reconciler of opposites: he is the fusion of the radiant solar enlightenment of Apollo and the somber subterranean knowledge of Dionysos."[66]

It is ironic, perhaps, that Henry Miller's most undisguisedly Orphic book, *The Colossus of Maroussi*, records a joyful trip to Greece which extended from July 19, 1939,[67] to December 27, 1939.[68] Throughout his five-month odyssey, the specter of another world war – this time the bloodiest war ever waged in human history – hangs over Miller's head. At the very outset, he writes that he had undertaken the trip in the conscious knowledge that he had "everything a man could desire, and I knew it. I knew too that I might never have it again. I felt the war coming on – it was getting closer and closer every day. For a little while yet there would be peace and men might still behave like human beings."[69]

But early in the book, a fatalistic feeling that even the most sensible men and women of his generation will be affected by the hysteria engendered by war sets in. Miller witnesses a quarrel about the war between Lawrence Durrell and his wife Nancy in Patras and observes that the thought of war "drives people frantic, makes them quite cuckoo, even when they are intelligent and far-seeing."[70] He remembers that in Corfu, where he had stayed earlier with the Durrells, "a superbly healthy young Englishman...who had intended to be a Greek scholar" had been driven to behave "like a chicken with its head off begging someone to put him in the front line where he could have himself blown to smithereens."[71] Miller himself has to struggle to maintain his equilibrium in the face of this collective insanity. He

66 *Descent and Return*, p. 18.

67 Henry Miller, *Letters to Anaïs Nin*, p. 169. Since Miller nowhere mentions the exact dates of his Greek pilgrimage in *Colossus*, it has been necessary to consult other sources. Because Anaïs Nin was regularly corresponding with Miller at the time of his trip and was keeping a daily diary in which his comings and goings figure prominently, she can be regarded as an accurate source of information.

68 Anaïs Nin, *The Diary of Anaïs Nin*, Vol. 3 (New York: Harcourt, Brace & World, 1969), p. 17.

69 *Colossus*, p. 13.

70 *Ibid.*, p. 25.

71 *Ibid.*, p. 25.

knows there is a war on, but he does not have "the faintest idea what it's about or why people should enjoy killing one another."[72] He intuits, however, that members of modern technological societies "are all part of a vast interlocking murdering machine."[73]

This is probably the reason why some of Miller's choicest anger and raillery in *The Colossus of Maroussi* are aimed[74] at contentious political ideologies (Catholicism, Capitalism, Communism) and unscrupulous political figures (Hitler, Mussolini, Stalin), those forces which mastermind the murdering machine while remaining completely oblivious to the sacredness of individual life. J.R. Watmough holds that Orphism was "a religion of revolt" which "discarded all traditional forms *qua* traditional forms and showed that, in the mind of a free and spiritually minded man, they can have no real meaning. They are only so much clap-trap – the ready tool of greedy ecclesiastics and unscrupulous politicans."[75] This is a tenet of Orphic doctrine with which Henry Miller is in complete agreement. He expatiates upon it at length after describing the transformative effect which the light inside the amphitheater at Epidaurus had on him:

> Our whole way of life has to alter. We don't want better surgical appliances, we want a better life. If all the surgeons, all the analysts, all the medicos could be withdrawn from their activity and gathered together for a spell in the great bowl at Epidaurus, if they could discuss *in peace and quiet* the immediate, drastic need of humanity at large, the answer would be forthcoming speedily, and it would be unanimous: REVOLUTION. A world-wide revolution from top to bottom, in every country, in every class, in every realm of consciousness. The fight is not against disease: disease is a by-product. The enemy of man is not germs, but man himself, his pride, his prejudices, his stupidity, his arrogance. No class is immune, no system holds a panacea. *Each one individually must revolt against a way of life which is not his own.* The revolt, to be effective, must be continuous and relentless. It is not enough to overthrow governments, masters, tyrants: *one must overthrow his own preconceived ideas of right and wrong, good and bad, just and unjust*. We must abandon the hard-fought trenches we have dug ourselves into and come out into the open, surrender our arms, our possessions, our rights as individuals, classes, nations, peoples. A billion men *seeking peace* cannot be enslaved (Italics mine).[76]

72 *Ibid.*, p. 42.
73 *Ibid.*, p. 51.
74 *Ibid.*, cf. esp. pp. 82-83, 124-125, 171-173, and 220.
75 J.R. Watmough, *Orphism* (London: Cambridge University Press, 1934), pp. 76-77.
76 *Colossus*, p. 82.

The major cause of humanity's distress, both according to "Father Orpheus" and his latter-day avatars, is the willingness to murder. As Henry Miller puts it: "There will be no peace until murder is eliminated from the heart and mind. Murder is the apex of a broad pyramid whose base is the self. That which stands will have to fall. Everything which man has fought for will have to be relinquished before he can begin to live as man."[77] Even though the function of the singer is to delight the hearts of his audiences with music, both Orpheus and Henry Miller seem to consider the problem of murder sufficiently urgent to be willing to risk resorting to "*preaching* the evil of murder to the men of Thrace." The most homiletic portions of *Colossus*, indeed, drone on in a seemingly inexhaustible and tendentious way about the blight of murder. The problem appears so crucial to Miller, and mankind seems so impervious to the pressing need for a solution, that the Orphic voice is impelled to suspend its capacity to weave enchantments and lapse into straight exhortation:

It is man's task to eradicate the homicidal instinct, which is infinite in its ramifications and manifestations. It is useless to call upon God, as it is futile to meet force with force. Every battle is a marriage conceived in blood and anguish, every war is a defeat to the human spirit. War is only a vast manifestation in dramatic style of the sham, hollow, mock conflicts which take place daily everywhere even in so-called times of peace. Every man contributes his bit to keep the carnage going, even those who seem to be staying aloof. We are all involved, all participating, willy-nilly. The earth is our creation and we must accept the fruits of our creation. As long as we refuse to think in terms of world good and world goods, of world order, world peace, we shall murder and betray one another. It will go on till the crack of doom, if we wish it to be thus. Nothing can bring about a new and better world but our own desire for it. Man kills through fear – and fear is hydra-headed. Once we start slaying there is no end to it.[78]

One might even suppose, in all charity, that it is the evil emanations given off by man's persistence in murder which interfere at this point with Orpheus' capacity to make pleasing music. In fact, elsewhere in *Colossus* Miller insists that as soon as man has ceased "to indulge in murder," he will inherit a "sublime peace" – a peace which is sheer perfection, "as in Mozart's music."[79]

77 *Ibid.*, p. 79.
78 *Ibid.*, pp. 82-83.
79 *Ibid.*, p. 76.

Paradoxically, the best instrument for "taming the wild beasts" lies ready to hand in Miller's own quite impressive gift for casting spells. Miller has written with enthusiasm in several of his books of the great affinity he feels with Saint Francis of Assisi, the Orpheus *redivivus* of the Middle Ages. He even goes so far as to list G.K. Chesterton's *St. Francis of Assisi* in his list of favorites, "The Hundred Books Which Influenced Me Most," in *The Books in My Life.*[80] In his essay on E. Graham Howe, the British psychoanalyst, Miller writes:

> Who...could feel sorry for St. Francis because he threw away his clothes and took the vow of poverty? He was the first man on record, I imagine, who asked for stones instead of bread. Living on the refuse which others threw away he acquired the strength to accomplish miracles, to inspire a joy such as few men have given the world, and, by no means the least of his powers, to write the most sublime and simple, the most eloquent hymn of thanksgiving that we have in all literature: *The Canticle to the Sun*. Let go and let be!...Being is burning, in the truest sense, and if there is to be any peace it will come about through being, not having.[81]

But in an essay on D.H. Lawrence, "Into the Future," Miller is more specific about what should be done to bring men closer to brotherhood. Calling Saint Francis of Assisi "second to Christ," he goes on to say that Francis "made a tremendous impression upon our world – perhaps like those Bodhisattvas who renounce Nirvana in order to aid humanity, he too elected to remain close to us."[82] This is undoubtedly the *askesis* which J.R. Watmough has in mind in *Orphism*, his useful study of the Orphic movement, when he calls the peace of Orpheus a "peace which flows naturally from the life of self-discipline and communion with the source of infinite *Eros*, losing its coldness in brotherly affection, and its austerity in tenderness to brute creation."[83] It calls for an all-embracing gesture of love which Miller himself finally is able to learn to make, toward the close of Part Two of *The Colossus of Maroussi:*

> I sent out a benediction in every direction – to old and young, to the neglected savages in the forgotten parts of the earth, to wild as well as domesticated animals, to the birds of the air, to creeping things, to trees and plants and

80 *Books*, p. 317.
81 *Wisdom*, pp. 38-39.
82 *Ibid.*, p. 161.
83 *Orphism*, p. 80.

flowers, to rocks and lakes and mountains. This is the first day of my life, said I to myself, that I have included everybody and everything on this earth in one thought. I bless the world, every inch of it, every living atom, and it is all alive, breathing like myself, and conscious through and through.[84]

The Orphic aftermath of this lyrical act of benediction occurs in the closing paragraph of Part Two of *Colossus*. Describing his own indignation at the bloody horrors of the Smyrna Massacre of 1922, Miller traces his disgust not only "to the savagery and barbarism of the Turks but to the disgraceful, supine acquiescence of the big powers." He speaks of the shock the world received at the realization that "governments, in the pursuit of their selfish ends, can foster indifference, can reduce to impotence the natural spontaneous impulse of human beings in the face of brutal, wanton slaughter." He is angered that "the armed forces of the great powers...stood idly by under strict command of their leaders while thousands of innocent men, women and children were driven into the water like cattle, shot at, mutilated, burned alive, their hands chopped off when they tried to climb aboard a foreign vessel...."[85]

This calculated indifference to the butchering of human beings reminds Miller of a preliminary warning which was projected on the screens of French movie theaters in the 1930's "whenever a newsreel was shown of the bombing of a Chinese city." The warning "urgently requested" the public "not to display any undue emotion."[86]

But the Orphic poet cannot stand idly by while his brothers and sisters (the contemporary Eurydices in Hades) are being engulfed in death. Once he has arrived at the insight that murder must be abolished, he must share "the image's truth" of this insight with other people. As Wallace Stevens has expressed it, the poet's "function is to make his imagination theirs and...he fulfills himself only as he sees his imagination become the light in the minds of others. His role, in short, is to help people to live their lives."[87] The failure of sympathy symbolized by the Smyrna Massacre and the warning notice in French cinemas are completely contrary to the Orphic spirit of brotherhood. Orpheus, by his very nature, *cares*. The Orphic poets of France,

84 *Colossus*, p. 161.
85 *Ibid.*, p. 172.
86 *Ibid.*, p. 173.
87 Wallace Stevens, *The Necessary Angel* (New York: Vintage Books, 1951), p. 29.

according to Eva Kushner, provide marvelous instances of such understanding. They have consistently displayed

> un immense désir de présence au monde, de participation à la souffrance d'autrui. L'Orphée moderne porte en lui la souffrance des multitudes comme l'Orphée antique, ou même celui que dépeignent les Parnassiens, ressentait la souffrance silencieuse des choses. Il est, d'après l'expression de Jouve, le "résonnateur" de l'histoire, c'est-à-dire qu'il s'efforce de subjuguer sa propre douleur pour pouvoir mieux exprimer celle des autres. Est-ce trop peu? Exprimer ces vicissitudes, c'est déjà signifier aux victimes qu'elles ont été comprises, c'est crier la nécessité de leur porter secours, c'est se montrer, comme l'écrivait Divoire, "poète fraternel." ...il n'y a pas de "complexe d'Orphée"... Souhaitons du moins que le mythe d'Orphée soit encore de temps en temps à l'avenir, comme il l'a été jusqu'à maintenant, l'expression de la fidélité du poète.[88]

Henry Miller's rejoinder to the passive French movie-goers of the 1930's and to those who commit the endless murders which they are being enjoined not to respond to with "undue emotion" occurs at the close of Part Two of *Colossus*, where he writes that "as long as human beings can sit and watch with hands folded while their fellowmen are tortured and butchered so long will civilization be a hollow mockery, a wordy phantom suspended like a mirage above a swelling sea of murdered carcases."[89] But he had put the matter in far more forceful terms near the end of Part One. The italics are Miller's:

> I say the whole world, fanning out in every direction from this spot, was once alive in a way that no man has ever dreamed of. I say there were gods who roamed everywhere, men like us in form and substance, but free, electrically free. When they departed this earth they took with them the one secret which we shall never wrest from them until we too have made ourselves free again. We are to know one day what it is to have life eternal – *when we have ceased to murder.*[90]

88 *Le mythe d'Orphée*, pp. 348-349.
89 *Colossus*, p. 173.
90 *Ibid.*, pp. 93-94.

5. *Orpheus Descending: the Katábasis Theme*

> *"Hell is a different place for each man, or each man has his own particular hell. My descent into the inferno is a descent into the irrational level of existence, where the instincts and blind emotions are loose, where one lives by pure impulse, pure fantasy, and therefore pure madness. No, that is not the inferno. While I am there, I am as unconscious of misery as a man who is drunk; or rather, my misery is a great joy. It is when I become conscious again that I feel unutterable pain."*
>
> Anaïs Nin in *The Diary of Anaïs Nin*

Although the ancient world knew Orpheus primarily as the master music-maker and prophet of the god Dionysos, the "outstanding fact about Orpheus" to the modern imagination – the most potent single episode of the myth – has been "his descent into the underworld"[91] to reclaim his lost Eurydice. This is the feature of the Orpheus story which Western European artists have characteristically seized upon and emphasized, both in the well-known operas on Orpheus (from Monteverdi's *Orfeo* and Gluck's *Orfeo ed Eurydice* to Offenbach's comic *Orphée aux enfers* and Darius Milhaud's *Les malheurs d'Orphée*) and in the poems of Rainer Maria Rilke and the plays and films of Jean Cocteau. And in view of the pervasive nostalgia throughout modern literature for lost states of communal belief or primal well-being, this is not surprising. For, as Walter A. Strauss rightly points out, the Orphic poet "seeks to regenerate himself particularly by means of the voyage downward, with its attendant self-recognition through remembrance and its mandatory self-transformation." According to Strauss, our own era – with its "modern pathos of time

91 E.M. Butler, *Rilke*, p. 341.

and history" and its uncertain sense of identity – has a particularly urgent need for this sort of voyage *downward* wherein the themes of regeneration and reminiscence go hand in hand. Seen in this perspective, the new Orphics are comparable to the Dante of the *Vita Nuova*, who experienced a personal renewal through the love and death of Beatrice very much in the way Orpheus "renews" himself (at least, according to the modern view) through his loss of Eurydice and his descent into hell.[92]

The Orphic *katábasis* (signifying, literally, an act of "downgoing" or "descent") involves, on the most obvious level, a willing confrontation with the dark, chthonic regions of the earth's hidden depths. Dionysos, whose cult Orpheus managed to reconcile with the Apollonian cult of sunlight and open spaces, was a chthonic god.[93] He is usually associated with the earth, with the instincts, and with the regions of darkness. Obviously, the appeal of *katábasis* to generations of modern artists cannot be limited to the literal denotation of the term alone. To the contemporary mind, it has managed to suggest a whole cluster of other meanings: the unknown, the female *mysterium*, the psychic or occult levels of being, even the unconscious mind. The Orphic poet, like the psychoanalyst, is in a position to re-establish the lost accord between human beings and their energies by assisting them to take the plunge into the heart of darkness within, where the lights which they yearn for always lie buried.

In assessing the performance of a modern Orphic writer, therefore, one need not strictly limit the name "Eurydice" to a particular woman who has been snatched into Hades by death. Even in Ancient Greece, W.K.C. Guthrie tells us, "this purely personal errand" had been "magnified into a reason for knowing all about the realms of the dead and possessing peculiar powers as advisor and intercessor." The reason which had originally prompted Orpheus to descend into Hades (fetching Eurydice) soon came to be regarded as secondary to the knowledge he could impart to his followers as to what "the fate of their souls would be."[94]

Nevertheless, it is interesting to note how often, both in art and in psychoanalysis, the efficacious descent into the "underworld" is associated with a woman. C.G. Jung provides a good illustration of

92 *Descent and Return*, pp. 12-13.

93 W.K.C. Guthrie, *Orpheus*, pp. 41-44.

94 *Ibid.*, p. 29.

this in his autobiography. Writing about the manner in which he made his discovery of the archetypes by daring to analyze some disturbing fantasies he was being troubled by in 1913, Jung says that "to grasp the fantasies which were stirring in me 'underground,' " he knew that he had

> to let myself plummet down into them, as it were. I felt not only violent resistance to this, but a distinct fear. For I was afraid of losing command of myself and becoming a prey to the fantasies – and as a psychiatrist I realized only too well what that meant. After prolonged hesitation, however, I saw that there was no other way out. I had to take the chance, had to try to gain power over them; for I realized that if I did not do so, I ran the risk of their gaining power over me.[95]

In the most crucial of a series of "steep" descents into a "cosmic abyss" that feels much like "the land of the dead," he comes upon "an old man with a white beard and a beautiful young girl." The old man, it turns out, is the prophet Elijah and the girl is a blind Salome. Jung explains that only "many years later" was he able to understand the meaning of these mythic figures:

> Salome is an anima figure. She is blind because she does not see the meaning of things. Elijah is the figure of the wise old prophet and represents the factor of intelligence and knowledge; Salome, the erotic element. One might say that the two figures are personifications of Logos and Eros. But such a definition would be excessively intellectual. It is more meaningful to let the figures be what they were for me at the time – namely, events and experiences.[96]

To anyone familiar with the *katábasis* of "Father Orpheus," this trio of figures (dreamer, Salome, Elijah) is immediately recognizable as a combination that crops up with unfailing consistency in Orphic writing and art: Orpheus the seeker, Hermes the *psychopomp* (who helps direct souls through the byways of Hades), and Eurydice the anima figure. Rilke has beautifully memorialized the configuration in his great poem, "Orpheus. Eurydike. Hermes," which describes the famous Attic bas-relief now in the Villa Albani in Rome. And Henry Miller brings Part One of *The Colossus of Maroussi* to a close with a vision of "two men and a woman" measuring off "a plot of land" (the all-important chthonian element) and the vision immediately prompts

95 *Memories*, p. 178.
96 *Ibid.*, p. 182.

him to conclude this section with the words:

> Yes, Lawrence Durrell, zero is what you make it: you take a piece of wet earth and as you squeeze it between your fingers you get two men and a woman standing in a field of Irish green measuring land. The wine has come. I raise my glass. *Salute, Larry me lad, and keep the flag at zero*! In a few more pages we shall revisit Mycenae together and Nancy will lead the way down the bat-slimed stairs to the bottomless well (Miller's italics).[97]

Here is one of those sudden moments of metamorphosis to which readers of Orphic writing are accustomed. Just as the messenger in Corinth on Christmas Eve was transformed, in Miller's imagination, into the messenger/composer of his New York days, so here the "two men and a woman" of the Orphic triad undergo a metamorphosis before our eyes: it is Durrell, at this moment, who is metamorphosed into Orpheus (because of his enthralling talk of "heraldic fields of Irish green" and "zero for pure vision") and his wife Nancy is Eurydice; Miller, at this point, is the Hermes/Elijah of the piece, the wise old "messenger" who has traveled much in Hell and can help others find their way about.

But the metamorphoses of Eurydice are also numerous throughout Henry Miller's writings, not only in the crucial Orphic text, *The Colossus of Maroussi*, but in the long-winded autobiographical trilogies as well. *Tropic of Cancer* and *Tropic of Capricorn* are manifestly patterned as descent-and-ascent narratives whose structures record a series of deaths and re-births. In *Cancer*, the descent is into the tawdry underworld of Paris bars and whore-houses and the ascent is into the author's eventual discovery of his freedom and vocation as a writer; in *Capricorn*, the descent is into the maelstrom of various hellish jobs in America and the ascent is into greater awareness and sympathy for the sufferers in that workaday world and an enlarged sense of himself as a human being. In fact, the design of these two books patently describes a series of upward arcs that move, invariably, from *katábasis* ("death" in one form or another) to *palingénesis* (a restorative "re-birth"). If both books are rather lavishly drenched in promiscuous sex, it should be remembered that sexual intercourse is a sort of physiological *katábasis*. "Dying," as the Elizabethans well understood, is a word that can signify the sexual climax that leads to

97 *Colossus*, pp. 96-97.

conception and the propagation of life.[98]

Tropic of Cancer opens with the words: "I am living at the Villa Borghese. There is not a crumb of dirt anywhere, nor a chair misplaced. We are all alone here and we are dead."[99] But it closes on a distinctly "high" note:

> Christ, before my eyes there shimmered such a golden peace that only a neurotic could dream of turning his eyes away. So quietly flows the Seine that one hardly notices its presence. It is always there, quiet and unobtrusive, like a great artery running through the body. In the wonderful peace that fell over me it seemed as if I had climbed to the top of a high mountain; for a little while I would be able to look around me, to take in the meaning of the landscape.[100]

Tropic of Capricorn, which is dedicated "To Her," opens with the words: "Once you have given up the ghost, everything follows with dead certainty, even in the midst of chaos."[101] It comes to a radiantly triumphant close with the words: "Everything above the horizon is clear to me. It is like Easter Sunday. Death is behind me and birth too. I am going to live now among the life maladies. ...Tack your womb up on my wall, so that I may remember you. We must get going. Tomorrow, tomorrow.."[102] If there is a strong sexual odor binding together the opening and close of these two books, it is only because they are the record of a struggle in the womb of death – dis-

98 There is evidence that Henry Miller also understood this. In a letter dated November 15, 1937, in his *Hamlet* correspondence with Michael Fraenkel (p. 313), Miller writes: "It is an old theme, this love and death. The Elizabethans were saturated with it." Miller dramatizes this knowledge at several points in *Tropic of Cancer*. Early in *Cancer* (p. 130) the narrator says of the character Van Norden: "His one fear is to be left alone, and this fear is so deep and so persistent that even when he is on top of a woman, even when he has welded himself to her, he cannot escape the prison which he has created for himself. 'I try all sorts of things,' he explains to me. 'I even count sometimes, or I begin to think of a problem in philosophy, but it doesn't work. It's like I'm two people, and one of them is watching me all the time. I get so goddamned mad at myself that I could kill myself...and in a way, that's what I do every time I have an orgasm.' " Later in the book (p. 244), Miller wakes up from a sound sleep "with curses of joy on [his] lips" as he repeats a litany of images evoked by his sleep that includes "the door of the womb always on the latch, always open, ready like the tomb."

99 *Cancer*, p. 11.

100 *Ibid.*, p. 305.

101 *Capricorn*, p. 9.

102 *Ibid.*, p. 348.

agreeable on that account, but understandable if the *nature* of the experience is kept in mind.

To the Orphic temperament, "good tidings" must flow inevitably from the tapping of Eurydicean well-springs. Edouard Shuré has pointed out how the Orphic dispensation differs from the Mosaic:

Moise, âprement, jalousement glorifie le Père, le Dieu mâle. Il confie sa garde à un sacerdoce fermé et soumet le peuple à une discipline implacable, sans révélation. Orphée divinement épris de l'Éternel-Féminin, de la Nature, la glorifie au nom de Dieu qui la pénètre et qu'il veut en faire jaillir dans l'humanité divine.[103]

And as every reader of the *Tropic* trilogy knows, the chameleon figure of Mona/Mara (the "Her" to whom *Capricorn* is dedicated) plays a pivotal role in the sequence of descents described in those books. The many-faceted nature of the Eternal-Feminine is a topic Miller never tires of.

The fascination with descent into darkness is easy enough to discern in the *Tropics* and the later *Rosy Crucifixion*, but it is interesting to observe that there is nothing "slapdash" about Miller's treatment of the *katábasis* theme in any of his writings. There is a conscious awareness of its imperatives as a literary and psychological device. Nor is there a narrowing restriction of the Eurydice motif to woman alone. In the chapter devoted to the English writer of romance, H. Rider Haggard, in *The Books in My Life*, Miller writes:

For a long time reality for me was Woman. Which is equivalent to saying – Nature, Myth, Country, Mother, Chaos. I expatiate – to the reader's amazement, no doubt – on a romance called *She*, forgetting that I dedicated the cornerstone of my autobiography to "Her." How very much there was of "She" in "Her"!.. Climbing down the slippery stairs to the pit, which I described in the book on Greece, I experienced the same sensation of horror which I did as a boy when descending into the bowels of Kôr. It seems to me that I have stood before many a bottomless pit, have looked into many a charnel house. But what is more vivid still, more awe-inspiring, is the remembrance that, whenever in my life I have gazed too long upon Beauty, particularly the beauty of the female, I have always experienced a sensation of fear. Fear, and a touch of horror too. What is the origin of this horror? *The dim remembrance of being other than I am now, of being fit (once) to receive the blessings of beauty, the gift of love, the truth of God.* (Italics mine) Why, do we not ask ourselves, why the fatidical beauty in the great heroines of love throughout the ages? Why do they seem so logically and naturally surrounded by death, bolstered by crime, nourished by evil?[104]

103 Edouard Shuré, *Les grands initiés* (Paris: Perrin & Cie. 1927), p. 246.
104 *Books*, pp. 96-97.

Perhaps there is an answer to Miller's question regarding the fascination exercised by "the bowels of Kôr" in his own reference to a "dim remembrance of being other than I am now." Perhaps the *descensus ad infernos* which impels the Orphic writer is not unrelated to what Mircea Eliade calls the *regressus ad uterum* desired by every child. Eliade's words make a compelling case:

> The child lives in a mythical, paradisal time. Psychoanalysis developed techniques capable of showing us the "beginnings" of our personal history, and especially of identifying the particular event that put an end to the bliss of childhood and determined the future orientation of our life... [T] hat "going back," of which Freud saw the importance in understanding man and, especially, in healing him, was already practiced in non-European cultures. After all that we have said concerning the hope of renewing the World by repeating the cosmogony, it is not difficult to grasp the basis for these practices: the individual's return to the origin is conceived as an opportunity for renewing and regenerating the existence of him who undertakes it.. From the structural point of view, the return to the womb corresponds to the reversion of the Universe to the "chaotic" or embryonic state. The prenatal darkness corresponds to the Night before Creation... [I] nitiation rituals involving a return to the womb have, of course, a mythical model. But even more interesting than the myths relating to initiation rites of *regressus ad uterum* are those that narrate the adventures of Heroes or shamans and magicians who accomplished the *regressus* in their flesh-and-blood bodies, not symbolically. A large number of myths feature (1) a hero being swallowed by a sea monster and emerging victorious after breaking through the monster's belly; (2) initiatory passage through a *vagina dentata*, or the dangerous descent into a cave or crevice assimilated to the mouth or the uterus of Mother Earth. All these adventures are in fact initiatory ordeals, after accomplishing which the victorious hero acquires a new mode of being.[105]

In other words, the perilous *katábasis* with which we have been concerned may be a journey consciously undertaken by someone with a view to finding life-giving answers to the nagging question of

105 Mircea Eliade, *Myth and Reality* (New York: Harper & Row, 1963), pp. 77-81. Certainly there are differences between the Orphic descent to regain a specific loss and the aching, compelled descent of a Freudian psychoanalytic search, especially inasmuch as the latter is clinically supervised by a medical specialist and the former is not. But the Orphic *katábasis* is also an aching descent and its aim is likewise to restore the sufferer's equilibrium. Henry Miller seems to have sensed the connection between the two, since in the mid-1930's he met and came under the spell of such practitioners as E. Graham Howe and Otto Rank and appears to have seriously worked as a lay analyst himself. Cf. F.-J. Temple, *Henry Miller*, p. 111, and Henry Miller's own extended chronology of his life in *My Life and Times* (New York: Playboy Press, 1971).

happiness that persist in the minds of all of us after the expulsion from the womb.

The symbol of the "cave," which Eliade associates with "Mother Earth," figures prominently in visions which have been experienced and written about by both C.G. Jung and Henry Miller – in Jung's case, at the threshold of the Elijah/Salome self-analysis which led to his discovery of the archetypes of the collective unconscious in 1913, and in Miller's case, just prior to his euphoric discovery at Phaestos in 1939 that all creation is "conscious through and through" and that he inhabits "the abode of the heavenly queens." Aside from slight differences in the sequence of the events recorded, the scenarios of these initiatory "nightmares" which the two men describe are so strikingly alike that I give them in parallel columns so as to better highlight their similarities:

I. (Jung)

I was sitting at my desk once more, thinking over my fears. Then I let myself drop. Suddenly it was as though the ground literally gave way beneath my feet, and I plunged down into dark depths. I could not fend off a feeling of panic. But then, abruptly, at not too great a depth, I landed on my feet in a soft, sticky mass. I felt great relief, although I was apparently in complete darkness....[I] waded knee deep... to the other end of the cave where, on a projecting rock, I saw a glowing red crystal. I grasped the stone, lifted it, and discovered a hollow underneath. ...Dazzled by the light, I wanted to replace the stone upon the opening, but then a fluid welled out. It was blood. A thick jet of it leaped up, and I felt nauseated. It seemed to me that the blood continued to spurt for an unendurably long time. At last it ceased, and the vision came to an end.[106]

II. (Miller)

I fell into a nightmare. I was being gently and endlessly rocked by the omnipotent Zeus in a burning cradle. I was toasted to a crisp and then gently dumped into a sea of blood. I swam ceaselessly amidst dismembered bodies marked with the cross and the crescent. I came at last to a rock-ribbed shore. It was bare and absolutely deserted of man. I wandered to a cave in the side of a mountain. In the shivery depths I saw a great heart bright as a ruby suspended from the vault by a huge web. It was beating and with each beat there fell to the ground a huge gout of blood. It was too large to be the heart of any living creature. It was larger even than the heart of a god. It is like the heart of agony, I said aloud, and as I spoke it vanished and a great darkness fell over me. Whereupon I sank down, exhausted, and fell into a sob that reverberated from every part of the cave and finally suffocated me.[107]

106 *Memories*, p. 179.
107 *Colossus*, p. 156.

Miller, the artist, leaves the vision unexamined in the form of a brief prose poem laid out on the page; Jung, the professional psychoanalyst, goes on to identify it as a "hero and solar myth, a drama of death and renewal."[108]

It is consequently appropriate that *The Colossus of Maroussi* should open, as I mentioned earlier, with a preliminary visit to the French valley of the Dordogne and the Cro-Magnon caves which are located there. Miller, it is worth recalling, had identified the "black, mysterious river at Dômme" (which sounds not unlike the mythical river Lethe in this evocative characterization) with the author of *Sonnets to Orpheus* and, in a letter of June 10, 1939, to Anaïs Nin, he even calls this region the place "where the 'gouffre' is" and "God's own country,"[109] a much more explicit confession of the quasi-religious feelings it inspired in him. The rest of Miller's description of the Dordogne region is a rather remarkable corroboration of what Jung has written about his own "cave" vision as a psychic re-enactment of a drama of death and renewal. Miller writes that "the fossilized evidences of the great caves...point to a condition of life rather bewildering and terrifying," but he goes on to call this spot an ideal place of renewal:

> I believe that this great peaceful region of France will always be a sacred spot for man and that when the cities have killed off the poets this will be the refuge and the cradle of the poets to come. I repeat, it was most important for me to have seen the Dordogne: it gives me hope for the future of the race, for the future of the earth itself. France may one day exist no more, but the Dordogne will live on just as dreams live on and nourish the souls of men. [110]

The imagery of death and re-birth is especially striking on this whole page. The artful conjoining of ancient *caves*, chthonic *abysses*, age-old *violence*, and flowing *water* strongly suggests a deliberate mosaic of metaphor exploited by Miller to foreshadow the death-and-birth processes which the book will deal with, literally as well as figuratively, later on. It is the first of a sequence of "bottomless pits" and Miller uses it skillfully at the beginning to adumbrate others to come.

Indeed, at the end of his first excursion, after he settles down in

108 *Memories*, p. 179.
109 *Letters to Anaïs Nin*, pp. 161-162.
110 *Colossus*, p. 5.

Corfu with the Durrells, Miller brings the self-same conjunction of symbols into play but to describe a much more somber and more dramatic setting:

> As we climbed a weird melody greeted us from above. Like the heavy mist sweeping up from the sea, it enveloped us in its *nostalgic* folds [the word "nostalgic" is derived from the Greek word *nóstos*, meaning "womb"] and then as suddenly *died away*. When we had risen another few hundred feet we came upon a clearing in the midst of which was a huge vat filled with a poisonous liquid, an insecticide for the olive trees, which the young women were stirring as they sang. It was a song of death which blended singularly with the mist-laden landscape. Here and there, where the vaporish clouds had rolled apart to reveal a clump of trees or a bare, *jagged fang-like snag of rocks*, the reverberations of their haunting melody sang out like a choir of brass in an orchestra. Now and then a great blue area of sea rose out of the fog, not at the level of the earth but in *some middle realm between heaven and earth*, as though after a typhoon.... We took spells of resting at the edge of the precipice, too fascinated by the spectacle to continue on *through the pass* into the *clear, bright work-a-day world* of the little mountain village beyond. In that operatic realm, where the Tao Teh King and the ancient Vedas fused dramatically in contrapuntal confusion, the taste of the light Greek cigarette was even more like straw.... Here the most frightful, vengeful massacres must have been perpetrated again and again throughout the endless *bloody* past of man. It is a trap devised by Nature herself for man's undoing. Greece is full of such *death*-traps.... Here too men of the Pythagorean stripe must have stopped to meditate in silence and solitude, gaining *fresh* clarity, *fresh* vision, from the dust-strewn place of carnage. All Greece is diademed with such antinomian spots; it is perhaps the explanation for the fact that Greece has *emancipated* itself as a country, a nation, a people, in order to continue as the luminous carrefour of a *changing humanity* (Italics mine).[111]

But Miller's many uses of *katábasis* are not limited merely to solemn re-enactments of sacramental (or quasi-sacramental) returns to "the bowels of Mother Earth" and the refreshenings that follow such returns. Several times in *The Colossus of Maroussi*, he resorts to literary strategies that poke wonderful fun at his obsessive descents in search of answers – parody, burlesque, even outright buffoonery. Here is a passage in which Miller describes himself watching Katsimbalis taking a nap, his mouth "pried open now in a prolonged mute gasp like the mouth of a fish suffocating with air." Notice that though Orpheus/Katsimbalis has been made to suffer this rather outrageous meta-

111 *Ibid*., pp. 20-22.

morphosis, his lost "Eurydice" (the eloquent voice now hidden inside him) still resides within specifically *chthonian* depths (the references to "earth" and "clay"). And the "descent" is, as ever, fraught with "perils":

By what miracle is the hot magma of the earth transformed into that which we call speech? If out of clay such an abstract medium as words can be shaped what is to hinder us from leaving our bodies at will and taking up our abode on other planets or between the planets? What is to prevent us from rearranging all life, atomic, molecular, corporeal, stellar, divine? Why should we stop at words, or at planets, or at divinity? Who or what is powerful enough to eradicate this miraculous leaven which we bear within us like a seed and which, after we have embraced in our mind all the universe, is nothing more than a seed – since to say universe is as easy as to say seed, and we have yet to say greater things, things beyond saying, things limitless and inconceivable, things which no trick of language can encompass. *You* lying there, I was saying to myself, where has that voice gone? Into what inky crevices are you crawling with your ganglionic feelers? Who are you, *what* are you now in drugged silence? Are you fish? Are you spongy root? Are you *you*? If I should bash your skull in now would all be lost – the music, the narcotic vapors, the glissandos, the rugged parentheses, the priapic snorts, the law of diminishing returns, the pebbles between stutters, the shutters you pull down over naked crimes? If I bore into you now with an awl, here at the temple, will there come out with the blood a single tangible clue?[112]

In addition to being a mock-*katábasis* into the depths of a man's speech-making powers, this passage offers an impressive example of the perennial mutations of Orpheus. When Miller uses the rhetorical appositive "I was saying to myself" – "*You* lying there, I was saying to myself, where has that voice gone?" – a subtle ambiguity is created. One gets the impression, for a moment, that the Katsimbalis whom Miller is talking to is merely a projection of his own garrulous self. And in fact, both the speaker and the sleeper are in a very real sense mere *alter ego's* of the unkillable Orpheus. "He comes and goes," as Rilke reminds us.

In each of the three major parts of *The Colossus of Maroussi*, Miller plays variations on the theme of *katábasis* that employ differing tonalities and intensities, at times comical and at times serious, depending on their context and on Miller's artistic aims of the moment. The manner in which he handles the motif of *descensus ad infernos* in

112 *Ibid.*, pp. 73-74.

each part, in fact, seems outwardly to jibe with a definite gradation of moods extending from Part One through Part Three: the infernal, the purgatorial, the paradisaical.

During much of Part One, Miller's mood is tinged with anxiety due to the approach of the war; it is also rather retrospective. And the strife-ridden modern world to which he is still close enough to look back persists in vexing Miller's spirit:

> The earth pullulates with adventurous spirits who populate it with death: these are the souls who, bent upon conquest, fill the outer corridors of space with strife and bickering. What gives a phantasmal hue to life is this wretched shadow play between ghoul and ghost. The panic and confusion which grips the soul of the wanderer is the reverberation of the pandemonium created by the lost and the damned.[113]

There is a prolongation, here, of the feelings of dread he had described early in Part One in connection with the "poison song" which he had heard the young women sing in Corfu. Despite the glimmerings of light and joy that obtrude here and there in Part One, the inferno-feeling cannot be altogether dispelled.

Even the crucial descent into the tomb of Agamemnon to which I alluded earlier, a "descent" efficacious enough to enable Miller upon "re-birth" (emergence) to "take flight...as pure spirit,"[114] leaves Miller deeply troubled concerning the fate of a world being menaced, at that very moment (Summer 1939), by a recurrence of terrible atavistic violence:

> Here at this spot, now dedicated to the memory of Agamemnon, some foul and hidden crime blasted the hopes of man. Two worlds lie juxtaposed, the one before, the one after the crime. The crime contains the riddle, as deep as salvation itself. Spades and shovels will uncover nothing of any import. The diggers are blind, feeling their way towards something they will never see. Everything that is unmasked crumbles at the touch. Worlds crumble too, in the same way. We can dig in eternally, like moles, but fear will be ever upon us, clawing us, raping us from the rear.[115]

On the previous page, Miller had referred to Mycenae as a veritable inferno, "the great shining bulge of horror, the high slope whence

113 *Ibid.*, p. 81.
114 *Ibid.*, p. 93.
115 *Ibid.*, p. 94.

man, having attained his zenith, slipped back and fell into the bottomless pit."[116]

It's for this reason that I feel that Part One of *Colossus* truly pivots upon the *katábasis* at Corinth, which Miller records around the midpoint of this section of the book. This is the descent into the chthonic depths – the realm of the crucified Dionysos, it must be remembered – which most evocatively brings together the hellish threads that bind the whole world in its web of common suffering:

> In each place I open a new vein of experience, a miner digging deeper into the earth, approaching the heart of the star which is not yet extinguished. The light is no longer solar or lunar; it is the starry light of the planet to which man has given life. The earth is alive to its innermost depths; at the center it is a sun in the form of a man crucified. The sun bleeds on its cross in the hidden depths. The sun is man struggling to emerge towards another light. From light to light, from calvary to calvary. The earth song....[117]

Part Two of *Colossus*, by contrast, may be thought of as "purgatorial." I have already pointed out how it is climaxed with a reference to the Smyrna Massacre and Miller's preachy insistence that the world must purge itself of the impulse to murder. But the chapter as a whole dwells on the varieties of *purity*, from the purity of the life-style he imagines once obtained in primaeval Knossos to the striking purity of the self-transforming light he himself experiences towards the close. In fact, one is even tempted to wonder whether the references to a severe case of diarrhoea which Miller conspicuously interjects at various points in this part of the book are not intended, in a semi-burlesque fashion, to fit into such a scheme of purification![118]

It's in Part Two of the book that Miller is decisively made aware that the purging light of Greece is a light in which "*all ugliness* is obliterated (my italics)"[119] and the crucial *katábasis* here is unquestionably the dazzling illumination achieved at Phaestos in the company of Kyrios Alexandros. The "light" he witnesses at that spot finally

116 Cf. Prof. George E. Mylonas, *Eleusis and the Eleusinian Mysteries* (Princeton: Princeton University Press, 1961), p. 268, note 179 *infra*, for a reference to "the bottomless pit" as an instance of specifically "Orphic" language used to designate Hell or Tartarus.
117 *Colossus*, p. 57.
118 *Ibid.*, pp. 128-129 and 130-131, where Mr. Tsoutsou appears to symbolize "corruption," whereas diarrhoea symbolizes self-purification or catharsis.
119 *Ibid.*, p. 133.

purges Miller of his own resentments, hatreds, and rivalries. In the benediction he sends out "in every direction," he becomes aware that this is "the first day of my life...that I have included everybody and everything on this earth in one thought."[120] From this vantage point, things take on for him a sort of prelapsarian purity:

From this sublime, serene height it has all the appearance of the Garden of Eden. At the very gates of Paradise the descendants of Zeus halted here on their way to eternity to cast a last look earthward and saw with the eyes of innocents that the earth is indeed what they had always dreamed it to be: a place of beauty and joy and peace. In his heart man is angelic; in his heart man is united with the whole world.[121]

The sense of paradisaical "hush"[122] pervading the whole of Part Three is so compelling that when the time arrives to return with the Durrells "down the bat-slimed stairs to the bottomless well" at Mycenae near the close of the book, Miller's new-found happiness and an apparent determination not to risk losing it induce him to resort outright to a comic travesty of *katábasis*, upon which he now turns his back. Through the use of telling comic exaggeration, he dramatizes his refusal to willingly accept a negation of the "light" which he loves so much:

Durrell went first, Nancy next, and I followed gingerly behind. About half-way down we halted instinctively and debated whether to go any further. I experienced the same feeling of terror as I had the first time with Katsimbalis, more, if anything, since we had descended deeper into the bowels of the earth. I had two distinct fears – one, that the slender buttress at the head of the stairs would give way and leave us to smother to death in utter darkness, and two, that a mis-step would send me slithering down into the pit amidst a spawn of snakes, lizards and bats. I was tremendously relieved when Durrell, after much persuasion, consented to abandon the descent. I was thankful that I was first now instead of last. When we reached the surface I was in a cold sweat and mentally still going through the motions of kicking off the demons who were trying to drag me back into the horror-laden mire. Thinking back on it now, after a lapse of months, I honestly believe I would rather be shot than forced to descend that staircase alone. In fact, I think I would die of heart failure before ever reaching the bottom.[123]

120 *Ibid*., p. 161.
121 *Ibid*., p. 162.
122 *Ibid*., p. 189.
123 *Ibid*., p. 215.

In a very real sense, however, Miller is conscious that the "veritable rebirth"[124] he had undergone earlier inside Agamemnon's tomb had bestowed on him a genuine immunity to such horrors, and the remaining thirty pages of *Colossus* attest eloquently to his awareness that he now possesses this immunity. In a letter he wrote to Anaïs Nin aboard the *Exochorda* dated January 12, 1940, just two weeks after leaving Greece, Miller makes even more explicit this personal conviction of imperviousness to the "darkness" which a successfully completed *katábasis* entails:

And now on the boat, in the midst of the American scene, I feel as though I am living with people who are not yet born, with monsters who escaped from the womb before their time. I am no longer in communication with anything. I am in a world of broken eggshells. Nothing is being hatched. Eggs are no longer in demand. It is like the after-death state which the Tibetans talk about. What is happening about me is just as real as if it were life, but it is not life. It is something somewhere between death and birth. We shall come to port like a cargo of well-nourished, well-preserved and exceedingly animated ghosts. Through the radio we are permitted to keep in touch with everything that is going on in the world, but the world seems always out of reach. It is the place where things have just happened or are about to happen. But for us nothing is happening. Dimly I seem to remember that but a short time ago I was alive, alive in full sunlight. There is another light which envelops me now. It is like the illumination from a cold mechanical reflector. The house is dark. Only the stage is lit up. The curtain is rising.[125]

What the curtain is "rising" upon, it can be argued, is what Orpheus – the Musician, the Voyager, the Peace-Maker, and the Down-Goer – had been reaching out for all along: "immortality."

124 *Ibid*., p. 237.
125 *Letters to Anaïs Nin*, p. 194.

6. *Orpheus as Divinity: the Immortality Motif*

"What fascinates me is that anything so dead and buried as I was could be resuscitated, and not just once, but innumerable times. And not only that, but each time I faded out I plunged deeper than ever into the void, so that with each resuscitation the miracle becomes greater. And never any stigmata! The man who is reborn is always the same man, more and more himself with each rebirth.... The identity which was lost is recovered. Man walks forth from his open wound, from the grave which he had carried about with him so long."

Henry Miller in *Tropic of Capricorn*

If the dark earth is the domain of Dionysos, the light (sun, open spaces, stars) is associated in the Greek mind with the god Apollo. Not only did Orpheus' music share with Apollo's the power to gather wild beasts around him and calm their wildness, but the Apollonian temper of Orpheus and his worship of the immortal sun (Helios) "support the opinion that he belonged at first to the sunny open-air religion of the Hellenes,"[126] which placed great emphasis on life after death. One of Orpheus' greatest achievements, as I have indicated earlier, was his brilliant reconciliation of the Dionysian death-instinct with the placid Apollonian celebration of everlasting life and light. Henry Miller shows an uncanny affinity with this Orphic resolution. One of the many ways he does this, in *The Colossus of Maroussi*, is by adumbrating the book's entire scheme of descent-and-re-emergence at the very outset by means of Betty Ryan's "peculiar" account of her travels about the world, an account in which both she and Miller are "lost" as they pass through China and North Africa (like Dante in his "dark

126 W.K.C. Guthrie, *Orpheus*, p. 29.

forest?") and then "found" – in the "blinding light of Greece," in "a world of light."[127]

The Orphics appear to have understood very well that the dangers of *katábasis* were merely a prelude to *palingénesis*, but they knew equally well that these hazards were an indispensable prelude. (This is no less true of their modern counterparts: Dante's *Paradiso* follows his *Inferno*, Saint John of the Cross' *Ascent of Mount Carmel* follows *The Dark Night of the Soul*, Rimbaud's *Illuminations* – some parts of it, at least, according to scholars like Ruff and Fowlie – follows *A Season in Hell*.) The special importance of the Orphics is that they grasped the problem of the tragic duality of body and soul; they tended to regard the body as a prison (*soma-sema*) from which the soul perennially strove to escape to some higher plane of reality.[128] Mircea Eliade provides an excellent analogue of this death-to-rebirth (or darkness-to-light) syndrome in terms of shamanistic initiation. According to Eliade, the shaman descends into the belly of a giant or a monster "in order to learn *science* or *wisdom*." He remains there for three years "to resolve the enigma of life and see into the future." Eliade speaks of this descent as "equivalent to a descent into Hell" during which "all personality is dissolved [the Dionysian dismemberment]" and "Death... symbolizes wisdom." It's for this reason, he maintains, that the dead have come to be considered omniscient and prophetic and that poets and visionaries seek inspiration "among the tombs":

> [T]he man of the archaic societies strove to conquer death by according it such an importance that, in the final reckoning, death ceased to present itself as a cessation and became a *rite of passage*. In other words, to the primitive one is forever dying to something that was not essential; one is dying to the profane life...[I]f one knows death already *here below*, if one is continually dying countless deaths in order to be reborn to *something else* – to something that does not belong to the Earth but participates in the sacred – then one is living, we may say, a *beginning of immortality* (Eliade's italics).[129]

The achievement of "immortality," as this passage by Eliade suggests, is posited on a willingness to foreswear "something that [is] not essential" – the profane, the gross, the merely somatic.

127 *Colossus*, pp. 3-4.
128 W.K.C. Guthrie, *Orpheus*, p. 84 *infra* and p. 157.
129 *Myths, Dreams, Mysteries*, pp. 225-227.

Henry Miller, whose shamanistic *askesis* (or method of spiritual self-discipline) was shaped in Brooklyn and some of the dingier precincts of 1930's Paris, would say it is posited on "surrender." There is a passage early on in *Colossus* which reads almost like a paraphrase of Eliade's description of the way of the shaman:

> Our diseases are our attachments, be they habits, ideologies, ideals, principles, possessions, phobias, gods, cults, religions, what you please. Good wages can be a disease just as much as bad wages. Leisure can be just as great a disease as work. Whatever we cling to, even if it be hope or faith, can be the disease which carries us off. Surrender is absolute: if you cling to even the tiniest crumb you nourish the germ which will devour you. As for clinging to God, God long ago abandoned us in order that we might realize the joy of attaining godhood through our own efforts.[130]

But the way of the shaman is also the way of Orpheus. Miller's concept is remarkably close to the Orphic eschatology, as expounded by W.K.C. Guthrie:

> The beginnings of salvation lie within every one of us, since they are identical with the germ of divinity which it is our nature as human beings to possess... To misuse the divine is to use it to our own damnation. Hence the believer will try to lead the Orphic life...which aims at the exaltation and purification of our Dionysiac nature in order that we may in the end shake off the last trammels of our earthly selves and become actually, what we are now potentially, gods instead of mortals.[131]

With the shaman and with Orpheus, Henry Miller believes in the imperative of "dying to something that was not essential" in order to accede to that "*something else*" which Mircea Eliade calls "*a beginning of immortality*."

Part Three of *The Colossus of Maroussis* – the part I have designated the most "paradisaical" in the book – actually culminates in a weird visit to an Athenian refugee quarter where an Armenian soothsayer completely unknown to Miller proclaims Miller *literally* "immortal"! But it is an interesting structural feature of the book that this rather extravagant episode, on which Miller dwells solemnly and at great length, is carefully led up to in the two previous sections. There is a clearly discernible integrative method to this doctrinal

130 *Colossus*, p. 78.
131 *Orpheus*, p. 156.

madness, if madness it be in the eyes of Miller's uninitiated readers.

Miller's first reference to immortality in *Colossus* occurs at the very beginning when he speaks of the Dordogne region as a place which will always "live on just as dreams live on and nourish the souls of men."[132] Soon after, he makes an oblique reference to immortality when he speaks of Greece as a place that "still remains under the protection of the Creator," a place where "God's magic is still at work."[133] In one of his earliest excursions in Greece – the trip to the island of Hydra – Miller readily identifies the promise of immortality with the place itself:

> After the uterine illumination comes the ordeal of rock out of which must be born the spark which is to fire the world. I speak in broad, swift images because to move from place to place in Greece is to become aware of the stirring, fateful drama of the race as it circles from paradise to paradise. Each halt is a stepping stone along a path marked out by the gods. They are stations of rest, of prayer, of meditation, of deed, of sacrifice, of transfiguration. At no point along the way is it marked FINIS. The very rocks, and nowhere on earth had God been so lavish with them as in Greece, are symbols of *life eternal*.[134]

At Mycenae, later, Miller feels certain that in a place so extraordinary "the gods once walked the earth," and he goes on to suggest that their faculties now "lie dormant" in us and we must await their return.[135] It's only a few pages later that, after making his own descent into Agamemnon's tomb, he arrives at this conclusion (quoted earlier): "I say there were gods who roamed everywhere, men like us in form and substance.... We are to know one day what it is to have life eternal – *when we have ceased to murder*!"[136] While the gods were still visible in Mycenae, Apollo's presence was felt everywhere. Miller's reverie, while standing over the ruins of Mycenae, inspires some of his most visionary lines: "A world of light is born. Man looks at man with new eyes. He is awed, smitten by his own gleaming image reflected everywhere."[137] In the afterglow of this "pure vision" ("the idea of Zero in the heraldic sense"), Miller brings Part One to a close.

132 *Colossus*, p. 5.
133 *Ibid.*, p. 15.
134 *Ibid.*, pp. 55-56.
135 *Ibid.*, p. 86.
136 *Ibid.*, pp. 93-94.
137 *Ibid.*, pp. 90-91.

Part Two virtually opens with a symbolically "sensational" visit with Durrell to the astronomical observatory in Athens, where Miller gets his first glimpse of the stars through an observatory telescope. Durrell's comment, on gazing at the Pleiades, is: "*Rosicrucian*!" Miller, hardly less enthusiastic, is almost at a loss to describe

> the effect of that first breathless vision of a splintered star world. The image I shall always retain is that of Chartres, an effulgent rose window shattered by a hand grenade. I mean it in a double or triple sense – of awesome, indestructible beauty, of cosmic violation, of world ruin suspended in the sky like a fatal omen, of the *eternality* of beauty even when blasted and desecrated. "As above, so below," runs the famous saying of Hermes Trismegistus (Italics mine).[138]

It's interesting to note that another famous mystagogue, C.G. Jung, shares Hermes Trismegistus' and Henry Miller's intuitive feeling about the "correspondences" that exist between the upper and lower: "Our psyche is set up in accord with the structure of the universe, and what happens in the macrocosm likewise happens in the infinitesimal and most subjective reaches of the psyche. For that reason the God image is always a projection of the inner experience of a powerful vis-à-vis."[139]

Miller had already referred, in a seemingly off-handed fashion early in Part One, to "studying the stars" with a small telescope on a beach in Corfu. He immediately drops the incident in *Colossus*. But in a letter that he wrote to Anaïs Nin right after the event, he tells her about this episode in much greater detail:

> [B]y a strange paradox, one evening, when we were studying the stars attentively, from gazing at them so long, so steadfastly, so earnestly, I suddenly realized that what we call light is really darkness, compared to that blaze which there must be when one gets off the earth and well out in space. The occultists speak of the sun behind the sun, the real sun. We see only the lens, as it were, of something so blazingly brilliant that it would annihilate us if we could see it. But again, the real thing isn't see-able. To apprehend the real glow of the sun one needs other senses.... I suddenly realized that the universe is nothing but light, light, light! I realized more – that actually there is no light and dark at all! In this great void – space – in which everything swims there in a nameless energy which is by turns light, heat, motion, etc., anything and everything we are capable of making or naming or using, once we comprehend. Whatever world we

138 *Ibid.*, pp. 102-103.
139 *Memories*, p. 335.

have represents the maximum of our penetration of this unceasing void – which again is not emptiness, but its very opposite.[140]

A true son of "Father Orpheus" could do no less than "comprehend" that star-stuff and soul-stuff – "this unceasing void" – are not unrelated. For W.K.C. Guthrie cites no less an authority than Aristotle on the Orphic belief that the soul is an imprisoned spark of *aither* which is destined "to fly to the stars, or become a star, for the *aither* is the substance of which the stars existing as they do in these pure outer regions, are made."[141] According to Plato's *Timaeus*, writes Guthrie, when the Creator first made individual souls, He created them "equal in number to the stars" and "assigned each one to a star." While the souls were still inhabitants of the stars, the Creator taught them "the nature of the Universe." Plato goes on to explain that as soon as the souls are placed in bodies "by the workings of necessity," they obtain, first of all, "the faculty of sensation...aroused in them as a result of violent impressions," and secondly "love, mingled with pleasure and pain, and in addition to these, fear and anger and all the passions which either result from these or are their contraries...."[142] And, not surprisingly, toward the close of Part Two of *Colossus*, in anticipation of his light-filled visit to Phaestos, Miller

felt that the earth was bearing me through a zone I had never been carried through before. I was a little *nearer to the stars* and the *ether* was charged with their *nearness*.... It was *nostalgic*; it awakened those ageless hordes of ancestral men who stand with eyes closed, like trees after the passing of a flood, in the *ever-moving* stream of the blood.... The earth became again that strange one-legged creature which pegs and wobbles through diamond-pointed fields, passing faithfully through all the habitations of its solar creation; became that which it will be to the end and which in becoming transmogrifies the obscene goat [Miller is a Capricorn] into the stillness of *that which always was*, since there is no other, not even the possibility of a simulacrum (Italics mine).[143]

This near-obsessive concern with immortality culminates, as I mentioned earlier, in Part Three of *Colossus* during a visit by Miller and Katsimbalis to the home of an Armenian soothsayer by the name of Aram Hourabedian. The Apollonian *core* of Hourabedian's modest

140 *Letters to Anaïs Nin*, pp. 186-187.
141 *Orpheus*, p. 185.
142 *Ibid.*, p. 186.
143 *Colossus*, pp. 152-153.

home, "in the heart of the labyrinth" of a neighborhood noted for its Dionysian disorder and confusion, is insisted upon in Miller's own carefully ordered description of the refugee quarter: "In the midst of the most terrible poverty and suffering there nevertheless emanated a glow which was holy... Nor did one have the slightest desire to laugh at seeing a squalid hut surmounted by an improvised *solarium* made of pieces of tin."[144] Prophecy, it will be remembered, was the special province of the sun-god Apollo. And while waiting for the soothsayer himself to appear, Miller launches into quasi-prophetic speculations (inspired by a volume of Jules Verne through which he is riffling while waiting) about the shape of the human future. The room Miller is finally ushered into is "extremely clean and orderly,"[145] qualities befitting the domicile of an avatar of Apollo.

Before quoting (at some length) Miller's account of Orpheus/Hourabedian's reading, it's worth mentioning that Miller had been consciously convinced, before accompanying Katsimbalis there, that such a consultation could only result in "a good or bad reading of *one's own mind* (Italics mine)."[146] The proof of the soothsayer's skills, in this strange episode, would simply lie in his ability to validate and confirm "the image's truth" of the immortality motif with which the subject of the reading had already acquainted his readers in the first two parts of his book. But in addition, Hourabedian is inordinately perceptive in his discernment of the Orphic "duality" in Henry Miller – light (Apollo)/earth (Dionysos):

He said that I had led not only *a dual life* (I believe he used the word schizophrenic) but a multiple life and that nobody really understood me, not even my closest friends. But soon, he said, all this was to cease. At a certain date, which he gave me, I would find a clear, open path ahead of me; before dying I would bring great joy to the world, to everybody in the world, he emphasized, and my greatest enemy would bow down before me and beg my forgiveness. He said that I would enjoy before my death the greatest honors, the greatest rewards which man can confer upon man. I would make three trips to the Orient where among other things, I would meet a man who would understand me as no one had and that this meeting was absolutely indispensable for the both of us. That on my last visit to the Orient I would never return, neither would I die, but vanish *in the light*. I interrupted him here to ask if he meant by that that I

144 *Ibid.*, p. 200.
145 *Ibid.*, p. 202.
146 *Ibid.*, p. 199.

would be immortal through my works or my deeds, and he answered solemnly and most significantly that he did not, that he meant simply and literally that I would never die. At this I confess I felt startled and I glanced at Katsimbalis, without saying a word, to make sure that I had heard correctly.

He went on to tell me that there were signs and indications given which he himself could not understand but which he would relate to me exactly as they were given. Not at all surprised by this I begged him to do so, adding that I would understand quite well myself. He was particularly baffled, and impressed, it seemed, by the fact that I had *all the signs of divinity* and at the same time my feet were *chained to the earth*. He paused to explain himself to Katsimbalis in Greek, obviously quite moved and obviously fearful to offer an interpretation of which he was not certain. Turning to me again he made it clear, both by his speech and by his words, that he considered it a rare privilege to be in the presence of such a one as myself. He confessed that he had never seen the indications for such a splendid career as now lay before me. He asked me pertinently if I had not escaped death several times. "In fact," he added, hardly waiting for confirmation, "you have always miraculously escaped whenever a situation became desperate or unbearable. You always will. You lead a charmed life. I want you to remember my words, when danger confronts you again – that however perilous the situation you must never give up, you will be saved. You are like a ship *with two rudders*: when one gives out the other will function. In addition, you are equipped with wings: you can take flight when those about you must perish. You are protected (Italics mine throughout)."[147]

Walter A. Strauss, as we have seen, calls Orpheus "truly a reconciler of opposites: he is the fusion of the radiant solar enlightenment of Apollo and the somber subterranean knowledge of Dionysos."[148] This is something Henry Miller understood somewhat better about himself after he had consulted an obscure Armenian soothsayer in the slums of Athens. I can think of no better way of illustrating this new understanding of his than by quoting freely from a letter he wrote to Anaïs Nin from Delphi on December 21, 1939, just a few days before leaving Greece. It's noteworthy that, in addition to reconciling Dionysos with Apollo, this revealing letter once more adverts to Miller's need to reconcile the outer with the inner – the spectacle with the spectator. The one way to fully experience the Greek miracle, he seems to suggest, is to *become* that miracle:

Here they held their chariot races – in the clouds, far above the Temple of Apollo and the spring whose waters brought the gift of prophecy.... From all

147 *Ibid.*, pp. 202-204.
148 *Descent and Return*, p. 18.

over the world the conquering nations sent their gifts to Apollo. Neptune played a part also – perhaps in the dim memory of Atlantean days. They say that the Minoans of Crete inaugurated the cult of Apollo.... For me the great experience began before I ever reached Delphi, before Thebes even. Before you come to the land of the Boeotians is a narrow and frightening pass, you descend into a vortex of agonized rocks, a veritable deathtrap near which somewhere was situated the famous Sphinx whom Oedipus questioned.... Suddenly the scene changes. You come into the great smiling plain of Thebes.... It is so lovely, so intimate, so silent, so peaceful, so beautifully luminous that I wring my hands with desperate joy. It is the maximum of bliss.... Suddenly there is a bend in the road and it takes my breath away. The earth is bubbling like a great cauldron of boiling water – only that this liquid mass is one endless patch of cultivated land – a sea of varied colors like great sails fastened down upon a swollen sea. I have no more words, no more emotion to expend. I am almost out of my mind. I am looking at the most civilized and yet the most savage, dynamic land imaginable. It is the quintessence of contradictions. This is Dionysian. And from this sprang the Apollonian – or else everything would have reverted to chaos and idiocy. What is contained in these few kilometres before Delphi expressed the inexpressible. It is the apotheosis of man vis-à-vis nature. Here he had to become godlike or perish.... From here on to Delphi the unifying conflict rises to a crescendo which lifts you completely out of the world and puts you in the clouds *among the immortals*.... Here the human modulates into the godly. It is not God with a capital G any more – it is the god spirit, *the god in man triumphing*. One has to get beyond ecstacy. One has to conquer all human emotions – even of worship and adoration. One has to *become that which one bows down before*.... This, I feel, is the secret of the Apollonian power and majesty – this rising above the conflict, above the drama, above one's very self, to *incarnate* a god, as a sublime and exalted spectator.[149] (Italics mine)

149 *Letters to Anaïs Nin*, pp. 191-193.

CHAPTER THREE

THE SYMBOLISTE PARALLELS: AN INTERLUDE

1. *"Une sorcellerie évocatoire"*

> *"Let me put it another way; Henry's work, in its ensemble, strikes me as a huge crossword puzzle which can only be solved correctly if solved differently by each of his serious readers. Our job is to give them the clues, the 6 across, and 3 down, etc. But they must fill in the words themselves; I dare say they prefer it this way."*
>
> Alfred Perlès in *Art and Outrage*

Literary criticism has grown perhaps too accustomed to thinking of the writings of Henry Miller in terms of their indebtedness to the literary techniques of Naturalism, of Surrealism and Dadaism, of Revolt – or of plain pornography. One recent critic has made a very telling case for Miller's affinities with the Romantic tradition;[1] another has argued convincingly that Miller's ideological and artistic stance has much in common with literary Existentialism, with its strategies of disintegration and silence.[2] But something important has managed to escape the attention of Miller scholars. A close examination of Henry Miller's works reveals how early and how *decisively* Miller's mind became steeped in the various literatures of the occult: theosophy, Rosicrucianism, yoga, Illuminism, Swedenborgism, astrology and alchemy – the rich and murky sub-soil out of which grew

1 Cf. William A. Gordon, *The Mind and Art of Henry Miller* (Baton Rouge: University of Louisiana Press, 1965), *passim*.

2 Cf. Ihab Hassan, *The Literature of Silence: Henry Miller and Samuel Beckett* (New York: Alfred A. Knopf, 1967), *passim*. Hassan also seems to intuit that there is a connection between Miller's work and the Orphic myth (cf. esp. pp. 17-19 of *The Literature of Silence*), but he does nothing to explore this possibility in his otherwise brilliant and provocative study.

much of the best writing of French *Symbolisme.*[3]

We know from his own testimony that Miller took the trouble, early in his career, to study the methods of such *Symboliste* writers as Rimbaud, Verlaine, Baudelaire, Huysmans, Maeterlinck, and Rilke. We know he was intimately acquainted with Poe, Whitman, Emerson, and Thoreau – the Transcendentalist visionaries whose outlook and methods were important fore-runners of the *Symboliste* school.[4] We also know that Miller had an abiding interest in the work of many other important precursors of French *Symbolisme*, especially Swedenborg (whose theory of "correspondences" decisively influenced Baudelaire) and the "voyant" novels of Balzac (about which Miller has written some illuminating pieces).[5]

The purpose of this chapter will be to establish, merely in the form of a framework of illustrative examples, the very important bridge that connects Miller "as" Orpheus with Miller "as" Rimbaud. It is fairly obvious, in fact, that literary Orphism has a great deal in common with what became known as *Symbolisme* during the closing decades of the nineteenth century. What Professor John Senior has called "the destructive element" of the *Symboliste* school – the conscious awareness and systematic application of the doctrine that

3 Cf. esp. John Senior, *The Way Down and Out: The Occult in Symbolist Literature* (Ithaca, New York: Cornell University Press, 1959), *passim*.
4 Henry Miller, *Letters to Anaïs Nin*, pp. 22 and 25, and *The Books in My Life*, pp. 15, 28, 62, 317-319, and *passim*. There can be no denying that Miller's extensive acquaintance with the works of the major American Transcendentalists contributed a good deal to shaping his vision of "reality." As early as *Tropic of Cancer*, Miller apotheosizes Whitman as "that one lone figure which America has produced in the course of her brief life" and the "first and the last poet" (pp. 232-233). He repeatedly refers in his books to Emerson, Whitman, Poe, and Thoreau (cf., especially, the full-length essays on Whitman and Thoreau in *Stand Still Like the Hummingbird*, pp. 107-118). But as Miller's own *Books in My Life* emphatically makes clear, his readings in the American forerunners of French *Symbolisme* were never anything but slapdash and unsystematic, whereas his apprenticeship to his favorite *Symboliste* writers – as I point out elsewhere in this study – was remarkably rigorous, indeed almost pedantic. Emerson's treatment of certain "Orphic" themes (e.g., the belief in "correspondences" and a universal language, the view of the poet as "seer," the problem of the macrocosm and microcosm, and the quest for the absolute of Selfhood) closely parallels that of the *Symbolistes*. But it is *Rimbaud*'s art which Miller confesses himself envious of, not Emerson's (Cf. *Assassins*, p. 108).
5 Cf. "Seraphita" and "Balzac and His Double" in *The Wisdom of the Heart*, pp. 192-250.

"*the way down*...is also *the way out* (Italics Senior's)"[6] – brings immediatcly to mind the related Orphic themes of *katábasis* and *palingénesis*. But, in addition, the devout and ritualistic Orphic *askesis* which was intended to restrain the debasing types of self-indulgence most men lived by (and thus assure them of "life ever-lasting") also suggests two major *Symboliste* concerns: the dissatisf-action with everyday reality and the preference for the Absoloute. I've consulted all of the well-known authorities on *Symbolisme* while writing my own book, but I found James L. Kugel's *The Techniques of Strangeness in Symbolist Poetry* particularly useful for two reasons: first, for the excellent synopsis Kugel provides of the typical preoccupations which define the *Symboliste* mentality; and second, for the manner in which he cleverly tracks down the effects of "strangeness" – which he quite correctly considers the essential feature of *Symboliste* writing – to very specific tricks employed by the *Symbolistes* to achieve this "strangeness."

According to Kugel, the *Symboliste* outlook can be reduced, at its most quintessential, to the following list of articles of faith: the rejection of the quotidian; the preference for the miraculous; the belief in a universal language, in evocativeness, in musicality, and in the theory of "correspondences;" and, ultimately its most important concern, the quest for the Absolute.[7] In this, Kugel is entirely in agreement with such respected authorities as Guy Michaud, Anna Balakian, and A.G. Lehmann. But Kugel's book goes much farther than the great pioneer studies in French *Symbolisme* in that it establishes a direct connection between the high-sounding *Symboliste* creed and some fairly simple tricks used by this school to create its aura of "strangeness" – tricks which no one had previously subjected to such careful scrutiny. These include: the use of "incompatible-union phrases" (such as Gérard de Nerval's "le soleil noir" in the poem "El Desdichado"), the use of "name-allusions without gloss" (biographical or otherwise *specifying* information withheld on purpose), and the use of "apparent references to an unknown story" (designed, with deliberate intent, to make the reader feel like an outsider).[8]

In his own random and free-wheeling way, I believe Henry Miller's

6 *Down and Out*, p. xxv.

7 James L. Kugel, *The Techniques of Strangeness in Symbolist Poetry* (New Haven and London: Yale University Press, 1971), pp. 10-11.

8 *Ibid*, pp. 37-39 and pp. 43-44.

more important writings reveal that he was consistently and uncannily susceptible not only to the atmospherics of the *Symboliste* doctrines but to precisely the same kind of verbal devices the *Symbolistes* typically made use of to give concrete embodiment to their special vision of reality. He certainly is in accord with the *Symboliste* view of the *aims* of literature, as the following passage from *The Colossus of Maroussi* illustrates, quite vividly:

I have always felt that the art of telling a story consists in so stimulating the listener's imagination that he drowns himself *in his own reveries* long before the end.... I never cease to marvel how it happens that, with certain individuals whom I know, within a few minutes after greeting them we are embarked *on an endless voyage* comparable in feeling and trajectory only to the *deep middle dream* which the practiced dreamer slips into like a bone into its socket. Often, after one of these supra-sensible séances, endeavoring to recapture the thread which had broken, I would work my way back as far as some trifling detail – but between *that bespangled point of repair* [symbol?] and the mainland there was always an impassable void, a sort of no man's land which *the wizardry of the artist* had encumbered with shell holes and quagmires and barbed wire.[9]

Writing about this sort of *Symboliste* evocativeness in *The Symbolist Movement*, Anna Balakian says that

when Mallarmé was proposing that the poet should *suggest* rather than *name* the object, that was his way of protesting against any word that gives dimensions to objects and puts them within the direct grasp of every man; in confining the object (a particular bouquet) he robs the perceptive reader of the possibility of expanding the symbol (the generalized notion of flower) to suit his mood (Balakian's italics).[10]

Edward Engelberg's description of the Symbolist method reads almost like a paraphrase of Henry Miller's views. In a brilliant critical anthology called *The Symbolist Poem*, Engelberg writes that the practitioner of this kind of poem "assumes no prior agreement with the reader as to the manner in which he will use his language or as to

9 *Colossus*, pp. 71-72. For an interesting early prose poem by Henry Miller which attempts, without much success, to embody this aesthetic ideal, cf. Walter Schmiele's *Henry Miller* (p. 71). The poem, entitled "Circe," is signed "June E. Mansfield." Miller explains in *Plexus* (pp. 154-164) that he was in the habit of signing his wife June's assumed name to his apprentice poems and of peddling them from door to door.
10 Anna Balakian, *The Symbolist Movement: A Critical Appraisal* (New York: Random House, 1967), p. 83.

how he will fashion his context to yield 'meaning.' " Engelberg contends that a Symbolist poem is "far more autonomous" than "a poem within a symbolic system" because the former uses language "to evoke and to suggest" rather than "to describe or to declare."[11] James L. Kugel states Henry Miller's case most succinctly, perhaps, when he writes that the aim of the writings of the Symbolist school is to

> provide a direction for the reader's imagination without offering it a means of satisfaction. These are not parables, nor are they allegories; perhaps the most we can say is that they are models of a thought situation, invented archetypes which, however they may resound in the reader's consciousness, leave him with the feeling of having witnessed something mysterious and utterly strange.[12]

When we bear these notions in mind, the genealogical line of descent that connects the two magicians, Charles Baudelaire and Henry Miller, becomes fairly evident. What Miller calls "the wizardry of the artist" in *The Colossus of Maroussi* – the reliance on specific literary tricks and strategies which Kugel lists in his book and which I intend to single out among Miller's own literary performances – is simply what Baudelaire, the seminal figure and chief theoretician of the *Symboliste* movement, referred to as "une sorcellerie évocatoire."[13] Miller often gives the impression of being merely an intuitive, somewhat strident, even careless *Symboliste*, but such writings of his as "Into the Night Life" (from the second volume of the *Tropics* trilogy, *Black Spring*) and the well-known clown fable, *The Smile at the Foot of the Ladder*, would surely pose no problem to a disciple of Baudelaire or Mallarmé. At the very worst, Miller's most characteristic work represents a freewheeling and, at times, pedestrian culmination of all that is most typical of the *Symboliste* aesthetic intent. But when he is most fully in command of his resources, there are elements in Miller's work –

11 Edward Engelberg, *The Symbolist Poem: The Development of the English Tradition* (New York: E.P. Dutton & Co., 1967), p. 25.

12 *Techniques of Strangeness*, p. 5.

13 Charles Baudelaire, *Oeuvres Complètes* (Paris: Bibliothèque de la Pléiade, 1961), p. 385. Miller may well turn out to have been merely a marginal *Symboliste*, but he is a highly eclectic writer and it is his very marginality which is so appealingly characteristic. He has often described himself as a man *en marge* and a life-long anarchist. Anarchists have a trying way of not adhering to codes or sets of rules, however admirable.

especially in the magical *Colossus* – which are akin to the very best in *Symboliste* literature. Before dealing in some detail with Miller's fidelity to the major tenets of the *Symboliste* creed, I offer some specific examples of his use of identifiably *Symboliste* methods to produce a deliberate aura of "strangeness." I'll limit myself to just enough examples to show that Henry Miller is fully aware that "strangeness" is a very particular literary *effect* and its achievement on the page calls for more than wishful thinking.

What James L. Kugel calls "incompatible-union phrases" (Nerval's "le soleil noir") Anna Balakian had referred to, some years earlier, as the "rarefaction" or "enrichment" of literary images. Writing of "the magic of indirect communication," Professor Balakian had said:

> Synesthesia is almost automatized in the regular coupling of the abstract with the concrete. The use of color to convey a unity of theme of a mood continues, as we get the "Blue Guitar" of Stevens, the "Blancura" of Jorge Guillèn, the "Sinfonía en gris mayor" of Ruben Darío, "Verde que te quiero verde" of Lorca, and too many others to warrant multiplication of examples. When the symbol itself finds it difficult to convey ambiguity, it is the image – consisting of several associated symbols – that is geared to express elliptic meaning. This is brought about in two opposite ways: through a distillation which makes the world outside become more rarefied and anemic, or an enrichment of detail, which makes it more sanguine, and in creating effects ends up by appealing to the sensuality rather than to the imagination of the reader.[14]

Later in her book, Professor Balakian cites Rimbaud's famous sonnet, "Voyelles," as the *source* of such incompatible-union phrases as Lorca's remarkably vivid "blue rose" and "green wind."[15]

By means of this self-same device, Henry Miller is often able to project symbols of potent ambiguity that trigger in the minds of his readers the kind of "suprasensible séance" which he himself credits to "the wizardry of the artist." Here are a few examples from "Into the Night Life" in *Black Spring* (a title which is itself a good example of the device): "The trains are racing over the frozen river in wreaths of fire"[16]; "written into the fleshless brow was the word sex stony as a lizard"[17]; "The bridge sways over gasoline lakes below"[18]; "un-

14 *The Symbolist Movement*, p. 164.
15 *Ibid.*, p. 184.
16 *Black Spring* (New York: Grove Press, 1963), p. 135.
17 *Ibid.*, p. 136.
18 *Ibid.*, p. 136.

speakably brown earth and men with green hair"[19]; "queer doglike women with furry heads and always an alarm clock or a jigsaw puzzle hidden in the wrong place"[20]; "celluloid athletes who burst like ping-pong balls when they shoot through the gaslight"[21]; "the air hums with insects and their powdered wings spread pollen and depravity."[22]

"Into the Night Life" is a Surrealistic *katábasis* into the realm of nightmare, and its incompatible-union phrases do justice to its dark concerns. Their counterparts in *The Colossus of Maroussi* generally reflect Miller's more exalted state of mind during the trip to Greece. Here are some of the more striking specimens in the latter book: "a sun in the form of a man crucified. The sun bleeds on its cross..."[23]; "plastic underwear and glass shoes and platinum teeth"[24]; "that feeling of the back pages of Dickens' novels, of a quaint, one-legged world illumined by a jade moon"[25]; "a field of pea green, a lake of waving champagne"[26]; "stars now and then soft as geraniums, or hard and splintery like riven pikes"[27]; "a breathless ride on the scenic railway through a tropical Iceland"[28]; "the sun...sputtering out like a rumsoaked omelette"[29]; "a green sunset"[30]; and "something rich, sensuous, and rosy about Corinth. It is death in full bloom, death in the midst of voluptuous, seething corruption. The pillars of the Roman temple are fat; they are almost Oriental in their proportions, heavy, squat, rooted to earth, like the legs of an elephant stricken with amnesia."[31] There can be no doubt that the element of "strangeness" in these images is achieved in the classic *Symboliste* fashion of yoking together two or more strangely incompatible aspects of reality: visual with auditory, concrete with abstract, or – as in the

19 *Ibid.*, p. 141.
20 *Ibid.*, p. 144.
21 *Ibid.*, p. 144.
22 *Ibid.*, p. 153.
23 *Colossus*, p. 57.
24 *Ibid.*, p. 143.
25 *Ibid.*, p. 152.
26 *Ibid.*, p. 158.
27 *Ibid.*, p. 171.
28 *Ibid.*, p. 191.
29 *Ibid.*, p. 192.
30 *Ibid.*, p. 208.
31 *Ibid.*, p. 212.

case of the elephant who cannot remember – by reversing a familiar expectation.

But Miller is equally like his *Symboliste* forebears in the way he makes use of name-allusions without gloss and apparent references to unknown stories in order to create a sense of mysteriousness. When one reads a *Symboliste* poem like Gérard de Nerval's "El Desdichado," James L. Kugel maintains, one "feels there is an essential bit of information which he does not have and which is necessary to full comprehension.... [T]he poet creates the strangeness by *not telling everything*, or, more precisely, by implying that not everything has been told." Kugel goes on to call this "the fundamental discovery of the Symbolist poets. They were the first to seek out systematically this effect of *withheld information*, recognizing in mystery a source of beauty and depth not known before (Italics Kugel's in the previous statement, mine in the latter)."[32]

There are dozens of passages in *The Colossus of Maroussi* in which an air of "mystery" is deliberately created by means of "withheld information," but one such passage seems to me so thoroughly consistent with the *Symboliste* practice described by Kugel and by Balakian as to serve as a *locus classicus*. I quote the passage in its entirety because only this can do justice to its deft and unassuming *Symboliste* "magic":

> We sat there talking about the wonderful winters in Montreal. Jim had a special drink prepared for me which he said would do me good. I was wondering where to get a good bowl of thick soupy rice. Beside me was a man puffing away at a nargileh; he seemed to be in a stony trance. Suddenly I was back in Paris, listening to my occult friend Urbanski who had gone one winter's night to a bordel in Montreal and when he emerged it was Spring. I have been to Montreal myself but somehow the image of it which I retain is not mine but Urbanski's. I see myself standing in his shoes, waiting for a street car on the edge of the town. A rather elegant woman comes along bundled in furs. She's also waiting for the street car. How did Krishnamurti's name come up? And then she's speaking of Topeka, Kansas, and it seems as if I had lived there all my life. The hot toddy also came in quite naturally. We're at the door of a big house that has the air of a deserted mansion. A colored woman opens the door. It's her place, just as she described it. A warm, cosy place too. Now and then the doorbell rings. There's the sound of muffled laughter, of glasses clinking, of slippered feet slapping through the hall....

32 *Techniques of Strangeness*, pp. 37-38.

I had listened to this story so intently that it had become a part of my own life. I could feel the soft chains she had slipped around him, the too comfortable bed, the delicious drowsy indolence of the pasha who had retired from the world during a season of snow and ice. In the Spring he had made his escape but I, I had remained and sometimes, like now, when I forget myself, I'm there in a hotbed of roses trying to make clear to her the mystery of Arjuna's decision.[33]

It is not necessary, while reading such a passage, to know that Urbanski is an important character in Miller's *Rosy Crucifixion* trilogy. Nor is it necessary to know that Krishna and Arjuna are the central figures of the Indian epic poem, the *Bhagavat-Gita*. Nor what, precisely, is the exact nature of "Arjuna's decision." Any reader acquainted with *Symboliste* procedures will simply assume that it is entirely in the nature of the oblique allusions of *Symbolisme* to set one free in "the deep middle dream" (Miller) rather than to embody specific or delimited thought content. As Anna Balakian puts it, the "purpose of the obscurity is not simply an invitation to the reader to decipher its meaning, but rather to open various, often divergent avenues to thought.... [T]he secret of the obscurity is not one of hidden source but of structural ellipsis, of the elimination of explanatory words."[34] What we are concerned with in the Miller passage is, quite simply, a technique of strangeness. We are concerned with a latter-day manifestation of Baudelaire's "sorcellerie évocatoire."

33 *Colossus*, pp. 129-130.
34 *The Symbolist Movement*, pp. 186-187.

2. *The Rejection of the Quotidian*

> *"It is not an artifice that the mind has added to human nature. The mind has added nothing to human nature. It is a violence from within that protects us from a violence from without. It is the imagination pressing back against the pressure of reality. It seems, in the last analysis, to have something to do with our self-preservation; and that, no doubt, is why the expression of it, the sound of its words, helps us to live our lives."*
>
> Wallace Stevens in *The Necessary Angel*

The wholesale rejection of the quotidian – the workaday, the pedestrian, the socially or artistically orthodox, the ordinary – which we generally associate with the *Symbolistes* is merely the negative side of a coin which has a very important positive side: an authentic determination to seek out the miraculous, a sublime belief in the attainability of the Absolute. I intend to deal with these difficult aspirations of theirs, which can also be found throughout Henry Miller's work, after dealing briefly with three important tenets of their poetic faith employed by the *Symbolistes* – as well as by Henry Miller – as means of reaching the Absolute: the theory of "correspondences," the belief in a universal language, and the efficacy of evocativeness and musicality. But I want to emphasize at the outset how thoroughly like the *Symbolistes* Henry Miller can be in the forcefulness with which he turns his back on the quotidian.

In *The Techniques of Strangeness*, James L. Kugel characterizes the typical hero of *Symboliste* literature as a "superhuman figure." He points out that Huysmans' character Des Esseintes, Villiers de l'Isle-Adam's Axël, the speaker of Rimbaud's *Illuminations* and *Une Saison en Enfer*, Lautréamont's Maldoror, Mallarmé's Igitur, and Valéry's Monsieur Teste are all heroes "possessed of a single-minded search into their own beings." They all live "on the outskirts of society," according to Kugel, and their views are continually pitted against those of "la foule":

[T] he Symbolist heroes can only laugh at those caught up in the relativity implicit in mundane existence. Society's values are continually mocked; and even love, for the Symbolist hero, is transformed into rape, perversion, and death. His search, contemporary to Nietzsche, inevitably leads him *jenseits von Gut und Böse.*[35]

What passes for "reality" among the majority of people has little or no significance for the *Symboliste* as a type. The French scholar, Pierre Martino, writes: "Chez Verlaine, chez Mallarmé, chez Rimbaud, chez beaucoup de symbolistes, on retrouve, à ces degrés de conviction divers, cette même croyance bien installée. La réalité, présente ou passée, et la traduction de la réalité sont de plus en plus *méprisées*."[36] Martino closes his chapter on the theater of Maurice Maeterlinck, one of Miller's greatest *Symboliste* idols, with words which could apply as well to Rimbaud or to Miller himself:

Presque toutes ces pièces se passent en des lieux inconnus, chimériques, à des époques qu'on ne saurait dater; il y a des palais magiques, des grottes mystérieuses, des événements inouis.... Le tumulte de la vie, la passion des foules ne peuvent rien pour troubler le mystère qui vit dans le sanctuaire de l'âme.[37]

Chez Miller, this characteristically *Symboliste* disdain for the grubbier dimensions of everyday reality reaches its luminous apogee in *Colossus*, without a doubt, but there were already numerous evidences of it as early as *Black Spring* in the long sketch, "The Tailor Shop" – the shop being in itself a place-symbol for some of the author's most discouraging youthful collisions with the tawdriness of the workaday:

I should be saying Good Morning now to Tom Jordan, but it hangs there on my lips trembling. What morning is this that I should waste in salutation? Is it good, this morning of mornings? I am losing the power to distinguish morning from morning. In the ledger is the world of the fast disappearing buffalo; next door the riveters are sewing up the ribs of the coming skyscrapers. Cunning Oriental

35 *Techniques of Strangeness*, pp. 21-22.
36 Pierre Martino, *Parnasse et symbolisme* (Paris: Librairie Armand Colin, 1970), p. 121.
37 *Ibid.*, p. 180.

men with leaden shoes and glass craniums are plotting the paper world of tomorrow, a world made entirely of merchandise which rises box on box like a paper-box factory, f.o.b. Canarsie. Today there is still time to attend the funeral of the recent dead; tomorrow there will be no time, for the dead will be left on the spot and woe to him who sheds a tear. This is a good morning for a revolution if only there were machine guns instead of firecrackers. This morning would be a splendid morning if yesterday's morning had not been an utter fiasco. The past is galloping away, the trench widens. Tomorrow is further off than it was yesterday because yesterday's horse has run wild and the men with leaden shoes cannot catch up with him. Between the good of the morning and the morning itself there is a line of pus which blows a stench over yesterday and poisons the morrow. This is a morning so confused that if it were only an old umbrella the slightest sneeze would blow it inside out.

My whole life is stretching out in an unbroken morning. I write from scratch each day. Each day a new world is created, separate and complete, and there I am among the constellations, a god so crazy about himself that he does nothing but sing and fashion new worlds. Meanwhile the old universe is going to pieces. The old universe resembles a busheling room in which pants are pressed and stains removed and buttons sewn on. The old universe smells like a wet seam receiving the kiss of the red-hot iron. Endless alterations and repairs, a sleeve lengthened, a collar lowered, a button moved closer, a new seat put in. But never a new suit of clothes, never a creation. There is the morning world, which starts from scratch each day, and the busheling room in which things are endlessly altered and repaired. And thus it is with my life through which there runs the sewer of night. All through the night I hear the goose irons hissing as they kiss the wet seams; the rinds of the old universe fall on the floor and the stench of them is sour as vinegar.[38]

Throughout *Black Spring*, Miller repeatedly reiterates the *cri de coeur* of Arthur Rimbaud: "La vrai vie est absente." But nowhere does he do this with a more Rimbaldian fervor and acridity than in "Megalopolitan Maniac." The thrust of the passage also recalls the desperate Baudelairean injunction: "n'importe où, pourvu que ce soit hors de ce monde":

Done with his underground life the worm takes on wings. Bereft of sight, hearing, smell, taste he dives straight into the unknown. Away! Away! Anywhere out of the world! Saturn, Neptune, Vega – no matter where or whither, but away, away from the earth! Up there in the blue, with firecrackers sputtering in his asshole, the angel-worm goes daft.[39]

38 *Black Spring*, pp. 100-101.
39 *Ibid.*, p. 204.

The whole of *Tropic of Capricorn* and the retrospective scenes in *Tropic of Cancer* which deal with the sordid realities of everyday life in America constitute Miller's most sustained and most ambitious exercises in the rejection of the quotidian, but there is a wonderfully comical short essay in *The Cosmological Eye* called "Glittering Pie" – which originally appeared in *The Harvard Advocate* in 1939 – that summarizes the feelings of extravagant tedium Miller experiences when he is exposed again, on a brief return to his native land, to the numbing actualities of everyday life in the States:

Everything seemed very familiar to me and very grim and very ugly – like coming out of a dream. This, I thought to myself, is the sensation people usually get when they talk about "reality." If going to Europe is a form of evasion, a running away from one's self, from *reality*, then I knew that I was back again and *that this was reality*.... The day is full of activity, the night full of nightmares. On the surface things function smoothly – everything oiled and polished. But when it comes time to dream King Kong crashes through the windows; he pushes the skyscrapers down with one hand. "Skyscraper souls!" That was the last message from America that I caught walking down the Champs Elysees the eve of my departure. Now I walk through the marvelous tunnels with the rest of the sewer rats and I read: "*It's good to change the laxative*!..." What I saw years ago on the magazine covers I see now in actuality. The women's faces more particularly. That sweet, vapid, virginal look of the American woman! So putridly sweet and virginal! Even the whores have these vapid, virginal faces. They correspond exactly to the titles of the books and magazines for sale. It's a victory for the editors and publishers, for the cheap illustrators and the inventive advertising gentry. No more sales resistance. It's a push-over. Palm Olive, Father John, Ex-Lax, Peruna, Lydia Pinkham – *these* have conquered (Miller's italics)![40]

The Colossus of Maroussi virtually gets under weigh with a spirited rejection of precisely the same emblems of the quotidian which "Glittering Pie" satirizes. On the boat from Marseilles to Piraeus, Miller has a conversation with a Turk, a Syrian, some students from Lebanon, and an Argentine man of Italian extraction – all of whom are hopelessly bogged down in the quotidian:

What they wanted was success – money, power, a place in the sun. None of them wanted to return to their own country; for some reason they had all of them been obliged to return against their will. They said there was no life for them in their own country. *When would life begin*?, I wanted to know. When

40 *Cosmological Eye*, pp. 338-344.

they had all the things which America had, or Germany, or France. Life was made up of things, of machines mainly, from what I could gather. Life without money was an impossibility: one had to have clothes, a good home, a radio, a car, a tennis racquet, and so on. I told them I had none of those things and that I was happy without them, that I had turned my back on America precisely because these things meant nothing to me. They said I was the strangest American they had ever met.[41]

This remains a favorite theme throughout the book: it is as inescapable, in the structure of *Colossus*, as its antithesis, Miller's ecstatic praise of the shimmering and other-worldy light of Greece. Part of the problem, as Miller sees it, is the nefarious influence of newspapers. He traces much of the heaviness of the quotidian burden to the newspapers' genius for merchandizing both the commonplace and the lethal, without discrimination:

The absence of newspapers, the absence of news about what men are doing in different parts of the world to make life more livable or unlivable is the greatest single boon. If we could just eliminate newspapers a great advance would be made, I am sure of it. Newspapers engender lies, hatred, greed, envy, suspicion, fear, malice. We don't need the truth as it is dished up to us in the daily papers. We need peace and solitude and idleness. If we could all go on strike and honestly disavow all interest in what our neighbor is doing we might get a new lease on life. We might learn to do without telephones and radios and newspapers, without machines of any kind, without factories, without mills, without mines, without explosives, without battleships, without politicians, without lawyers, without canned goods, without gadgets, without razor blades even or cellophane or cigarettes or money.[42]

It's interesting how, once again, the antipathy to the journalistic in Miller is completely in keeping with the *Symboliste* ethos. If we bear in mind that both "quotidian" and "journalistic" are derived from cognate etymons that mean "day" (Latin *quoties* and French *journée*), the reason for this is not far to seek. Undoubtedly, it is the sheer *dailiness* of the newspapers' concerns that offends Miller's *Symboliste* temperament. Anna Balakian records Stéphane Mallarmé's belief that when a poet is accused of being obscure, he is actually being chided for "not being journalistic." According to Mallarmé, the poet's very identity pivots upon his *not* being journalistic. Mallarmé's words to his English friend, Edmund Gosse, are quoted by Balakian in support of this view:

41 *Colossus*, pp. 6-7.
42 *Ibid.*, pp. 42-43.

[N]o, dear poet, except by awkwardness, I am not obscure, as soon as people read me in terms of the principles I maintain, or as an example of the manifestations of an art which happens to utilize language, and I become obscure, it is true, if people are misled and think that they are opening the pages of a newspaper.[43]

There is a moment of genuine humor in *Colossus* when a tedious Greek vice-consul who has written a book on Crete insists on eliciting a critical opinion of it from Miller:

He kept telling his wife that I was a journalist, an insult which normally I find hard to swallow, but in this case I found it easy not to take offense since the vice-consul considered all writers to be journalists.... He spoke in his pompous, ornate, highly fatuous way about his masterpiece. He said that a journalist like myself would be one of the few to really appreciate what he had done for the cause of Crete et cetera. He handed me the book to glance at. He handed it over as if it were the Gutenberg Bible. I took one glance and realized immediately that I was dealing with one of the "popular masters of reality," a blood-brother to the man who had painted "A Rendezvous with the Soul."... [H]e informed me that if I came to his office in the morning he would bestow one upon me as a gift, as a memento of this illustrious occasion which had culminated in the meeting of two minds thoroughly attuned to the splendors of the past. This was only the beginning of a cataract of flowery horse shit which I had to swallow before going through the motions of saying good-night.[44]

This episode comes to an even zanier conclusion a few pages later in an extended spoof by Miller on the latest bellicose headlines in a Greek newspaper which another person quotes to him aloud, followed by Miller's comic dismissal of "an American book" – the ultimate repository of quotidian wisdom, it turns out – which another unsavory type brings out while Miller is waiting for a bus and lavishly praises to him: the almanach!

It is not that Miller, like the *Symbolistes* before him, is not attuned to "the splendors of the past." Some pages earlier in *Colossus*, a visit to Eleusis prompts him to write:

At Eleusis one realizes, if never before, that there is no salvation in becoming adapted to a world which is crazy. At Eleusis one becomes adapted to the cosmos. Outwardly Eleusis may seem broken, disintegrated with the crumbled

43 *The Symbolist Movement*, p. 84.
44 *Colossus*, pp. 118-120.

past; actually Eleusis is still intact and it is we who are broken, dispersed, crumbled to dust. Eleusis lives, lives eternally in the midst of a dying world.[45]

It is simply that, like a true *Symboliste*, Miller expects all "reality" to bestow a greater measure of awareness, of ecstacy, on its beholder – a greater measure of "life." At Nauplia, what he objects to is reminiscent of the things against which Arthur Rimbaud fulminated so savagely: "red tape, lawyers and judges everywhere, with all the despair and futility which follows in the train of these blood-sucking parasites." He notices that the fortress and the prison "dominate the town," and concludes: "Warrior, jailer, priest – the eternal trinity which symbolizes our fear of life. I don't like Nauplia. I don't like provincial towns. I don't like jails, churches, fortresses, palaces, libraries, museums, nor public statues to the dead."[46] Only a few pages after this, in the diatribe on "REVOLUTION" quoted in Chapter One, Miller writes: "Each one individually must revolt against a way of life which is not his own."[47] It is pure Rimbaud.

The rejection of the quotidian is an insistent theme which Miller never tires of invoking in all three parts of *Colossus*. It even appears, with a compellingly blunt formula for achieving it, toward the close of Part Three, where Miller writes:

People seem astounded and enthralled when I speak of the effect which this visit to Greece produced upon me. They say they envy me and that they wish they could one day go there themselves. Why don't they? Because nobody can enjoy the experience he desires until he is ready for it. People seldom mean what they say. Any one who says he is burning to do something other than he is doing or to be somewhere else than he is is lying to himself. To desire is not merely to wish. To desire is to *become* that which one essentially is. Some men, reading this, will inevitably realize that there is nothing to do but act out their desires. A line of Maeterlinck's concerning truth and action altered my whole conception of life.[48]

This theme is a constant in Miller. He had written about it before taking his trip to Greece, perhaps most eloquently in an essay on D.H. Lawrence:

45 *Ibid.*, pp. 45-46.
46 *Ibid.*, p. 75.
47 *Ibid.*, p. 82.
48 *Ibid.*, p. 237.

The artist's dream of the impossible, the miraculous, is simply the resultant of his inability to adapt himself to reality. He creates, therefore, a reality of his own – in the poem – a reality which is suitable to him, a reality in which he can live out his unconscious desires, wishes, dreams.... He lives out his dream of Paradise. He transmutes his real experience of life into spiritual equations. He scorns the ordinary alphabet, which yields at most only a grammar of thought, and adopts the symbol, the metaphor, the ideograph. *He writes Chinese*. He creates an impossible world out of an incomprehensible language, a lie which enchants and enslaves men. It is not that he is incapable of living. On the contrary, his zest for life is so powerful, so voracious that it forces him to kill himself over and over. He dies many times in order to live innumerable lives (Miller's italics).[49]

Put in somewhat less hyperbolic terms, this is simply a reformulation of the *Symbolistes*' indefatigable quest for the Absolute – complete with a direct reference to the *Symbolistes*' rejection of "the ordinary alphabet" and their partiality to "the symbol." I plan to return to the search for the Absolute, at the close of this chapter, after dealing briefly with three of the specific means used by *Symbolisme* to break through to the Absolute.

49 *Wisdom*, p. 4.

3. *The Theory of "Correspondences"*

> *"It is important to believe that the visible is the equivalent of the invisible; and once we believe it, we have destroyed the imagination; that is to say, we have destroyed the false imagination, the false conception of the imagination as some incalculable* vates *within us, unhappy Rodomontade. One is often tempted to say that the best definition of poetry is that poetry is the sum of its attributes. So, here, we may say that the best definition of true imagination is that it is the sum of our faculties."*
>
> Wallace Stevens in *The Necessary Angel*

According to Baudelaire's great preceptor, Emanuel Swedenborg, all cosmic phenomena exist in intimately related series and appear as scales on different planes of being. The components of one series are linked to those of another in their essence as well as in their ultimate meaning. Therefore, "all things which exist in nature from the least to the greatest are correspondences. The reason they are correspondences is that the natural world with all that it contains exists and subsists from the spiritual world, and both worlds come from the Divine being." It was also Swedenborg's belief that the verbal and phenomenal spheres were very strictly interconnected. Because the union "of heaven with the world is effected by correspondences, therefore a Word was provided in which everything down to the minutest detail has its correspondence."[50]

It is a well-established fact of literary history that Swedenborg's theory of "correspondences" played a crucial role in shaping the *Symboliste* aesthetic in France, not only through Baudelaire but

50 Cf. Emanuel Swedenborg, *Heaven and Hell* (New York: E.P. Dutton, 1911), pp. 44-50 and *passim*.

through Balzac somewhat earlier. Guy Michaud's magisterial study, *Message poétique du symbolisme*, gives an excellent synopsis of the manner in which *Symbolisme* assumed fixed relationships (or "correspondences") between the material and spiritual worlds. The *Symbolistes* made it their aim, according to Michaud, to recover the primordial sense of unity which had been lost to man. Taking the nostalgic ideal of "unity in multiplicity" as their point of departure, the *Symboliste* poets set out on the "démarche incessante" of bringing together the sundered realms of Being. Not only was microcosmic man the image and mirror of the macrocosmic universe, but material reality was nothing but an analogical projection of spiritual reality, according to the *Symboliste* creed. Since the harmony of nuances and sounds symbolized the harmony of souls and worlds, the human and cosmic planes were merely replicas of the divine plane:

> Et le role du Symbolisme est de produire la synthèse suprême, où s'inscrira "le dogme," c'est-à-dire la doctrine transmise par les traditions et dans laquelle la vérité se manifeste à l'homme, doctrine dont l'essentiel tient dans cet "Evangile des Correspondences" et dans cette "loi de l'analogie" dont les poètes se feront précisément les servants et grâce auxquels, selon Charles Morice, ils "donneront, selon les forces de leur esprit et la bonne foi de leur coeur, en de vastes synthèses, une explication mélodieuse et lumineuse des mystères."[51]

Henry Miller's exposure to the doctrine of "correspondences" seems to have taken place chiefly by way of the adaptations of Swedenborgian science which he found in the works of Rimbaud and Balzac. Anna Balakian calls Balzac's trilogy, *Recherche de l'Absolu* (consisting of *Séraphita, Livre mystique*, and *Louis Lambert*) "Balzac's version of the Divine Comedy,"[52] and Miller's illuminating analyses of these works (which he absorbed just before his trip to Greece) contain, among other things, his own glowing agreement with the central tenet of the Swedenborgian synthesis, viz., that there exist, in Balzac's words, "certain affinities between the constituent elements of matter and those of mind, which proceed from the same source." Miller then goes on to implicitly affirm his own faith in "the existence of magic and the evidences of the miraculous, the *relation of God to man* through Desire, the notion of *hierarchies in every realm of life*, as well

51 Guy Michaud, *Message poétique du Symbolisme* (Paris: Librairie Nizet, 1947), pp. 412-413.
52 *The Symbolist Movement*, p. 17.

as the belief in transmutation, all these manifestations of the spiritual attributes of man" which Balzac's trilogy brilliantly "summed up (Italics mine)."[53]

Miller nowhere employs the word "correspondence" outright in *The Colossus of Maroussi*, but it is everywhere evident that he espouses the doctrine to which Swedenborg gave a name. As in the letters which Lawrence Durrell had written to him to entice him to Greece, "the dream and the reality, the historical and the mythological," are "artfully blended" in *Colossus.*[54] Early in the book, for example, Miller alludes to the subjective desires we all have and the power of "God's magic" to realize them on the plane of objective reality:

[T]here were even greater moments to come, something beyond bliss even, something which if anyone had tried to describe to me I would probably not have believed. I didn't know then that I would one day stand at Mycenae, or at Phaestos, or that I would wake up one morning and looking through a port hole see with my own eyes the place I had written about in a book but which I never knew existed nor that it bore the same name as the one I had given it in my imagination.[55]

What Miller is referring to here is a hallucinating scene in *Tropic of Capricorn* where he becomes absolutely sure, in a flash, that he will reach a point at which he will achieve self-fulfillment as a writer *right after he has thought up a sufficiently fanciful name* for that place! In effect, the name-giving gesture would magically conjure up the reality. The scene is worth quoting, *in toto*, as a telling instance of Miller's belief in the "correspondence" that exists between a word and what it designates:

It was at Far Rockaway where this took place. After we had dressed and eaten a meal I suddenly decided that I wanted to be alone and so, very abruptly, at the corner of a street, I shook hands and said good-bye. And there I was! Almost instantaneously I felt alone in the world, alone as one feels only in moments of extreme anguish. I think I was picking my teeth absentmindedly when this wave of loneliness hit me full on, like a tornado. I stood there on the street corner and sort of felt myself all over to see if I had been hit by something. It was inexplicable, and at the same time it was very wonderful, very exhilarating, like a double tonic, I might say. When I say that I was at Far

53 *Wisdom*, p. 248.
54 *Colossus*, p. 4.
55 *Ibid.*, p. 15.

Rockaway I mean that I was standing at the end of the earth, at a place called Xanthos, if there be such a place, and surely there ought to be a word like this to express no place at all. If Rita had come along then I don't think I would have recognized her. I had become an absolute stranger standing in the very midst of my own people. They looked crazy to me, my people, with their newly sunburned faces and their flannel trousers and their clockwork stockings. They had been bathing like myself because it was a pleasant, healthy recreation and now like myself they were full of sun and food and a little heavy with fatigue. Up until this loneliness hit me I too was a bit weary, but suddenly, standing there completely shut off from the world, I woke up with a start. I became so electrified that I didn't dare move for fear I would charge like a bull or start to climb the wall of a building, or else dance and scream. Suddenly I realized that all this was because I was really a brother to Dostoeveski, that perhaps I was the only man in all America who knew what he meant in writing those books. Not only that, but I felt all the books I would one day write myself germinating inside me: they were bursting inside like ripe cocoons. And since up to this time I had written nothing but fiendishly long letters about everything and nothing, it was difficult for me to realize that there must come a time when I should begin, when I should put down the first word, *the first real word*. And this time was now! That was what dawned on me.

I used the word Xanthos a moment ago. I don't know whether there is a Xanthos or not, and I really don't care one way or another, but there must be a place in the world, perhaps in the Grecian islands, where you come to the end of the known world and you are thoroughly alone and yet you are not frightened of it but rejoice, because at this dropping off place you can feel the old ancestral world which is eternally young and new and fecundating. You stand there, wherever the place is, like a newly hatched chick beside its eggshell. This place is Xanthos, or as it happened in my case, Far Rockaway.[56]

But after his arrival in Greece, the attainment of "Xanthos" becomes a regular feature of Miller's life. On his very first night in Athens, he visits the Zapion – the beautiful public garden adjacent to the Temple of Zeus – which later remains in his memory "like no other park I have known. It is the quintessence of park, the thing one feels sometimes in looking at a canvas or dreaming of a place you'd like to be in and never find."[57]

And Miller's feeling for "correspondences" extends not only to places but to persons and wines as well. When he meets the poet Seferis' sister, Jeanne, in Athens, Miller immediately notices her "queenliness," a quality which he feels attracted to at once. He senses it's a quality which "all Greek women share to a greater or lesser

56 *Capricorn*, pp. 210-211.
57 *Colossus*, p. 11.

degree" and asserts that it's "the counterpart, or shall I say the *corresponding* human virtue, which goes with the *supernal light*. One would have to be a toad, a snail, or a slug not to be affected by this radiance *which emanates from the human heart as well as from the heavens* [i.e., from within and without simultaneously] (Italics mine)."[58] At Phaestos, Kyrios Alexandros treats him to a delicious wine which he later remembers "was called *mavrodaphne*." He is not entirely sure of the name, however, and adds:

If not it *should* have been because it is a beautiful black word and describes the wine perfectly. It slips down like molten glass, firing the veins with a heavy red fluid which expands the heart and the mind. One is heavy and light at the same time; one feels as nimble as an antelope and yet powerless to move. The tongue comes unloosed from its mooring, the palate thickens pleasurably, the hands describe thick, loose gestures such as one would love to obtain with a fat, soft pencil. One would like to depict everything in sanguine or Pompeiian red with splashes of charcoal and lamp black.[59]

The Greek word *mavrodaphne* derives from the two root words *mávros*, meaning "black," and *daphné*, meaning "reddish nymph." Daphnes are the bright pink-red flowers of the laurel bush and their name can be traced back to the Sanskrit word "ahanâ," which means "redness of dawn." The myth of Phoebus and Daphne describes the rising of the sun-god Apollo, the fading of the dawn at the touch of his rays, its descent into the bosom of Mother Earth, and its rebirth all-aflame the next day. If the wine Miller was served was not *mavrodaphne*, its effects "correspond" very strikingly with the name he assigns to it. Surely a wine that can produce such a resonance in an exponent of *katábasis* deserves to be re-named *mavrodaphne* forthwith, if it doesn't already bear that name! But for Miller, the "correspondences" between things is no joking matter. He believes *literally*, it seems, in the power of the word to incarnate reality. During Katsimbalis' nap, earlier in the book, Miller muses like a true Swedenborgian on the miracle of "speech":

Why should we stop at words, or at planets, or at divinity? Who or what is powerful enough to eradicate this miraculous leaven which we bear within us like a seed and which, after we have embraced in our mind all the universe, is

58 *Ibid.*, pp. 48-49.
59 *Ibid.*, p. 163.

> nothing more than a seed – since to say universe is as easy as to say seed, and we have yet to say greater things, things beyond saying, things limitless and inconceivable, things which no trick of language can encompass.[60]

Professor Hugh Kenner appears to have precisely these "mysterious, sacerdotal psychic rituals" in mind when he writes about two vastly different *Symbolistes*, Mallarmé and James Joyce:

> Mallarmé's Master, capitalized like Christ, is the "priest of the eternal imagination," composing the trouble leaves and waves have sighed to enunciate since Eden's loss terminated their radiant declarations. He gives voice on behalf of the voiceless flowers, and common words, rose and lily, acquire in his utterance "le mystère d'un nom," the value of each word discriminated and released. So the word finds speech. So *speech* finds speech. Common expressions are transubstantiated: Joyce found no more eloquent metaphor for the artist than the priest, in whose hands "the bread and wine of common experience" alter nothing of their appearance but nevertheless are changed, to afford spiritual as well as bodily food.

The author of *The Colossus of Maroussi* would find no difficulty in agreeing with Hugh Kenner that the *Symbolistes*' "psychic rituals, transcending science, can blend our vocables with the remote impulse which licit speaking no longer satisfies."[61]

The "correspondence" between inner and outer is as obvious to Miller as the "correspondence" between subjective and objective. Epidaurus, he feels, is

> merely a place-symbol: the real place is in the heart, in every man's heart, if he will but stop and search it. Every discovery is mysterious in that it reveals what is so unexpectedly immediate, so close, so long and intimately known. The wise man has no need to journey forth; it is the fool who seeks the pot of gold at the rainbow's end.... Voyages are accomplished inwardly, and the most hazardous ones, needless to say, are made without moving from the spot.[62]

And if there are "correspondences" between inner and outer, to a Rimbaldian/Swedenborgian hermeticist like Henry Miller there are even more obvious "correspondences" between upper and lower. I've

60 *Ibid.*, p. 73.
61 Hugh Kenner, *The Pound Era* (Berkeley and Los Angeles: University of California Press, 1971), pp. 106-107.
62 *Colossus*, pp. 80-81.

already quoted part of Miller's description of the "splintered star world" which he saw through the telescope of the astronomical observatory in Athens, but that passage is worth quoting at greater length here to substantiate in greater depth Miller's capacity to give poetic expression to his belief in "correspondences." It should be borne in mind that Hermes Trismegistus is the patron saint of two occult sciences which have had a life-long appeal to Miller: astrology and alchemy, the latter a subject to which I plan to devote much more attention in Chapter Four. The image Miller retains of his "look through the telescope" is a stunningly artful blend of the devout and the destructive, that of

> Chartres, an effulgent rose window shattered by a hand grenade. I mean it in a double or triple sense – of awesome indestructible beauty, of cosmic violation, of world ruin suspended in the sky like a fatal omen, of the eternality of beauty even when blasted and desecrated. "As above so below," runs the famous saying of Hermes Trismegistus. To see the Pleiades through a powerful telescope is to sense the sublime and awesome truth of these words. In his highest flights, musical and architectural above all, for they are one, man gives the illusion of rivalling the order, the majesty and the splendor of the heavens; in his fits of destruction the evil and the desolation which he spreads seems incomparable until we reflect on the great stellar shake-ups brought on by the mental aberrations of the unknown Wizard.[63]

There is no reason why a "sorcellerie évocatoire" should not be practiced above *as well* as below.

And as if to emphasize that even the most awesome celestial beauty must have its ugly side, Miller passes on – without using any rhetorical device whatever to indicate a logical transition – to his lengthy evocative soliloquy on Saturn (quoted in the previous chapter), to which he adds this discursive comment:

> This is the emotional photograph of a planet whose unorthodox influence still weighs heavily upon the almost extinct consciousness of man. It is the most cheerless spectacle in the heavens. It *corresponds* to every craven image *conceived in the heart of man*; it is the single *repository* of all the despair and defeat to which the human race from time immemorial has succumbed. It will become invisible only when man has purged it from his consciousness (Italics added).[64]

63 *Ibid*., pp. 102-103.
64 *Ibid*., p. 106.

It is a thought entirely worthy of any believer in "correspondences," but the hope he expresses here is not wholly disinterested since, astrologically, Miller is a Capricorn whose special planetary nemesis is Saturn!

But the terrors of Saturn are a concern solely of Miller the astrologist. Miller the illuminist knows that if men and cities are the vessels of the light within them, it is only because the light really exists *without*. There are intimations of this belief in a description of the city of Athens sparkling "like a chandelier" at night, which occurs toward the end of *Colossus:*

> It is as if the sky, becoming more liquescent, more tangible, has lowered itself to fill every crevice with a magnetic fluid. Athens swims in an electric effluvia which comes directly from the heavens. It affects not only the nerves and sensory organs of the body but the inner being. On any slight eminence one can stand in the very heart of Athens and feel the very real connection which man has with the other worlds of light.[65]

C.G. Jung, a hermeticist from the scientific community, would understand the Swedenborgian poet perfectly. Jung's thinking is totally in agreement with the theory of "correspondences," although he states his case in somewhat more austere terms. According to Jung, the human psyche is set up "in accord with the structure of the universe," and what happens "in the macrocosm" likewise happens "in the infinitesimal and most subjective reaches of the psyche." This is the reason why the God-image is "always a projection of the inner experience of a powerful *vis-à-vis*," says Jung:

> This is symbolized by objects from which the inner experience has taken its initial impulse, and which from then on preserve numinous significance, or else it is characterized by its numinosity and the overwhelming force of that numinosity. In this way the imagination liberates itself from the concretism of the object and attempts to sketch the image of the invisible as something which stands behind the phenomenon.[66]

But the effulgent image of Athens which Henry Miller beheld on the objective plane and the "Xanthos" which he had brought to Greece in his own mind can finally crystallize into a state of "correspondence"

65 *Ibid.*, p. 209.
66 *Memories*, pp. 335-336.

in the *reader's* mind only through the efficient formulary of Miller's own words. The magic lies in the arrangement of the words on the page. It is the same with all authentic poetry: the mind of the poet, like the poem itself, is made of words. But words, to the believer in "correspondences," have the power to make the invisible visible. Ernst Cassirer has brilliantly described this metamorphosis. Writing about poets endowed with "the mythic power of insight" (he gives Hölderlin and Keats as examples), Cassirer says:

> Word and mythic image, which once confronted the human mind as hard realistic powers, have now cast off all reality and effectuality; they have become a light, bright ether in which the spirit can move without let or hindrance. This liberation is achieved not because the mind throws aside the sensuous forms of word and image, but in that it uses them both as *organs* of its own, and thereby recognizes them for what they really are: forms of its own self-revelation.[67]

67 Ernst Cassirer, *Language and Myth* (New York: Dover Publications, 1946), p. 99.

4. *The Belief in a Universal Language*

> *"But if you have prayed earnestly for certain powers you recognize them when you witness them, even though you yourself may never have been granted these powers. I wonder if I make myself clear? All I mean is that I am truly humble in the presence of art, whether on a cultural level, a primitive level or a child's level. Spirit can shine through an idiot as well as through a saint, what! I never turned my back on art; I may have been defiant, nothing more. I may only have believed (naively) that art is capable of more than men have dared hope for."*
>
> Henry Miller in *Art and Outrage*

The encounter between Henry Miller and Alexandros Venetikos which takes place toward the close of Part Two of *The Colossus of Maroussi* is one of the most moving scenes in the book. The degree of contact which the two men succeed in achieving is extremely affecting and appears to have survived the occasion itself by at least twenty years.[68] Yet when the two strangers met, all alone, on that day in late 1939, neither spoke much more than a handful of words of the other's language. How, then, did they manage to "communicate"? Miller is uncharacteristically laconic on the subject: "I sat and talked with Alexandros in the deaf and dumb language of the heart."[69]

Much earlier in the book, when Miller had been in Greece only a

68 Cf. Alexandros Venetikos, "Letter to Henry Miller from Phaestos," in *Wanderlust*, I, No. 4, January 1959, and Lawrence Durrell, Alfred Perlès, and Henry Miller, *Art and Outrage* (New York: E.P. Dutton, 1961), pp. 20-21.
69 *Colossus*, p. 164.

few days and knew even less Greek than he had acquired by the time he reached Phaestos, he gives his readers a much more graphic illustration of this "language of the heart." This occurs in the description of a "conversation" he enjoyed with the inquisitive mayor of a mountain village near Kalami, in Corfu, where Miller was staying with the Durrells:

I knew about ten words of Greek and he knew about three words of English. We had a remarkable colloquy, considering the limitations of language. Seeing that he was half-cracked I felt at ease and, since the Durrells were not there to warn me against such antics, I began to do my own cracked song and dance for him, which was to imitate male and female movie stars, a Chinese mandarin, a bronco, a high diver and such like. He seemed to be vastly amused and for some reason was particularly interested in my Chinese performance. I began to talk Chinese to him, not knowing a word of the language, whereupon to my astonishment he answered me in Chinese, his own Chinese, which was just as good as mine. The next day he brought an interpreter with him for the express purpose of telling me a whopping lie, to wit, that some years ago a Chinese junk had been stranded on this very beach and that some four hundred Chinamen had put up on the beach until their boat was repaired. He said he liked the Chinese very much, that they were a fine people, and that their language was very musical, very intelligent. I asked did he mean *intelligible*, but no, he meant intelligent. The Greek language was intelligent too. And the German language. Then I told him I had been in China, which was another lie, and after describing that country I drifted to Africa and told him about the Pygmies with whom I had also lived for a while. He said they had some Pygmies in a neighboring village. It went on like this from one lie to another for several hours, during which we consumed some wine and olives. Then someone produced a flute and we began to dance, a veritable St. Vitus' dance which went on interminably to finish in the sea where we bit one another like crabs and screamed and bellowed in all the tongues of the earth.[70]

Although Miller's treatment of this scene has the effect of spoofing the more earnest side of Swedenborg's theory, once again authentic "communication" is achieved without benefit of ordinary linguistic means. It makes little difference whether we refer to this vibrant "performance" as "Chinese," as Miller does, or simply "Orphic."

It is well known that Baudelaire was much taken with Swedenborg's views on "the universal language" spoken by the angels and that Rimbaud, after reading Baudelaire, was enabled to shape some

70 *Ibid.*, pp. 18-19.

striking postulates of his own (in the famous *Voyant* letters) regarding the urgent need to achieve a universal language.[71] Swedenborg believed that there existed an archetypal language to which all the earthly languages, in a greater or lesser state of corruption, corresponded. He had described this language in the chapter entitled "The Speech of Angels" in *Heaven and Hell*: "In the whole of heaven all have one language, and they understand one another, from whatever society they are, whether near or distant. This language does not require to be learnt by them, but is natural to everyone, for it flows from their very affection and thought."[72] Gwendolyn Bays surmises that Rimbaud might even have read some popular commentaries on Swedenborg by Daillant de Latouche with which Balzac was familiar. These maintained that the universal language

> was related to the idea of correspondence in this way: man before the fall made use of the universal language and enjoyed by means of it immediate revelation and communication with higher beings. After the fall, revelation took place by means of correspondence, and when, still later, men forgot the knowledge of correspondence, the Word was written. This written Word, which possessed an external meaning apparent to men and an internal or spiritual sense for purposes of communication with heaven, constituted man's chief bond with heaven. Swedenborg identifies the "internal sense of the word" and the universal language in his *Dictionary of Correspondences.*[73]

One can easily imagine the impression such daring thoughts must have made on Rimbaud. His biographer, Enid Starkie, asserts that Rimbaud became convinced that his own fuliginous visions of the Absolute could not possibly be rendered in the threadbare language available to the poet and that a new language would have to be found, a language not bound by logic and syntax and therefore capable of expressing the ineffable. "A language must be found!" she quotes Rimbaud as saying, "and moreover, every word being an idea the time for a universal language will come." Professor Starkie goes on to explain that this opinion was also held by the occult philosopher Pierre-Simon Ballanche. According to Ballanche, language was gifted from its very beginning with a kind of transcendant intuition; our modern sense of

71 Anna Balakian, *The Symbolist Movement*, p. 58.
72 Emanuel Swedenborg, *Heaven and Hell*, p. 147.
73 Gwendolyn Bays, *The Orphic Vision: Seer Poets from Novalis to Rimbaud* (Lincoln, Nebraska: University of Nebraska Press, 1964), pp. 198-199.

language can give us no notion of the value put on language among primitive people, "for the word originally was able to give the full image of the object named. It had a kind of 'illumination' of its own of which the dead signs which we use to-day can give us no idea."[74]

Rimbaud's ardent yearning for a new language seems to have permeated the entire *Symboliste* movement. We have Guy Michaud's authority in support of the *Symbolistes*' belief that behind the individual unconsciousness, there exists an unconscious more profoundly and more universally human "qui vibre et vit à l'unisson des rythmes fondamentaux et des images primordiales de l'univers." Michaud goes on to say that in this collective unconsciousness there exist unsuspected powers capable of transforming the world, provided one knows how to recognize and seize them. He argues that man must come to understand, once again, the importance of the intuitive, prelogical, analogical, spontaneous thought latent in the great rhythms and symbols of creation:

> Mais il importe de la restituer à l'état pur, et l'on n'y saurait parvenir que par une discipline rigoureuse. Pour cela, ce qu'il nous faut, ce n'est pas seulement une révolution matérielle, ni une révolution poétique, mais comme l'avaient pressenti les Symbolistes, une véritable révolution spirituelle, une conversion à l'unité.... C'est enfin, ayant capté les forces inconscientes, savoir les transmettre et rendre au langage une partie au moins de ses pouvoirs. Alors la poésie, cessant d'être un jeu gratuit de mandarins, pourra redevenir un guide efficace.[75]

Alain Mercier traces back to a Rosicrucian poem of the early seventeenth century the frenetic craving for the "mot perdu"[76] which the *Symbolistes* later came to believe might restore man to his lost "unity," a scholarly discovery that is not entirely devoid of interest in a study devoted to the author of *The Rosy Crucifixion*.

Henry Miller's antic use of language to break down barriers in *The Colossus of Maroussi* – perhaps, in all fairness, I should be talking of his use of "language" – very frequently lapses into the sub-verbal or the anti-verbal. The following madcap example shows how his way of establishing unity between people is entirely in the nature of a pure "performance":

74 Enid Starkie, *Arthur Rimbaud* (New York: New Directions, 1961), p. 126.
75 *Message poétique*, pp. 641-642.
76 Alain Mercier, *Les sources ésotériques et occultes de la poésie symboliste* (Paris: A.G. Nizet, 1969), p. 19.

> After dinner Karamenaios would drop in. We had about fifty words with which to make lingual currency. We didn't even need that many, as I soon discovered. There are a thousand ways of talking and words don't help if the spirit is absent. Karamenaios and I were eager to talk. It made little difference to me whether we talked about the war or about knives and forks. Sometimes we discovered that a word or phrase which we had been using for days, he in English or I in Greek, meant something entirely different than we had thought it to mean. It made no difference. We understood one another even with the wrong words.... Now and then I would get excited and, using a mélange of English, Greek, German, French, Choctaw, Eskimo, Swahili or any other tongue I felt would serve the purpose, using the chair, the table, the spoon, the lamp, the bread knife, I would enact for him a fragment of my life in New York, Paris, London, Chula Vista, Canarsie, Hackensack or in some place I had never been or some place I had been in a dream or when lying asleep on the operating table. Sometimes I felt so good, so versatile and acrobatic, that I would stand on the table and sing in some unknown language or hop from the table to the commode and from the commode to the staircase or swing from the rafters, anything to entertain him, keep him amused, make him roll from side to side with laughter. [77]

Obviously, there is art in evidence here (albeit of a low order) but it is essentially an art grounded in improvisation. It is a performance in which subjective feeling calls out, with primitive verve, to subjective feeling. The most insistent example Miller gives us of this in *Colossus* is the Negro jazz "cadenza" which occurs in the middle of Part Two. The cast of performers which Miller features in this linguistic jam session includes a Boogie Woogie man named Agamemnon, Louis the Armstrong, a Count (Basie), a Duke (Ellington), Fats and Ella, Lionel the golden boy, and Meemy the Meemer. The Count, we are told, "always began – *bink-bink*! Bink for poison, bink for arson. He was quiet and steady-like, a sort of introverted gorilla who, when he got bogged in the depths of the gerundive, would speak French like a marquis or babble in Polish or Lithuanian. He never started twice the same way."[78] The other musicians all perform in their diversely zany ways, but the style of Meemy the Meemer ("little and low, sort of built up from the ground") must be quoted to be appreciated:

> Jam to-day, jam to-morrow. Nobody care, nobody worry. Nobody die sad no more. 'Cause the old glad land is full of torque. Blow wind! Blow dust in the eye! Blow hot and dry, blow brown and bare! Blow down them orchards, blow down them walls. Boogie Woogie's here again. Boogie Woogie go bink-bink.

77 *Colossus*, p. 41.
78 *Ibid*., p. 140.

Bink for poison, bink for arson. He ain't got no feet, he ain't got no hands. Boogie Woogie scream. Boogie Woogie scream again. Boogie Woogie scream again, again, again, again. No trees, no walls, no nuthin'. Tish and pish and pish and tish. Rats movin'. Three rats, four rats, ten rats. One cockerel, one rat. Locomotive make choo-choo. Sun out and the road is hot and dusty. Trees jell, leaves shell. No knees, no hands, no toes between his fingers. Makin' hominy, that's all. He's comin' down the road with a banjo on his knees. He's a-tappin' and a-slappin'. Tappin' the Tappahanna, rappin' the Rappahanna.[79]

Passages like this clearly underscore Miller's belief that it's through the rhythmic and incantatory uses of *sounds as such* that the "walls" between people can be broken down; it's, in short, through poetry. In this connection, the philosopher Ernst Cassirer again has some very illuminating things to say:

The modern science of language, in its efforts to elucidate the "origin" of language, has indeed gone back frequently to Hamann's dictum, that poetry is "the mother-tongue of humanity"; its scholars have emphasized the fact that speech is rooted not in the prosaic, but in the poetic aspect of life, so that its ultimate basis must be sought not in preoccupation with the objective view of things and their classification according to certain attributes, but in the primitive power of subjective feeling.[80]

Even a sober aesthetic analyst like R.G. Collingwood would concur with Cassirer's and Miller's view that the artist binds men into a community through the "universal language" of *art itself* because, as Collingwood points out,

no community altogether knows its own heart; and by failing in this knowledge a community deceives itself on the one subject concerning which ignorance means death. For the evils which come from that ignorance the poet as prophet suggests no remedy, because he has already given one. The remedy is the poem itself. Art is the community's medicine for the worst disease of the mind, the corruption of consciousness.[81]

But to appreciate how successfully Miller himself has succeeded in mastering this "universal language" of art, we must take a closer look at his artistic use of the devices of evocativeness and musicality.

79 *Ibid.*, pp. 141-142.

80 *Language and Myth*, pp. 34-35.

81 R.G. Collingwood, *The Principles of Art* (London: Oxford University Press, 1938), p. 336.

5. The Efficacy of Evocativeness and Musicality

> *"The general attitude of the youthful Mallarmé is not unlike that of Vigny and of Baudelaire's dilettante. Everything sacred, he says, is enveloped in mystery. Poetry, like religion, has its own secrets which it should protect. Mallarmé laments the fact that a page of poetry (he cites* Les Fleurs du Mal *as example) is not like a page of music, incomprehensible to those who are not competent, who are not trained in the art of deciphering. Since poetry is the greatest of the arts, Mallarmé wants to claim for it the deepest secrecy."*
>
> Wallace Fowlie in *Mallarmé*

I've already written about Henry Miller as "musician" at some length in the section of Chapter Two that deals with Orpheus as Musician, but I believe it's possible to expand significantly on Miller's mastery of the energies of performance by focusing attention on his calculated use of evocativeness and musicality as specifically *Symboliste* forms of virtuosity. Evocativeness is, in fact, the structural device with which Miller opens *The Colossus of Maroussi*. The three figures (two men and a woman) whom he places as emblematic journey-guides in the two prologue-like paragraphs at the very beginning of Part One are all masters of evocativeness: Betty Ryan, who is "an artist of some sort because nobody has ever given [Miller] the *ambiance* of a place so thoroughly as she did Greece"; Lawrence Durrell, whose letters to Miller about Greece "caused *a certain confusion* in [Miller] owing to the fact that the dream and the reality...were so artfully blended"; and Rainer Maria Rilke, the poet with whose extraordinary awareness of the interplay between dream and reality Miller associates "the black, *mysterious* river at Dômme" (Italics mine throughout).

I have explicitly drawn attention to the fact that Miller opens Part

One with two men and a woman because this is precisely the way he brings this part *to a close*. There's an unmistakably artful symmetry to the manner in which Miller constructs this chapter, beginning and ending it with the same "heraldic" grouping. After rhapsodizing over "the field of Irish green" in front of Agamemnon's inn at Mycenae – "a Lawrence Durrell field, heraldic in every sense" – Miller recalls the letters which Durrell used to send him at the Villa Seurat in Paris to entice him to Greece. One of these heraldic messages, as Miller calls them, contained a "fulsome sheaf which looked like prose" entitled "Zero." Miller realizes that he had been unable to understand "the idea of Zero in the heraldic sense" until he had come to this spot. It's here that he gives a strangely poetic description (which looks "like prose") of the two men and a woman going "down" to measure land, which I compared in Chapter Two with the Rilkean frieze-figures of Orpheus, Hermes, and Eurydice. The closing words of this description go like this:

> Yes, Lawrence Durrell, *zero is what you make it*: you take a piece of wet earth and as you squeeze it between your fingers you get two men and a woman standing in a field of Irish green measuring land. The wine has come. I raise my glass. *Salute, Larry me lad*, and keep the flag at zero! In a few more pages we [i.e., Miller and Lawrence Durrell] shall revisit Mycenae together and Nancy will lead the way down the bat-slimed stairs to the bottomless well (First italics mine, second Miller's).[82]

At this point in my exposition, I think it would be useful to quote again the Millerian formula for effective story-telling:

> I have always felt that the art of telling a story consists in so stimulating the listener's imagination that he drowns himself in his own reveries long before the end.... [He is] embarked on an endless voyage comparable in feeling and trajectory only to the deep middle dream which the practiced dreamer slips into like a bone into its socket.[83]

In these "suprasensible séances," Miller goes on to say, there is always "an impassable void" between the "bespangled point of repair" and "the mainland" created by "the wizardry of the artist."[84] This is perfectly sound *Symboliste* thinking. Anna Balakian speaks of the

82 *Colossus*, pp. 96-97.
83 *Ibid.*, p. 71.
84 *Ibid.*, pp. 71-72.

Symboliste process of "intervention of communication between the poet and the reader through an image or series of images that have subjective as well as objective value. While their objective existence is unilateral, their subjective meaning is multidimensional, and therefore suggestive rather than designated."[85] But Guy Michaud speaks of this special ability to launch the reader into what Henry Miller calls "the deep middle dream" as "la véritable découverte du Symbolisme":

> Il s'agit...de créer chez le lecteur ce même état d'illumination dont le poète a fait l'expérience, ou du moins un état équivalent, puisqu'une telle expérience est proprement indicible. Il s'agit exactement de "donner aux gens le souvenir de quelque chose qu'ils n'ont jamais vu." Comment? Si un semblable état ne peut se décrire, il faudra donc le *suggérer*. "Nommer un object, dit Mallarmé, c'est supprimer les trois quarts de la jouissance du poème qui est faite du bonheur de deviner peu à peu; le suggérer, voilà le rêve." Tel est le secret de la poésie. Suggérer (Michaud's italics).[86]

By providing the reader with the necessary "objective" counters (two men and a woman "going down" into Mystery) and by simultaneously refraining from interfering with the reader's "subjective" freedom to dream and imagine at will, Miller's evocative archetypes succeed in launching the reader on his own Orphic reverie. This is an instance of a *Symboliste* stratagem which even the most carping member of Mallarmé's critical *cénacle* would have considered entirely *en règle*.

One could point to numerous other moments like this in *Colossus*. Here is Miller describing Ghika's house on the island of Hydra:

> From the terrace, which was distinctly Oriental in flavor, we could look out on the sea in drunken stupefaction. The house had forty rooms, some of which were buried deep in the earth. The big rooms were like the saloon of an ocean liner; the little rooms were like cool dungeons fitted up by temperamental pirates. The maids were of divine origin and one of them, at least, was descended directly from the Erectheum though she bore the name of a sacred cereal. [What the name of the cereal is Miller never tells us.][87]

Here is Miller's account of the poet Seferis describing a piece of land on which the latter is thinking of building himself a bungalow:

85 *The Symbolist Movement*, p. 38.
86 *Message poétique*, p. 409.
87 *Colossus*, p. 58.

There was nothing extraordinary about the place – it was even a bit shabby and forlorn, I might say. Or rather it *was*, at first sight. I never had a chance to consolidate my first fleeting impression; it changed right under my eyes as he led me about like an electrified jelly-fish from spot to spot, rhapsodizing on herbs, flowers, shrubs, rocks, clay, slopes, declivities, coves, inlets and so on. Everything he looked at was Greek in a way that he had never known before leaving his country. He could look at a headland and read into it the history of the Medes, the Persians, the Dorians, the Minoans, the Atlanteans. He could also read into it some fragments of the poem which he would write in his head on the way home while plying me with questions about the New World. He was attracted by the Sibylline character of everything which met his eye. He had a way of looking forwards and backwards, of making the object of his contemplation revolve and show forth its multiple aspects.[88]

And here is Miller himself describing Katsimbalis' mysterious gift for evocative babbling which transmutes base metal into gold:

Many a time, as Katsimbalis talked, I caught that look on the face of a listener which told me that the invisible wires had been connected, that something was being communicated which was over and above language, over and above personality, something magical which we recognize in dream and which makes the face of the sleeper relax and expand with a bloom such as we rarely see in waking life. Often when meditating on this quality of his I thought of his frequent allusions to the incomparable honey which is stored by the bees on the slopes of his beloved Hymettos. Over and over again he would try to explain the reasons why this honey from Mount Mymettos was unique. Nobody can explain it satisfactorily.[89]

Zero is indeed what you *make* it!

And in the final analysis, it is the art of the "maker" (poetry, verbal architectonics, music) which must concern us if we are ever to get the right perspective on the art of Henry Miller. Anna Balakian has pointed out that it was Baudelaire who pioneered in foreseeing "the two uses to which the notion of 'music' " would be applied in poetry: "the massive, sensual use, to assuage the poetic anguish and provoke the dream release; and the intellectual uses of music, considered as a form of non-objective thinking, activating the mind to suggest rather than to dictate concepts and visions."[90] Perhaps the most blatant form which the "sensual" application of the devices of music took in *Symboliste* poetry was the conscious use of musical

88 *Ibid.*, pp. 46-47.
89 *Ibid.*, pp. 31-32.
90 *The Symbolist Movement*, p. 43.

instruments as readily identifiable auditory symbols to "provoke the dream release." Professor Balakian enumerates a whole gamut of such instruments which became familiar emblems of *Symboliste* wizardry: Mallarmé's Pan's flute, Verlaine's violin that sobbed, clarions, harps, guitars, bells, even the harmonium of our Connecticut insurance executive/*Symboliste*, Wallace Stevens.[91]

I've already referred to the haunting and evocative strains of the flute which Henry Miller uses in all three parts of *The Colossus of Maroussi*. It must not be imagined that the appearance of the flute in all three contexts is purely the product of Miller's having casually overheard the strains of that lovely instrument in the course of his travels through Greece. Miller is, in my opinion, much too conscious an artist and *Symboliste* for such a premise to be allowed. There is convincing evidence of Miller's conscious awareness of the symbolic uses to which a musical instrument might be put in a letter of August 10, 1933, in which he writes to Anaïs Nin about the D.H. Lawrence novel, *Aaron's Rod*, which he was reading at the time:

> When Lawrence created himself a *flautist* and Salavin [a Benda character and occultist of decidedly "Orphic" proclivities] was one too – not so remarkable, the coincidence!), it was for a very good reason. I used to ask you if Lawrence ever mentioned music. I said it was a strange omission. Well now – and behold! – music enters in *Aaron's Rod*. It has to be a very pure music, too – not literary, not program, not plastic. The choice of flute is very very wise – excellent taste. You have only to think a minute, to realize how cheap, how vulgar it would have been to introduce a pianist, or a violinist, or an orchestra conductor. He has the Marchesa (being more intelligent, more cultured, more withered than himself) say her say, or *his* say, about the "noisy" symphonies, etc.... But the flautist – Aaron, Salavin – the flautist is a genuine lover of music. He plays alone, in the dark. He improvises. It is the instrument of meditation – the solitary man's delight. I should not be surprised if Nietzsche played the flute!.... I hope to make some red-hot notes on *Aaron's Rod* before it is too late. The flute – music – very important. (So much here I can't dwell on it. But – think of it: the spirit of tragedy and the double theme. Schizophrenia. Narcissism. Flute. Masturbation the great sin! Toccata and fugue on the self. Aaron's letter has a terrific meaning then.)[92]

This excerpt from Miller's letter serves as a suggestive critical com-

91 *Ibid*., p. 108.
92 *Letters to Anaïs Nin*, pp. 113-114.

mentary on his own use of the flute in several places in *Colossus*, entirely within the framework of "the spirit of tragedy and the double theme" as he describes it above. But the jazz "cadenza" in the middle of Part Two of *Colossus* also overtly employs this device of making a particular musical instrument radiate a complex of directed feeling to a particular literary end, only here the instrument Miller has chosen is the "golden torque" (trumpet) of Louis the Armstrong, which dominates the entire "barbarious passacaglia" section of the book. The artistic appropriateness of Miller's choice is pretty self-evident. The aim of Miller's hectically gladsome prose poem is clearly to blow down Madame's resistant "walls of Jericho," and Louis' radiant and noisesome trumpet serves that purpose admirably.[93] It certainly incarnates the criteria Baudelaire envisioned for the first *Symboliste* application of "musical" power: massiveness and sensuality. In contrast with the somberness and solitude which Miller associates with the flute, the "torque" evokes the radiance and raucousness which Miller needs in the "passacaglia."

But the "*intellectual* uses of music" which Baudelaire foresaw are much more difficult to assess. The non-objective thinking a *Symboliste* writer can set in motion (referred to by Anna Balakian above) is especially problematical in view of the fact that words possess restrictive denotations which the verbal artist must confront and somehow transcend in order to produce his uniquely *Symboliste* musical effects. This is what Guy Michaud appears to have in mind when he writes that there can be no perfect equivalence between language and thought. Between the "mot essentiellement statique"

93 It might be noted, in passing, that Miller's own literary compositions have not escaped the attention of a composer. The works of the *Symbolistes* in general (with their heavy emphasis on "musicality") have lent themselves with conspicuous frequency to settings by composers. There are, to cite only a few well-known examples, memorable settings of Rimbaud's *Illuminations* by Benjamin Britten, of Maeterlinck's *Pelléas et Melisande* by Edgar Fauré, Claude Debussy, and Jan Sibelius, of several of Hofmansthal's magical libretti by Strauss, and of Mallarmé's *L'Après-midi d'un faune* by Claude Debussy (who also did numerous settings of short lyrics by *Symboliste* poets such as Verlaine and Jean Moréas – whose original Greek name was Ioánnis Papadiamantópoulos). In April 1965, an opera by the composer Antonio Bibalo based on Henry Miller's *The Smile at the Foot of the Ladder* – a little clown fable which incorporates all the salient features of the *Symboliste* mystique – was premièred in Hamburg, Germany.

and the "flux incessant de nos états d'âme," there can be mere approximation. The word, says Michaud, can never be more than a Bergsonian "repère dans la durée."[94]

Henry Miller's way of dealing with this problem, like Walt Whitman's and Mark Twain's before him, is to put his trust largely in voice rhythms and the truthfulness of emotive "speech" (allusion has already been made to his own and Katsimbalis' free-wheeling, Eurydice-seeking monologues). It's a particularly *American* solution to the problem of "musicality," which has provided such diverse figures as Ezra Pound, William Carlos Williams, Lawrence Ferlinghetti, Charles Olson, and Denise Levertov, with a sustaining faith. Wallace Stevens, writing about T.S. Eliot's "Rhapsody on a Windy Night," has characterized this "solution" as only an Orpheus acquainted with the worksday voice-rhythms of the American milieu could do it:

> Yet the passage from Eliot was musical. It is simply that there has been a change in the nature of what we mean by music. It is like the change from Haydn to a voice intoning. It is like the voice of an actor reciting or declaiming or of some other figure concealed, so that we cannot identify him, who speaks with a measured voice which is often disturbed by his feeling for what he says. There is no accompaniment. If occasionally the poet touches the triangle or one of the cymbals, he does it only because he feels like doing it. Instead of a musician we have an orator whose speech sometimes resembles music. We have an eloquence and it is that eloquence that we call music every day, without having much cause to think about it.[95]

In short, it's the "solution" of the solo voice, improvising its "performances" out of *inner* rhythmic resources that *call out* to the silences of its attentive counterparts. Henry Miller describes the style in his own fashion in *The Colossus of Maroussi:*

> I like the monologue even more than the duet, when it is good. It's like watching a man write a book expressly for you: he writes it, reads it aloud, acts it, revises it, savours it, enjoys it, enjoys your enjoyment of it, and then tears it up and throws it to the winds. It's a sublime performance, because while he's going through with it you are God for him – unless you happen to be an insensitive and impatient dolt. But in that case the kind of monologue I refer to never happens.[96]

94 *Message poétique*, p. 411.
95 *Necessary Angel*, pp. 125-126.
96 *Colossus*, p. 28.

I will limit myself to perfunctory analyses of two such heraldic monologues from Miller's books, which aptly objectify the *Symboliste* capacity which pure sound has to release that evocative form of "nonobjective thinking" (Balakian) which can activate the mind "to *suggest* rather than to dictate concepts and visions." The first is a particularly somber passage from *Black Spring* in which Miller heightens the atmospheric somberness by means of a simple O-assonance pattern of sound throughout. The negative feeling of the passage is enhanced, in addition, by means of an insistent repetition of the word "no":

N*o*where in the wh*o*le wide world have I seen a cemetery blossom like this. N*o*where in the wh*o*le wide world such rich, steaming manure. Street of early sorr*o*ws, I embrace you! N*o* more pale white faces, n*o* Beethoven skulls, n*o* crossb*o*nes, n*o* spindle shanks. I see nothing but corn and maize, and g*o*ldenrods and lilacs; I see the common h*o*e, the mule in his traces, flat broad feet with t*o*es spread and rich silky l*o*am of earth sloshing between the t*o*es. I see red handkerchiefs and faded blue shirts and broad sombrer*o*s glistening with sweat. I hear flies dr*o*ning and the dr*o*ne of lazy voices. The air hums with careless, reckless joy; the air hums with insects and their powdered wings spread pollen and depravity. I hear n*o* bells, n*o* whistles, n*o* gongs, n*o* brakes grindling; I hear the clink of the h*o*e, the drip of water dripping, the buzz and quiet pandem*o*nium of toil. I hear the guitar and the harmonica, a soft tam-tam, a patter of slippered feet; I hear the blinds being l*o*wered and the braying of a jackass in his *o*ats.[97]

The poetic device of parallelism which Miller uses in this passage ("I see...I see...I hear...I hear...") is one he is especially partial to. He uses it with even greater effectiveness and versatility, however, in the splendid *voyant* monologue with which he brings *The Colossus of Maroussi* to an exuberant close. In this instance, he achieves a greater homogeneity of effect by employing the phrase "I see..." alone at the start of each line. He also achieves a much greater richness of texture by superbly echoing the sounds "aye" and "ee" of "I see" in assonantal permutations throughout the passage, creating an effect of high-pitched blissfulness quite in keeping with the scenes he is describing – a superlative blending of luminous *mantras* and *yantras* (magical vocal and visual designs), to put it in Yogic terms. (I offer the testimony of an authority on Yoga who claims that the *mantra* "e-e-e-e-e--" has the effect of stimulating "the brain and all the glands

97 *Black Spring*, p. 153.

in the skull, leaving one with a very pleasant feeling of well-being, rather like the effect of a little champagne"![98]) In addition to the assonantal pattern of "aye" and "ee" sounds discernible here, there's also a remarkable incidence of liquid alliterative l's, to which (alas) Yogic science offers no key. Their very "liquidity," however, is suggestive since what Miller is offering his readers at this point is a luminous flow of stream-of-consciousness images:

> *I see* again the soft, low mounds in which the illustrious dead were hidden away; *I see* the violet light in which the stiff scrub, the worn rocks, the huge boulders of the dry river beds *gleam* like mica; *I see* the miniature islands floating above the surface of the *sea*, ringed with dazzling white bands; *I see* the eagles swooping out from the dizzy crags of inaccessible mountain tops, their sombre shadows slowly staining the bright carpet of earth below; *I see* the figures of solitary men trailing their flocks over the naked spine of the hills and the fleece of their beasts all golden fuzz as in the days of legend; *I see* the women gathered at the wells amidst the olive groves, their dress, their manners, their talk no different now than in Biblical times; *I see* the grand patriarchal figure of the priest, the perfect blend of male and female, his countenance serene, frank, full of peace and dignity; *I see* the geometrical pattern of nature expounded by the earth itself in a silence which is deafening. The Greek earth opens before me like the Book of Revelation.[99]

The concluding page of *Colossus* is dense with *Symboliste* evocativeness and musicality, but three summarizing comments about it seem to be in order: first, Miller's parting offerings to his readers in the last sentence of *Colossus* following the "Book of Revelation" soliloquy are "peace" (ee) and "life" (aye); second the word "Revelation" on which the soliloquy proper ends (since it's a word which reinforces and *clinches* the sense of the epiphanic which so strongly characterizes the whole passage) is immediately echoed by the word "revolution" (the wheel, the perfect "circle of destiny") to whose "real meaning," Miller tells us, the light of Greece opened his eyes and helped him find "the true center"; and third, it's from the vantage point of this "true center" that Miller comes to "refuse categorically to become anything less than the citizen of the world which I silently declared myself to be when I stood in Agamemnon's tomb. From that day forth my life was dedicated to the recovery of the divinity of man."[100]

98 James McCartney, *Yoga: The Key to Life* (New York: E.P. Dutton, 1969), p. 147.
99 *Colossus*, pp. 240-241.
100 *Ibid.*, p. 241.

To put it in more "objective" terms, the book's tripartite form comes to a full circle (since according to geometrical science it takes three points to "specify" any circle) with Miller's reaffirmation of the decision to pursue his quest for the Absolute.

6. *The Quest for the Absolute*

> *"Ordinary life does not interest me. I seek only the high moments. I am in accord with the surrealists, searching for the marvelous.*
>
> *I want to be a writer who reminds others that these moments exist; I want to prove that there is infinite space, infinite meaning, infinite dimension.*
>
> *But I am not always in what I call a state of grace. I have days of illuminations and fevers. I have days when the music in my head stops. Then I mend socks, prune trees, can fruits, polish furniture. But while I am doing this I feel I am not living."*
>
> Anaïs Nin in *The Diary of Anaïs Nin*

Any discussion of the Absolute must perforce involve us in some consideration of the terms "real" and "unreal." What *is* the "real"? And what is the "*un*real"? In the section on *katábasis* in Chapter Two, I referred to Henry Miller's comical unwillingness to go back down "the slippery staircase" at Mycenae for fear of losing the "light" which he had already grasped and made his own. The fear Miller depicts in this scene is not an instance of unmitigated comedy, pure and simple. In one of his most suggestive books, *Images and Symbols: Studies in Religious Symbolism*, Mircea Eliade has some very instructive things to say about "staircases":

> We now know why the idea of fear, for Julien Green, was associated with the image of a staircase, and why all the dramatic events he described in his works – love, death, or crime – happened upon a staircase. The act of climbing or ascending symbolises *the way toward the absolute reality*; and to the profane consciousness, *the approach towards that reality arouses an ambivalent feeling, of fear and of joy, of attraction and repulsion*, etc. The ideas of sanctification,

> of death, love and deliverance are all involved in the symbolism of stairs. Indeed, each of these modes of being represents a cessation of the profane human condition; that is, breaking of the ontological plane. Through love and death, sanctity and metaphysical knowledge, man passes – as it is said in the *Brihadaranyaka Upanishad*, from the "unreal to the reality (First italics Eliade's, second my own)."[101]

The descent clearly signifies the loss of the "real," according to Eliade, whereas the *ascent* symbolizes the climber's accession to it. But the two ways, as Eliade also suggests, are inextricably intertwined. There may be two *directions*, but there is only one staircase. And a real knowledge of one's own depths (Jung's "collective unconscious" is one of the names these depths have been given) is a necessary prelude to an authentic acquaintance with the Absolute, Henry Miller would argue.

This paradox is undoubtedly what Pierre Trahard has in mind when he writes, in *Le mystère poétique*, that only a small minority of people are aware of the possibilities of "la vie secrète." The majority live in a state of blissful unawareness. Yet they also participate, without realizing it, in the collective unconscious which takes the shape of fables, legends, myths, and imagination, the repositories of such eternal forms as werewolves and will-o'-the-wisps, monsters and magicians, devils and gods. In this way they are related to the poet, whose concern is with the mystery of the unconscious, which becomes

> le mystère de la poésie même. Ce mystère, chaque effort l'éclaircit, sans le dégager, complètement, de ses ombres; les choses qui ne sont pas vraies aujourd'hui le seront peut-être demain. Une aurore monte du fond de l'inconscient, et le poète la salue avec une joie tremblante.[102]

The poet, in brief, faces the perilous responsibility of appropriating, on behalf of the less conscious members of the tribe of man, as much of the still "unreal" as he possibly can into the sphere of the so-called "real"; he faces the task of *making* the "real." Baudelaire is the archetypal modern poet, according to Guy Michaud,

101 Mircea Eliade, *Images and Symbols: Studies in Religious Symbolism* (New York: Sheed and Ward, 1969), p. 51.
102 Pierre Trahard, *Le mystère poétique* (Paris: A.G. Nizet, 1969), p. 86.

parce qu'il s'avance au delà du Romantisme dans les âpres sentiers de la mauvaise conscience et de la quête d'absolu. Et il est poète moderne, parce que, le premier, il lie la cause de la poésie à celle de l'homme, qu'il s'engage totalement dans l'aventure poétique, et qu'il demande désespérément à cette poésie la solution de ses conflits et l'acces à un monde véritable.[103]

We've seen already that the *Symbolistes* found little to admire and cherish in the quotidian as such, but it is an unavoidable fact of human existence that their work should be deeply *rooted* in the quotidian. Both Baudelaire's *Les fleurs du mal* (with its "fourmillante cité") and Rimbaud's *Illuminations* (with its "métropole crue moderne") display, at every turn, a great – even voracious – dependency on the realities of everyday existence. Henry Miller is very much like them in this respect. His *Tropic* trilogy literally grows out of the teeming sub-soil of the "fourmillante cité." But, as is the case with Baudelaire and Rimbaud, the raw materials of the quotidian *chez* Miller have a way of being alchemically transmuted into the "miraculous." Here is a passage about Brooklyn in *Black Spring:*

From the tops of the skyscrapers plumes of smoke soft as Cleopatra's feathers. The air beats thick, the bats are flapping, the cement softens, the iron rails flatten under the broad flanges of the trolley wheels. Life is written down in headlines twelve feet high with periods, commas and semicolons. The bridge sways over the gasoline lakes below. Melons rolling in from Imperial Valley, garbage going down past Hell Gate, the decks clear, the stanchions gleaming, the hawsers tight, the slips grunting, the moss splitting and spelching in the ferry slips. A warm sultry haze lying over the city like a cup of fat, the sweat trickling down between the bare legs, around the slim ankles. A mucous mass of arms and legs, of halfmoons and weather vanes, of cock robins and round robins, of shuttlecocks and bright bananas with the light lemon pulp lying in the bell of the peel. Five o'clock strikes through the grime and sweat of the afternoon, a strip of bright shadow left by the iron girders. The trolleys wheel round with iron mandibles, crunching the papier-mâché of the crowd, spooling it down like punched transfers.[104]

103 *Message poétique*, p. 44.
104 *Black Spring*, pp. 136-137. In this regard, Miller again resembles the American Transcendentalists – who also had a knack for turning the commonplace into the miraculous. But this may simply be another case of parallel tendencies. In *The Mind and Art of Henry Miller*, William A. Gordon gives ample attention to Miller's concern with the major revelations which are latent in everyday reality. But the conclusion this leads Gordon to is that Miller belongs in the camp of William Wordsworth – a poet whom Miller has barely read and can't abide!

There's something akin to an *epiphany* in such a moment; the "unreal" of everyday life is on the verge of taking a leap into "the absolute real." And *Black Spring* abounds in such moments. One of the most unforgettable occurs in "The Fourteenth Ward," an account of Miller's young manhood in Brooklyn and the first chapter of the book:

> And then one day, as if suddenly the flesh came undone and the blood beneath the flesh had coalesced with the air, suddenly the whole world roars again and the very skeleton of the body melts like wax. Such a day it may be when first you encounter Dostoevski. You remember the smell of the tablecloth on which the book rests; you look at the clock and it is only five minutes from eternity; you count the objects on the mantelpiece because the sound of numbers is a totally new sound in your mouth, because everything old and new or touched and forgotten, is a fire and a mesmerism. Now every door of the cage is open and whichever way you walk is *a straight line toward infinity*, a straight mad line over which the breakers roar and great rocs of marble and indigo swoop to lower their fevered eggs. Out of the waves beating phosphorescent step proud and prancing the enamel horses that marched with Alexander, their tight-proud bellies glowing with calcium, their nostrils dipped in laudanum. Now it is all snow and lice, with the great band of Orion slung around the ocean's crotch.[105]

The chiliastic fever which Miller refers to as "only five minutes from eternity" is a familiar item in the *Symboliste* lexicon. James L. Kugel cites a passage in Andrej Belyj's *Recollections of A. Blok* to show how the Russian *Symbolistes* were especially affected by this sense of "the perception of the dawn, the fact of daybreak" which they had inherited from their French forebears (cf. e.g., Rimbaud's scintillating "L'aube" in *Illuminations*). He goes on to explain that for this school of writers

> to write a poem in the new "strange" style was to say in their poetry precisely the same thing they said in expository prose when they wrote about their alienation from contemporary standards and their sense of the coming apocalypse... That which is mysterious is always set off, separate from us, foreign; and with mysteriousness the Symbolists created a barrier parallel to those present in their thinking about a New Age....[106]

This *Symboliste* infatuation with a "New Age" is one of the keystones of Henry Miller's work. No critic has yet remarked that it is the

105 *Ibid.*, pp. 12-13.
106 *Techniques of Strangeness*, pp. 27-29.

central theme of *Black Spring*; it figures crucially in all ten of that book's pointedly eschatological sketches. The coda of the second sketch, "Third or Fourth Day of Spring," begins with the words:

> From now on, ladies and gentlemen, you are entering Mexico. From now on everything will be wonderful and beautiful, marvelously beautiful, marvelously wonderful. Increasingly marvelously beautiful and wonderful. From now on no more washlines, no suspenders, no flannel underwear. Always summer and everything true to patterns.[107]

The next-to-last piece, a hilariously looney and hallucinating account of a revival-meeting entitled "Burlesk," climaxes with Miller travestying the enthusiastic *élan* of the revivalist:

> Well, you are right and you are wrong, Brother Eaton. Wrong because the law of hypothecation does not permit of what is known as doing the duck; wrong because the equation is carried over by an asterisk whereas *the sign points clearly to infinity*; right because all that is wrong has to do with incertitude and in clearing away dead matter an enema is not sufficient. Brother Eaton, what you see on the horizon line is neither a homunculus nor a plugged hat. It is the shadow of Praxus. It shrinks to diminutive proportions in the measure that Praxus waxes great. As Praxus advances beyond the palc of the tertiary moon he disembarrasses himself more and more of his terrestrial image. Little by little he divests himself of the mirror of substantiality. When the last illusion has been shattered Praxus will cast no shadow. He will stand on the 49th parallel of the unwritten eclogue and waste away in cold fire. There will be no more paranoia, everything else being equal. The body will shed its skins and the organs of man will hold themselves proudly in the light. Should there be a war you will please rearrange the entrails according to their astrologic significance. *The dawn is breaking* over the viscera. No more logic, no more liver mantic. *There will be a new heaven and a new earth...* (Italics mine).[108]

I've already demonstrated how, in the sermon on "REVOLUTION" in *The Colossus of Maroussi*, Miller traces the failure of this "New Age" to dawn on schedule to man's *fear*: "Nothing can bring about a new and better world but our own desire for it. Man kills through fear – and fear is hydra-headed."[109] But Miller is as sanguine about the imminence of the "New Age" as were the Russian and French *Symbolistes* of the *fin de siècle*. In Part Three of *Colossus*, he writes:

107 *Black Spring*, p. 28.
108 *Ibid.*, p. 200.
109 *Colossus*, p. 83.

The world which passed away with Delphi passed away as in a sleep. It is the same now. Victory and defeat are meaningless in the light of the wheel which relentlessly revolves. We are moving into a new latitude of the soul, and a thousand years hence men will wonder at our blindness, our torpor, our supine acquiescence to an order which was doomed.[110]

Like the *Symbolistes*, Miller espouses the belief that it is the tribe of man ("the indestructible morsels of living flesh") who must appropriate the absolute real – "an absolutely new condition of life," as he puts it in *The Wisdom of the Heart*, an "entirely new cosmos."[111]

Henry Miller's quest for the Absolute began very early in his boyhood. Its first manifestation, not surprisingly for an Orphic type, was woman: the lost Eurydice. The French scholar, F.-J. Temple, has pointed out an interesting parallel between Henry Miller and D.H. Lawrence in this respect:

On ne peut s'empêcher de remarquer que presque à la même époque un drame analogue se jouait en Angleterre, [pour] une autre raison: D.-H. Lawrence quittait "comme un homme frappé par une sentence d'exil" son amie d'enfance, Jessie Chambers (la Miriam de *Sons and Lovers*). Là aussi, un amour avorté, un fiasco, devait se terminer par un hurlement de terreur. Miller évoquera dans *Tropic of Capricorn* cet épisode de sa vie [the painful loss of his childhood sweetheart, Cora Seward, whom he calls Una Gifford in *Capricorn*], pour se demander ce qui a bien pu arriver alors. Qu'est-ce que la fonction sexuelle sans la tendresse? Pourquoi a-t-il fui cet amour?... Pas plus que Lawrence n'oubliera Jessie, Miller n'a oublié Cora Seward. Pour tous deux, ces femmes furent la personnification d'un absolu. Ils n'imaginaient pas qu'il leur fût donner de l'atteindre.[112]

Miller himself readily confirms this explanation that it was a woman who provided the primal impulse to desire to connect with the Absolute (in the earlier *Tropic of Cancer*):

Going back in a flash over the women I've known. It's like a chain which I've forged out of my own misery. Each one bound to the other. A fear of living separate, of staying born. The door of the womb always on the latch. Dread and longing. Deep in the blood the pull of Paradise. The beyond. Always the beyond. It must have all started with the navel. They cut the umbilical cord,

110 *Ibid.*, p. 195.
111 *Wisdom*, p. 163.
112 F.-J. Temple, *Henry Miller* (Paris: Editions Universitaires-Classiques du XXe Siècle, 1965), pp. 21-22.

give you a slap on the ass, and presto! you're out in the world, adrift, a ship without a rudder.[113]

Later, exactly like Arthur Rimbaud (as I will demonstrate in Chapter Four), Miller's craving for the paradisaical was to take the form of a frenzied mystique of Childhood-as-an-absolute. The revolt of the unsullied child against its parents is the earliest and purest response to a world that's always striving, with the unfair advantages of its greater years and social power, to make the child's soul a quotidian replica of its own finished habits and usages. As long as the child remains a child, it can fend off "responsibility" and pleasantly enjoy the cosy womb of its privileged "beyond."

But how successful has Miller been, as a writer, at catching the Absolute on the printed page? Is it possible to measure "success" or "failure" in dealing with such an elusive quantum as the Absolute? Professor John Senior wittily observes that such "successes and failures are relative only to each other, not to the Absolute. No one has more or less of the Absolute; no method can be perfected and passed on, like an industrial process, to succeeding generations."[114] The major *Symbolistes*, as we have already seen, made systematic use of sounds to create their "miraculous" effects. They also used colors. (Rimbaud provides the *locus classicus* in his notorious "Sonnet des voyelles.") Stephane Mallarmé's use of the color blue to articulate the difficult concept of the Absolute finds expression in his own equally difficult term, "l'azur." This beautiful word, which denotes both "blue" and "sky" in French, is virtually untranslatable and perhaps for this reason it became common linguistic coin in the *Symboliste* purse:

> En vain! l'Azur triomphe, et je l'entends qui chante
> Dans les cloches. Mon âme, il se fait voix pour plus
> Nous faire peur avec sa victoire méchante,
> Et du métal vivant sort en bleus angélus!
>
> Il roule par la brume, ancien, et traverse
> Ta native agonie ainsi qu'un glaive sûr;
> Où fuir dans la révolte inutile et perverse?
> *Je suis hanté*. L'Azur! l'Azur! l'Azur! l'Azur![115]

113 *Cancer*, pp. 275-276.
114 *Down and Out*, p. 115.
115 Stéphane Mallarmé, *Oeuvres Complètes* (Paris: Bibliothèque de la Pléiade-Editions Gallimard, 1945), p. 38.

Greece, with its uncanny hazeless light that gives one the impression that everything within sight has a greater degree of *proximity* than elsewhere, was an ideal choice for Miller to make in order to come into contact with "l'azur." In one of the earliest walks he describes in *Colossus* (in the direction of Mount Hymettos on the outskirts of Athens), he tells us:

> One is impelled to keep walking, to move on towards the mirage which is ever retreating. When one comes to the edge, to the great wall of mountains, the light becomes even more intoxicating; one feels as if he could bound up the side of the mountain in a few giant strides, and then – why then, if one did get to the top, clear into the sky, one clear headlong flight into the blue and Amen forever.... Here the light penetrates directly into the soul, opens the doors and windows of the heart, makes one naked, exposed, isolated in a metaphysical bliss which makes everything clear without being known. No analysis can go on in this light: here the neurotic is either instantly healed or goes mad.[116]

Much later, during the memorable trip to Phaestos (which he explicitly calls "a piece of the Absolute"[117]), Miller gives us a description of "l'azur" which has a near-Mallarméan *élan:*

> The rain has stopped, the clouds have broken; the vault of blue spreads out like a fan, the blue decomposing into that ultimate violet light which makes everything Greek seem holy, natural and familiar. In Greece one has the desire to bathe in the sky. You want to rid yourself of your clothes, take a running leap and vault into the blue. You want to float in the air like an angel or lie in the grass rigid and enjoy the cataleptic trance. Stone and sky, they marry here. It is the perpetual dawn of man's awakening.[118]

But a *Symboliste* poet, as Mallarmé well knew, doesn't need the "actual" blue of the Greek sky to body forth his sense of the Absolute in a work of art. Three years before he ventured to Greece, Henry Miller published an extraordinary prose sketch called "The Angel is My Watermark!" in which he minutely describes the process of painting a watercolor which starts out as a "horse's ass" and ends up as a "blue angel." Though the essay has all the outward trappings of improvisation and sheer delirium, in reality it moves with the inexorable inner "logic" of a *Symboliste* prose poem towards the

116 *Colossus*, pp. 44-45.
117 *Ibid.*, p. 158.
118 *Ibid.*, p. 159.

revelation of its final *mysterium*: the "blue angel frozen by the glaciers." (One cannot help being reminded immediately of Mallarmé's swan with its feet frozen in the ice). It is an angel in "a cold blue spotlight which throws into relief his fallen stomach and his broken arches. The angel is there to lead you to Heaven, where it is all plus and no minus."[119] Miller's angel must pass through a series of transmutations before it finally emerges as an angel and a door thus abruptly opens out on the Absolute. Likewise, the final *epiphany* is foreshadowed in another shape earlier in the sketch:

> When you find the plus equivalent you have – *nothing*. You have that imaginary, momentary something called "a balance." A balance never is. It's a fraud, like stopping the clock, or like calling a truce. You strike a balance in order to add a hypothetical weight, in order to create a reason for your existence.
>
> I have never been able to draw a balance. I am always *minus* something. I have a reason therefore to go on. I am putting my whole life into the balance in order that it may produce nothing. To get to nothing you have to lay out an infinitude of figures. That's just it: in the living equation the sign for myself is infinity.[120]

Clearly the way to the Absolute can be found only through an infinite series of subtractions. We are back at Lawrence Durrell's "Zero in the heraldic sense." Or, as Miller words it at the close of Part One of *Colossus*, "Zero is Greek for pure vision."[121] And in fact the emphasis on a series of strongly *visual* images which culminates in the radiant ikon of the "blue angel" in "The Angel is My Watermark" is one of Miller's most vividly artful exemplifications of the Illuminist paradox he propounds later in *Colossus*.

One of the reasons Henry Miller was so deeply impressed with Rimbaud is that the great French *illuminé* had the awesome daring to wish for the actualization of his quasi-heroic vision of the Absolute in the realm of everyday life. As early as the Fall of 1937, Anaïs Nin records in her *Diary* that Miller had told her "whoever reaches an absolute and dies for it, sainthood, or Rimbaud's madness, is *right*."[122] This may explain why, in *The Colossus of Maroussi*, Miller so zestfully reproduces Katsimbalis' stirring monologue about Pericles

119 *Black Spring*, pp. 66-67.
120 *Ibid.*, pp. 65-66.
121 *Colossus*, p. 96.
122 Anaïs Nin, *The Diary of Anaïs Nin*: 1934-1939, Vol. 2 (New York: Harcourt, Brace & World, 1967), p. 248.

Yannopoulos – a legendary Greek poet/art critic who committed suicide, spectacularly, in 1910 and whom the aged Katsimbalis described to me on April 4, 1974, as "a Greek Ruskin who *acted*!" Katsimbalis' vibrant delineation tempts one, at every turn, to substitute the name of Rimbaud for that of Yannopoulos:

"I'll read you some of Yannopoulos when we get back to Athens. I'll read you what he says about the rocks – just the rocks, nothing more. You can't know what a rock is until you've heard what Yannopoulos has written. He talks about rocks for pages and pages; he *invents* rocks, by God, when he can't find any to rave about. People say he was crazy, Yannopoulos. He wasn't crazy – he was *mad*. There's a difference. His voice was too strong for his body: it consumed him. He was like Icarus – the sun melted his wings. He soared too high. He was an eagle. These rabbits we call critics can't understand a man like Yannopoulos. He was out of proportion. He raved about the wrong things, according to them. He didn't have *le sens de mesure*, as the French say. There you are – *mesure*. What a mean little word! They look at the Parthenon and they find the proportions so harmonious. All rot. The human proportions which the Greek extolled were superhuman. They weren't *French* proportions. They were divine, because the true Greek is a god, not a cautious, precise, calculating being with the soul of an engineer...."[123]

The secret of men like Yannopoulos and Rimbaud, both on the human and artistic planes, is that they seemed equally capable of making terrible *descents* and terrible *ascents*. Earlier in this section, I characterized the symbol of the staircase as having two directions but as remaining one staircase. It is this *ying/yang* principle derived from Chinese philosophy, it would appear, that provides the surest access to the Absolute. Henry Miller makes unquestionably clear in *Colossus* that, humanly speaking, he was able to achieve a reconciliation of warring opposites in himself: heaven/earth, light/dark, love/hate, here/there, ascent/descent, chronos/keiros. And the clue he gives us to this achievement lies in a reference to Balzac's *Séraphita:*

123 *Colossus*, p. 68. The suicide of Pericles Yannopoulos (1869-1910), like that of Vladimir Majakovskij in Russia, is part of one of the most famous legends in contemporary Greek literature. Yannopoulos, whose career as a writer had apparently reached an impasse, had also been experiencing romantic troubles with a mysterious woman about whom, even in 1974, Katsimbalis would not talk with me on one of several visits to his house. On a beautiful day in 1910, the statuesquely handsome Yannopoulos, completely dressed in white, rode on horseback into the Sea of Salamis near Eleusis and drowned.

There is only one analogy I can make to explain the nature of this illuminating voyage which began at Poros and ended at Tripolis perhaps two months later. I must refer the reader to the ascension of Seraphita, as it was glimpsed by her devout followers. It was a voyage into the light. The earth became illuminated by her own inner light.[124]

In an even more suggestive essay called "Balzac and His Double," Miller had written:

Balzac's whole life and work....represents a veritable "search for the absolute." The *sustained antagonism* in the very heart and core of life is the key-note; it is the same passionate quest, the same struggle to wrest from life the secret of creation, which influenced D.H. Lawrence in writing *The Crown*. "For Balzac," to quote Curtius..., "unity is a mystic principle, the mark, *the seal of the Absolute*." In the book called *The Search for the Absolute* this secret of the philosopher's stone is discovered by the hero only when he is dying.[125]

Mircea Eliade calls Balzac's *Séraphita* "the last great work of European literature that has the myth of the androgyne [a mythic being which combines the two sexes in one] as its central theme."[126] I think it's worth quoting at length what Eliade implies about the relationship between the two-in-one and the Absolute. There is, he maintains,

a parallel between the "Prologue in Heaven" of *Faust* [a work which is known to have enthralled both Rimbaud and Henry Miller] and Balzac's *Séraphita*. Both works are concerned with the question of the *coincidentia oppositorum* and with totality. The mystery is hardly perceptible in the "sympathy" that binds God to Mephistopheles, but it is perfectly recognizable in the myth of the Androgyne borrowed by Balzac from Swedenborg.... It is well known that for Nicholas of Cusa the *coincidentia oppositorum* was the least imperfect definition of God. It is well known also that one of the sources of his inspiration was the Pseudo-Areopagite. Now, as the Areopagite said, the union of opposites in God constitutes a mystery.... I will not dwell...on the importance of the concept of totality in the work of C.G. Jung. It is sufficient to recall that the expressions, *coincidentia oppositorum*, *complexio oppositorum*, union of opposites, *mysterium coniunctionis*, etc., are frequently used by Jung to describe the totality of the Self and the mystery of the dual nature of Christ. According to Jung the process of individualization essentially consists of a sort of *coincidentia oppo-*

124 *Colossus*, pp. 56-57.
125 *Wisdom*, p. 244.
126 Mircea Eliade, *The Two and the One* (New York and Evanston: Harper & Row, 1965), p. 99.

> *sitorum*, for the Self comprises both the whole consciousness and the contents of the unconscious. In *Die Pyschologie der Uebertragung* and the *Mysterium Coniunctionis* are to be found the most complete exposition of the Jungian theory of the *coincidentia oppositorum* as the ultimate aim of the whole psychic activity [or, in less strictly scientific terms, the realization of the Absolute at the individual level].[127]

Indeed a cursory look at *Mysterium Coniunctionis* will convince anyone (cf. Volume 14, Bollingen Series) that to C.G. Jung the union of opposite tendencies in human life is the *ne plus ultra*, an Absolute of psychic activity.

One of Henry Miller's most succinct statements on the subject of the reconciliation of opposites occurs in the middle of Part Three of *Colossus*. Miller had yet to encounter the Armenian soothsayer who described his "dual life" (heaven/earth) to him, at that point, but he had already experienced the "terrific synchronization of dream and reality" outside of Thebes and had drunk from the waters of the Castellian Spring (past/present):

> In the museum I came again upon the colossal Theban statues which have never ceased to haunt me and finally we stood before the amazing statue of Antinous, last of the gods. I could not help but contrast in my mind this most wonderful idealization in stone of *the eternal duality of man*, so bold and simple, so thoroughly Greek in the best sense, with that literary creation of Balzac's, *Séraphita*, which is altogether vague and mysterious and, humanly speaking, altogether unconvincing. Nothing could better convey the transition from light to darkness, from the pagan to the Christian conception of life, than this enigmatic figure of the last god on earth who flung himself into the Nile [shades of Rimbaud and Yannopoulos!]. By emphasizing the soulful qualities of man Christianity succeeded only in disembodying man; as angel the sexes fuse into the sublime spiritual being which man essentially is. The Greeks, on the other hand, gave body to everything, *thereby incarnating the spirit and eternalizing it*. In Greece one is ever filled with *the sense of eternality* which is expressed in the here and now.[128]

But there exists an even more succinct statement of this "miracle" in modern literature: "Elle est retrouvée./Quoi? – L'Éternité./C'est la mer allée/Avec le soleil (Arthur Rimbaud)."[129] Which brings us to the

127 *Ibid.*, pp. 80-81.
128 *Colossus*, p. 196.
129 Arthur Rimbaud, *Oeuvres Complètes* (Paris: Bibliothèque de la Pléiade-Editions Gallimard, 1954), p. 133.

question of how *artistically* successful Henry Miller has been in bodying forth his great human vision of the crucial unification of *ying* and *yang*. It's one thing to achieve union with the Absolute in one's life; it's quite another to give an apprehensible account of it in literature. If Miller is to be considered a genuine artist of the *Symboliste* stripe, how effectively does he manipulate the *Symboliste's* stock-in-trade – symbols?

There are a number of important Illuminist/alchemist symbols (such as gold, water, fire, blood, and light) which I intend to deal with in my chapter on Miller and Rimbaud. But I believe a strong case can be made for Miller's attainment of something verging on "the Absolute" in the handling of literary symbols by focusing on three powerful and suggestive symbols he deploys in *The Colossus of Maroussi*: the *colossus*, the *flower*, and the *rooster*. I will start with the last of these – the rooster – which figures merely in an appendix to *Colossus* in the form of a splendid anecdote quoted by Miller from a letter written to him by Lawrence Durrell after Miller had left Greece. Durrell ends his letter by saying that the event it describes is "part of the mosaic" and should be included in Miller's book; the *Symboliste* poet in Miller readily agreed. This is the way Orpheus/Durrell sings it:

We all went up to the Acropolis the other evening very drunk and exalted by wine and poetry; it was a hot black night and our blood was roaring with cognac. We sat on the steps outside the big gate, passing the bottle, Katsimbalis reciting and G – weeping a little, when all of a sudden K. was seized with a kind of fit. Leaping to his feet he yelled out – "Do you want to hear the cocks of Attica, you damned moderns?" His voice had a hysterical edge to it. We didn't answer and he wasn't waiting for one. He took a little run to the edge of the precipe, like a faery queen, a heavy black faery queen, in his black clothes, threw back his head, clapped the crook of his stock into his wounded arm, and sent out the most blood-curdling clarion I have ever heard. Cock-a-doodle-doo. It echoed all over the city – a sort of dark bowl dotted with lights like cherries. It ricochetted from hillock to hillock and wheeled up under the walls of the Parthenon.... We were so shocked that we were struck dumb. And while we were still looking at each other in the darkness, lo, from the distance silvery clear in the darkness a cock drowsily answered – then another, then another. This drove K. wild. Squaring himself, like a bird about to fly into space, and flapping his coat tails, he set up a terrific scream – and the echoes multiplied. He screamed until the veins stood out all over him. Looking like a battered and ravaged rooster in profile, flapping on his own dunghill. He screamed himself hysterical and his audience in the valley increased until all over Athens like bugles they were calling and calling, answering him. Finally between laughter and hysteria we had to ask him to stop. The whole night was alive with cock-crows – all Athens, all Attica, all Greece, it seemed, until I almost imagined you being woken at your desk late in New York to hear these terrific silver peals: Katsimbaline cock-crow in Attica.[130]

Both the Orphics and the *Symbolistes* programmatically set themselves the mission of "waking up" mankind, it's well known. It was as a sort of *Symboliste*/Orphic "awakener" that Henry Thoreau placed the words: "I do not propose to write an ode to dejection, but to brag as lustily as chanticleer in the morning, standing on his roost, if only to wake my neighbors up"[131] as an epigraph to the first edition of *Walden*. Juan Eduardo Cirlot, whose masterful lexicon/treatise on symbols Sir Herbert Read calls a "profound study of symbolism in all its aspects,"[132] throws light on the dedicated wakener's partiality to the rooster as a symbol. (I consider Señor Cirlot's brilliant study definitive; its interpretations cogently synthesize the collective findings of such symbologists as Bachelard, Frobenius, C.G. Jung, Briffault, Zimmer, Cumont, Sir James Frazer, Bachofen, and Freud). Cirlot writes:

As the bird of dawn, the cock is a sun-symbol, and an emblem of vigilance and activity. Immolated to Priapus and Aesculapius, it was supposed to cure the sick. During the Middle Ages it became a highly important Christian image, nearly always appearing on the highest weathervanes, on cathedral towers and domes, and was regarded as an allegory of vigilance and resurrection. Davy comments that vigilance in this context must be taken in the sense of "tending towards eternity and taking care to grant first place to the things of the spirit, to be wakeful and to greet the Sun – Christ – even before it rises in the East" – illumination.[133]

130 *Colossus*, pp. 243-244.
131 Henry David Thoreau, *Walden, or Life in the Woods* (New York: Holt, Rinehart & Winston, 1948), p. xiii.
132 *Dictionary of Symbols*, p. ix.
133 *Ibid.*, p. 49. I would agree that there are real differences between the *Symboliste* use of the single extended symbol which gives organic unity and structure to a particular poem and the Jungian symbological, *archetypal* analysis to which I refer several times in this study. The latter deals with materials that are often as diffuse as Henry Miller's less controlled *Symboliste* constructs. However, there are intriguing similarities between the two and these have been identified in Jane Nelson's *Form and Image in the Fiction of Henry Miller* (cf. pp. 14-15, p. 94, and *passim*).

Henry Miller could not have been unaware of the potent suggestiveness of the cock as a symbol. It will be remembered that his own last words in *The Colossus of Maroussi*, just before incorporating Durrell's anecdote of the cocks of Attica into the book, is the lusty, visionary "Book of Revelation" cock-crow on behalf of the "life more abundant."

Flowers also play an extremely evocative role in the structure of *Colossus*. At a number of luminous (indeed *numinous*) moments in the book,[134] Miller invokes flower-symbolism in order to make an important point, quietly and without commentary. But his most suggestive use of such symbolism occurs at the end of Part Three and serves as the specific catalyst that precipitates his radiant "Book of Revelation" soliloquy:

> But the most trivial incident, if it happened to Katsimbalis, had a way of blossoming into a great event. It might be nothing more than that he had picked a flower by the roadside on his way home. But when he had done with the story that flower, humble though it might be, would become the most wonderful flower that ever a man had picked. That flower would remain in the memory of the listener as the flower which Katsimbalis had picked; it would become unique, not because there was anything in the least extraordinary about it, but because Katsimbalis had immortalized it by noticing it, because he had put into that flower all that he thought and felt about flowers, which is like saying – a universe.
> I choose this image at random but how appropriate and accurate it is! When I think of Katsimbalis bending over to pick a flower from the bare soil of Attica, the whole Greek world, past, present and future rises before me. I see...[135]

And at this point Miller intones his beautiful litany of images of Greece, brilliantly summarizing all the major themes of his book (from voyages to light, from Solitude to the Androgyne) – all, it would appear, because of a "humble" flower.

This "appropriate and accurate" symbol, as Miller himself terms it – with a *délicatesse de Symboliste* that does no more than hint – is, because of its shape, an image of the "Centre," and hence "an archetypal image of the soul." According to Cirlot, meteorites and shooting stars are given the name "celestial flower" by the alchemists and the flower was, for them, "symbolic of the work of the sun." The "blue flower" is a familiar symbol of the impossible, while the "golden

134 Cf. *Colossus*, esp. pp. 17, 49, 92, 125 and 141.
135 *Ibid*., p. 240.

flower" is a famous parallel in Chinese mysticism, a non-existent flower which is "also spoken of in alchemy." It is sometimes given the name of "the sapphire-blue flower of the Hermaphrodite."[136] The refusal to offer the reader any exegetical data about Katsimbalis' "flower," other than to call it "appropriate and accurate," is a good example of what James L. Kugel calls the device of "withheld information." It patently makes for a lovely "strangeness."

Miller's third great symbol, the colossus, implicitly and explicitly dominates the entire book. It rather "obviously" applies to all of Miller's Orphic avatars in *Colossus*, especially George Katsimbalis of Maroussi. But it is in reality Miller's most elusive and most "evocative" symbol. Lest the derivation of this now utterly hackneyed word[137] be entirely forgotten, I venture to remind the reader that the term derives from the original Ancient Greek Colossus of Rhodes – which not only colossally "bestrode the narrow world" in the shape of a bronze statue of Apollo (the god of *light*), but as a *lighthouse* whose function was to lead ships safely home to harbor! Miller's cunning use of the word, therefore, not only serves to designate his own heroic music-makers as larger-than-life beings but as light-bringers and direction-setters towards "home" (the Homeric *nóstos*). Even before writing *The Colossus of Maroussi*, Miller had compared himself to a lighthouse whose ever-glowing eye was "wide-awake" in *Tropic of Capricorn.*[138] Light, of course, is traditionally "equated with the spirit" and "the All"; the sunlight which shines from the East symbolizes "illumination."[139]

136 Cirlot, *Dictionary of Symbols*, p. 105.

137 Interestingly, when Duke Ellington died in May, 1974, *Time* Magazine's obituary (June 3, 1974, p. 47) referred to him as a "colossus of jazz." *Vide* what Henry Miller has to say about the colossal "Duke of Ellington" in the jazz cadenza of *Colossus* (pp. 138-145) in 1941!

138 *Capricorn*, pp. 75-76. Miller may well be indebted for his lighthouse metaphor to a book he has written about with boundless enthusiasm, Elie Faure's *The Dance Over Fire and Water*. In this book, the French writer (whom Miller regards as one of the unsung colossi of modern literature) says the following: "Heroes are lighthouses for the multitude, and toward them all souls push on in the night.... The glow of great souls revolves around the horizon only to show men how to fly from the tempest, or to govern their ship in the tempest." Cf. Elie Faure, *The Dance Over Fire and Water* (New York: Harper & Brothers, 1926), p. 11.

139 Cirlot, *Dictionary of Symbols*, p. 179.

Authentic symbols are the keys to new modalities of reality which are not revealed to us at once on the plane of quotidian existence. True symbols are surcharged with a numinous glow which can link the "real" and the "unreal" and thus unlock for us the passageway to the Absolute. Anyone who uses or understands symbols not only establishes links with the objective world, but can also leap out of its constraining boundaries and achieve communion with others and with the Absolute. Henry Miller is conscious of as much when he writes in his study of Rimbaud, *The Time of the Assassins*, that the symbol is a key "which the creator alone possesses. It is the alphabet of the soul, pristine and indestructible. By means of it the poet, who is the lord of imagination and the unacknowledged ruler of the world, communicates, holds communion, with his fellow man."[140] And what important key-meaning do Miller's three symbols of *rooster, flower*, and *colossus* bear in common in *The Colossus of Maroussi*? It's very simple. All three are *sun*-symbols. All three point, in their powerfully wordless way, to the transcendent truth of "illumination." All three serve also to remind us, among other things, that a close bond of kinship exists between Henry Miller and that other "fils du soleil," Arthur Rimbaud.

140 Henry Miller, *The Time of the Assassins: A Study of Rimbaud* (New York: New Directions, 1962), p. 92.

CHAPTER FOUR

THE RIMBAUD FACTOR

1. "Une fatalité de bonheur"

> *" 'So you think Rimbaud is greater than all the American poets put together?' said one young man challengingly.*
>
> *'Yes, I do. I think he's greater than all the French poets put together too.' "*
>
> Henry Miller in *The Colossus of Maroussi*

Few American writers have been as enthusiastic in openly admitting to a passion for books as Henry Miller. Miller's voracious and life-long appetite for books and his devotion to those who make it their life's work to write them are essential and recurrent themes in his own writings. And there is something that can only be called a Chaucerian joyfulness to the verve and meticulousness with which Miller has chronicled his early encounters with the world of "olde bookes" and has documented the impact upon his greedy imagination of such writers as Rabelais, Boccaccio, Maeterlinck, Walt Whitman, and Dostoevsky in *The Books in My Life*. Each new author Miller came in touch with seemed to suggest to him a possible new self-metamorphosis which would enable him to become more fully himself by means of the favorite author. But for the phenomenal young author of *Illuminations* and *Une saison en enfer*, Arthur Rimbaud, Miller professes a devotion that borders on sheer idolatry – a predictably Narcissistic sort of idolatry:

> In Rimbaud I see myself as in a mirror. Nothing he says is alien to me, however wild, absurd or difficult to understand. To understand one has to surrender, and I remember distinctly making that surrender the first day I glanced at his work. I read only a few lines that day, a little over ten years ago [i.e., around 1933-1934], and trembling like a leaf I put the book away. I had the feeling then, and I have it still, that he had said *all* for our time. It was as though he had put a tent over the void. He is the only writer whom I have read and reread with undiminished joy and excitement, always discovering something new in him, always profoundly touched by his purity.... He is the one writer whose genius I envy; all the others, no matter how great, never arouse my jealousy.... Had I

read Rimbaud in my youth I doubt that I would ever have written a line.... What interests me extremely in Rimbaud is his vision of Paradise regained, Paradise *earned*. This, of course, is something apart from the splendor and the magic of his words, which I consider incomparable.[1]

It is clear from the foregoing that Miller considers himself little less than the twentieth-century *alter ego* of Rimbaud, a sort of bald-headed Rimbaud *redivivus*.

Miller's claim may not be as extravagant as it appears to be on the face of it. But the critical question for comparative scholarship is: In what ways, specifically, does Miller's own work evince genuinely measurable lines of connection with that of Rimbaud? How extensive are Miller's resemblances to and adaptations of the great themes and techniques of Rimbaud? I think a good case can be made for a high degree of ideological and artistic consanguinity between Rimbaud and Miller, particularly between the former's *Illuminations* and the latter's *The Colossus of Maroussi*. It is obvious that Miller devoted a good deal of time to the study of Rimbaud's techniques. *Colossus* contains numerous references, implicit and explicit, to Rimbaud and Rimbaud's influence.[2] *The Time of the Assassins*, devoted entirely to the meaning of Rimbaud's life and works, traces the French poet's direct influence back to the years 1933-1934, a full five years before Miller's trip to Greece.[3] In a letter of February 7, 1932, to Anaïs Nin, Miller expresses a desire "to become acquainted with the poetry of Rimbaud and Verlaine"[4] and Anaïs Nin's own diary for that month mentions the pleasure she derives watching Miller "writing a hundred pages after our talks together" after exploring, among other things, "the illuminations of Rimbaud."[5]

In general, it can be said that both *Illuminations* and *The Colossus of Maroussi* deal with the problem of "being an artist" in a world which is either hostile to or baffled by artists. Stylistically, Rimbaud's book takes the form of a series of ingenious gnomic images or anecdotes which are often deliberately opaque or oracular, whereas Miller makes use of the *superficially* more accessible genre of the intimate

1 *Assassins*, pp. 108-109.
2 Cf. *Colossus*, esp. pp. 45, 53, 75, 115, 131, 132, and 138.
3 *Ibid.*, pp. 1-3.
4 *Letters to Anaïs Nin*, p. 22.
5 *Diary* (Vol. 1), p. 60.

travel narrative. But Sibyl or Baedeker, both writers are concerned with the same dilemmas and their symbologies are, not surprisingly, quite similar. In fact, after making close comparative scrutinies of the two books, back to back, I have come to think of *Colossus* as Henry Miller's *Illuminations*.

There's an abundance of symbolic material used by Rimbaud and Miller in identically the same ways – water, fire, light, darkness, blood, gold, angels, heaven, hell. All of these symbols will be examined in their appropriate places in the course of this chapter. But what both writers have in common, fundamentally, is that frenetic thirst for happiness which Rimbaud called "une fatalité de bonheur" in *Une saison en enfer*. In order to *achieve* this happiness, Rimbaud believed he would have to change himself utterly. He was prepared to adopt a number of crucial disguises or psychic roles which alone, he believed, would enable him to translate his dream into reality:

> Je devins un opéra fabuleux: je vis que tous les êtres ont une fatalité de bonheur: l'action n'est pas la vie, mais une façon de gâcher quelque force, un énervement. La morale est la faiblesse de la cervelle.
>
> A chaque être, plusieurs *autres* vies me semblaient dues. Ce monsieur ne sait ce qu'il fait: il est un ange. Cette famille est une nichée de chiens. Devant plusieurs hommes, je causai tout haut avec un moment d'une de leurs autres vies. – Ainsi, j'ai aimé un porc.
>
> Aucun des sophismes de la folie, – la folie qu'on enferme, – n'a été oublié par moi: je pourrais les redire tous, je tiens le système.[6]

This tactic of transforming life by first transforming oneself also found a ready acceptance in Miller. The *Tropics* and *The Rosy Crucifixion* abound in examples of tactical chameleon-play. And *The Colossus of Maroussi*, aside from being a grab-bag of prose poems which record a journey of discovery (like Rimbaud's *Illuminations*), adopts most of the major poses of Rimbaud's "opéra fabuleux" to achieve the desired end of "changing life." For the sake of cogency, I have reduced the metamorphoses which the two men most characteristically adopt – not only in *Illuminations* and *Colossus* but in other important works as well – to the five following: the poet as Demon, as Angel, as Dromomaniac, as Alchemist, and as *Voyant*. These themes, I believe, are the most original in Rimbaud and they appear

6 *Oeuvres*, p. 237.

to have been the most instructive to Miller in his perusal of Rimbaud's work.

The Demon in both Rimbaud and Miller is usually provoked into the open by the city, the supreme symbol of "civilization," with its limitless chaos and violence. As far back as *Tropic of Cancer*, Miller was writing about cities in language which is reminiscent of Rimbaud's angry diatribes:

> An eternal city, Paris! More eternal than Rome, more splendorous than Ninevah. The very navel of the world to which, like a blind and faltering idiot, one crawls back on hands and knees. And like a cork that has drifted finally to the dead center of the ocean, one floats here in the scum and wrack of the seas, listless, hopeless, heedless even of a passing Colombus. The cradles of civilization are the putrid sinks of the world, the charnel-house to which the stinking wombs confide their bloody packages of flesh and bone.[7]

The violence of "civilization" is a constant in Rimbaud and Miller. The outwardly nihilistic excesses in their writings can be regarded as protective *counter*-violence, tactical attempts of the threatened artist to fight fire with fire. The analogy is exact. Fire is an important symbol in *Illuminations* and *The Colossus of Maroussi*. It is perhaps a curious coincidence (although neither writer believes in "coincidence") that both Rimbaud and Miller composed their respective *Illuminations* in the face of devastating and fiery wars which had profound effects on their lives. In Rimbaud's case, the French débâcle of 1870 provided the trauma; in Miller's, World War Two. Miller was driven out of his Grecian "land of light" by the on-coming Germans in 1939, Rimbaud out of his new-found "ville lumière," Paris, by their ancestors in 1870 after having successfully made his escape from the restrictiveness of his mother's provincial Charleville.

The sensitivity of the two writers to the disintegrative aspects of the "chaos" which often goes by the name of "life" tends to bring out the demon/rebel in them, but it also instills in them a terrific craving for a change to its opposites: "cosmos," heaven. Rimbaud's heartbreaking "Vite! est-il d'autres vies?"[8] is paraphrased by Henry Miller almost a century later with undiminished naiveté and impatience: "*When would life begin*?"[9] One cannot help being impressed by the

7 *Cancer*, p. 179.
8 *Oeuvres*, p. 224.
9 *Colossus*, p. 6.

consistency with which both Miller and Rimbaud adopted the roles of angel, dromomaniac, alchemist, and *voyant* (merely the *dominant* "magical" roles in their respective "opéras fabuleux") as concerted programmatic gestures to help them attain the "paradise" they both longed for all their lives. Miller's "millennial" book, *Big Sur and the Oranges of Hieronymus Bosch* (1957), is merely a projection upon a California landscape of all the good things he had found in his Rimbaldian/Illuminist paradise in Greece, just as the hallucinatingly beautiful *topoi* Rimbaud invents in *Illuminations* are projections of the blissful world of brotherhood he had glimpsed briefly during his period of enthusiasm for the Paris Commune of 1871.[10] (I will be using the word "paradise" throughout this chapter in accordance with its Old Persian etymology, as defined in Webster's Third New International Dictionary – "pairi-daeza" being derived from the components *pairi* [meaning "around"] and *daeza* [meaning "wall"], which signify an "enclosed park, garden, orchard," "a place of bliss...characterized by favorable conditions" – i.e., a place clearly demarcated, recognizably set apart from other places, a pleasant and carefully defined enclave as opposed to an amorphous or indefinite locale – a definition which, I believe, accounts also for some of the specifically "paradisaical" emotions one experiences while reading any piece of artfully executed or "enclosed" writing.)

All the exemplary characters whom Henry Miller celebrates in *The Colossus of Maroussi* are marked by an aggressively child-like, Rimbaldian nostalgia for paradise. They are all "angels," but angels in the special sense in which Wallace Fowlie defines the term in his brilliant study of Rimbaud. They are exiles from their own legitimate sphere of being, "pure spirits functioning as intermediaries between God and the world...able to exert influence on men."[11] As exiles, they perpetually yearn to return to their lost realm of happiness – they suffer from "une fatalité de bonheur" which they can satisfy only by moving. The word "angel" means literally "messenger" – as Rimbaud and Miller were both aware – but it refers to someone who moves, who travels, who can escape. That Rimbaud's and Miller's inordinate love of walking – which, because of its obsessiveness, I shall dub "dromomania" (from Greek *drómos* [road] and *manía* [craze], i.e., a

10 Wallace Fowlie, *Rimbaud: A Critical Study* (Chicago and London: The University of Chicago Press, 1965), p. 22.
11 *Ibid.*, p. 254.

maniacal love of the open road) – is a special stratagem employed by both poets to dramatize their desire to escape "hell" and reach "heaven" will, I believe, be made evident later on in this chapter.

Finally, I will address myself to the problems posed by the adoption of the related functions of "alchemist" and "voyant" in the works of Arthur Rimbaud and Henry Miller. Rimbaud's theory of "l'alchimie du verbe" has been thoroughly analyzed by Rimbaud scholars. As for his belief that the poet should make himself a "voyant" ("seer") by a "long, immense et raisonné *dérèglement de tous les sens*,"[12] it is one of the notorious literary formulas of our time. What has not been sufficiently appreciated to the present day is that Rimbaud's mid-twentieth-century counterpart, Henry Miller, has been no less systematically bent on resolving his own "fatalité de bonheur" by also making himself both "alchemist" and "voyant." As literary mystagogues, both Rimbaud and Miller fiercely resist analytical exegesis in the usual sense. Both achieve the kind of "untranslatability" which is befitting to the seer/illuminist through the use of such orthodox *Symboliste* techniques as name-allusions without gloss and cryptic allusions to esoteric truths designed to make the reader feel like an outsider. Both, in short, have that vexatious respect for the element of "mystery" latent in all things which is the earmark of *soi-disant* "initiates." And even though they both possess the radical generosity which often produces in the alchemist a willingness to share his "elixir" of happiness and, in the seer, a desire to communicate his "beatific vision," Rimbaud and Miller adhere fixedly to the hermeticist's code: the ultimate Mystery (both in life and in literature) must remain ungraspable and intact. This, unfortunately, does not make things easy for their readers. From the point of view of the "common reader," happiness frequently *is* a fatality!

12 Arthur Rimbaud, *Oeuvres*, p. 270.

2. *The Poet as Demon*

> *"It is not merely the neurotic whose right hand does not know what the left hand is doing. This predicament is a symptom of a general unconsciousness that is the undeniable common inheritance of all mankind.*
>
> *Man has developed consciousness slowly and laboriously, in a process that took untold ages to reach the civilized state (which is arbitrarily dated from the invention of script in about 4000 B.C.). And this evolution is far from complete, for large areas of the human mind are still shrouded in darkness."*
>
> C.G. Jung in *Man and His Symbols*

The obscurities of style and substance which their readers habitually encounter in the writings of Rimbaud and Miller are partly the product of willful hermeticism, partly the result of certain erosions or diminutions which both writers believe life and literature have undergone since the golden beginnings that have now disappeared from the earth. The strain of "demonic" anger that runs through the works of both poets perhaps unconsciously reiterates their deep-rooted resentment at the loss of a primeval felicity to which they feel entitled. Miller is sensitively aware of this grievance in the work of his predecessor, Rimbaud, when he writes:

At the very beginning of his career he understood what others only understand at the end, if at all, that the sacred word no longer has validity. He realized that the poison of culture has transformed beauty and truth into artifice and deception. He takes Beauty on his knees and he finds her bitter. He abandons her. It is the only way he can still honor her. What is it again that he says in the depths of hell? "*Des erreurs qu'on me souffle: magies, faux parfums, musique puérile.*" (For me this is the most haunting, baffling line in the *Season*). When he boasted that he possessed all talents, he meant *on this phony level*! Or – with this "lying cultural mask." In this realm he was, of course, a master. But this is the realm of confusion, the *Mamser* world. Here everything is of equal value and therefore of no value. Do you want me to whistle? Do you want a *danse du ventre*? Okay! Anything you wish. Just name it (Italics Miller's)![13]

Whether consciously or unconsciously, Miller's choice of the analogy of a nihilistic belly-dance (*danse du ventre*) as Rimbaud's putative response to being cast out of the snug womb of ancient certainties has a deadly symbolic accuracy. Both men are fiercely nostalgic writers. It is not with genuine gaiety or insouciance but with *ferocity* that Rimbaud and Miller react to their dispiriting expulsion from early Paradises.

The unrestrained fury with which Rimbaud opens *Une saison en enfer* is well-known. His rejection of "Beauty" as an abstraction, as a blatant example of the fossilization of "the sacred word," is one of the truly great demonic moments in modern literature:

Jadis, si je me souviens bien, ma vie était un festin où s'ouvraient tous les coeurs, où tous les vins coulaient.

Un soir, j'ai assis la Beauté sur mes genoux. – Et je l'ai trouvé amère. – Et je l'ai injuriée.

Je me suis armé contre la justice.

Je me suis enfui. O sorcières, ô misère, ô haine, c'est à vous que mon trésor a été confié!

Je parvins à faire s'évanouir dans mon esprit toute l'espérance humaine. Sur toute joie pour l'étrangler j'ai fait le bond sourd de la bête féroce.[14]

"To-day the magic has gone out of the alphabet; it is a dead form to express dead thoughts," writes Henry Miller in *The Colossus of Maroussi.*[15] His own first book, *Tropic of Cancer*, had opened with a vehement Rimbaldian rejection of "phony" abstractions that serve dead souls as substitutes for pristine "reality":

This is not a book. This is a libel, slander, defamation of character. This is not a book, in the ordinary sense of the word. No, this is a prolonged insult, a gob of

13 *Assassins*, p. 134.
14 *Oeuvres*, p. 219.
15 *Colossus*, p. 122.

spit in the face of Art, a kick in the pants to God, Man, Destiny, Time, Love, Beauty...what you will. I am going to sing for you, a little off key perhaps, but I will sing. I will sing while you croak, I will dance over your dirty corpse....[16]

Presumably, there was a season "once upon a time" ("jadis") when happiness was truly accessible and death was far less in evidence. It was possible, "*in illo tempore*," for humanity to lay claim to its angelic heritage of life and happiness. But that time is no longer.

There's an excellent analysis of the "paradisiac myth" in Mircea Eliade's book, *Myths, Dreams, and Mysteries*. Eliade cites Herman Baumann's account of African myths relating to the primordial paradisiac epoch as stories in which "men knew nothing of death; they understood the language of animals and lived at peace with them; they did no work at all, they found abundant food within their reach."[17] Eliade explains that the paradisiac myth occurs "all over the world" and "always includes a certain number of characteristic features" besides the supreme paradisiac element, *immortality:*

When Heaven had been abruptly *separated* from the earth, that is, when it had become *remote*, as in our days; when the tree or the liana connecting Earth to Heaven had been cut; or the mountain which used to touch the sky had become flattened out – then the paradisiac stage was over, and man entered into his present condition.

In effect, all these myths show us primordial man enjoying a beatitude, a spontaneity and freedom, which he has unfortunately lost in consequence of the *fall* – that is, of what followed upon the mythical event that caused the *rupture* between Heaven and Earth. *In illo tempore* ["at that time"], in the paradisiac age, the gods came down to earth and mingled with men; and men, for their part, could go up to Heaven by climbing the mountain, the tree, creeper or ladder, or might even be taken up by birds (Italics Eliade's throughout).[18]

It's this unfortunate "fall" – from Heaven, from the womb of the mother, from the primieval "bonheur" of eternity – that accounts for the cries of rebellious rage in Rimbaud and Henry Miller. "Hell," as

16 *Cancer*, p. 11-12.
17 *Myths, Dreams and Mysteries*, p. 59.
18 *Ibid.*, pp. 59-60.

John Senior defines it, in *The Way Down and Out*," is the realization of how far we are from Heaven."[19]

The archetypal elements of Eliade's paradisiac myth are outlined with remarkable precision at the close of "The Tailor Shop" in Henry Miller's *Black Spring*. I have italicized all the key phrases:

> Once I thought there were *marvelous things in store* for me. Thought I could build *a world in the air*, a castle of pure white spit that would *raise me above the tallest building*, between the tangible and the intangible, put me in a space like music where everything collapses and perishes but where I would be *immune, great, god-like, holiest of the holies*. It was *I* imagined this, I the tailor's son! I who was born from a little acorn *on an immense and stalwart tree*. In the hollow of the acorn even the faintest tremor of the earth reached me: I was part of the great tree, part of the past, *with crest and lineage*, with *pride, pride*. And when I *fell to earth* and was buried there I remembered who I was, *where* I came from. Now I am *lost*, do you hear?[20]

This painful "fall" from felicity is also one of the two or three most insistent themes in Rimbaud's *Illuminations* (which Miller had been carefully studying just before writing *Black Spring*), but nowhere is it stated with greater poignancy than in the poem which Rimbaud editors have usually placed at the beginning of the sequence, "Après le déluge." The breathless delicacy and innocence of the poet's youthful desire for a restoration of the conditions that anteceded the devastations of the flood are powerfully contrasted by Rimbaud with the violations implicit in much of his imagery:

> Aussitôt que l'idée du Déluge se fut rassise, un lièvre s'arrêta dans les sainfoins et les clochettes mouvantes, et dit sa prière à l'arc-en-ciel à travers la toile de l'araignée.
>
> Oh! les pierres précieuses qui se cachaient, – les fleurs qui regardaient déjà.
> . . . .
>
> Le sang coula, chez Barbe-Bleue, – aux abatoirs, – dans les cirques, où le sceau de Dieu blêmit les fenêtres. Le sang et le lait coulèrent.
> . . . .
> Dans la grande maison de vitres encore ruisselante les enfants en deuil regardèrent les merveilleuses images.
> . . . .

19 *Down and Out*, p. 203.
20 *Black Spring*, pp. 111-112.

Les caravanes partirent. Et le Splendide-Hôtel fut bâti dans le chaos de glaces et de nuit du pôle.

. . . .

Sourds, étang! Écume, roule sur le pont et pardessus les bois; – draps noirs et orgues, – éclairs et tonnerre, – montez et roulez; – Eaux et tristesses, montez et relevez les Déluges.[21]

In the poem's last three paragraphs, "Eucharis" tells the poet "que c'était le printemps," but it is paradoxically a black Spring which is alluded to – a Spring under "draps noirs" or "black drapes" –presided over by a Witch (usually identified with Rimbaud's mother, whom the poet had nicknamed "la Bouche d'Ombre" – "the Murky Oracle" or, more literally, "the Shadowy Mouth") who knows something which is *being kept from the poet* and which might provide a key:

Depuis lors, la Lune entendit les chacals piaulant par les déserts de thym – et les églogues en sabots grognant dans le verger. Puis, dans la futaie violette, bourgeonnante, Eucharis me dit que c'était le printemps.

Sourds, étang! – Écume, roule sur le pont et pardessus les bois; – draps noirs et orgues, – éclairs et tonnerre, – montez et roulez; – Eaux et tristesses, montez et relevez les Déluges.

Car depuis qu'ils se sont dissipés, – oh! les pierres précieuses s'enfouissant, et les fleurs ouvertes! – c'est un ennui! et la Reine, la Sorcière qui allume sa braise dans le pot de terre ne voudra jamais nous raconter ce qu'elle sait, et que nous ignorons.[22]

Henry Miller's indebtedness to Rimbaud is extensive and pervasive, but there is a passage in *Black Spring* which seems to me to be little more than an echo-filled adaptation of Rimbaud's "Après le déluge." Although the sequence of Miller's images differs from Rimbaud's, the very same phantasmagoric effects are produced by means of a selection and manipulation of materials that are strikingly similar (flood, woman, precious stones, innocence, ice, night, transformation, mourning, and a desolating sense of loss):

21 *Oeuvres*, p. 175.
22 *Ibid.*, pp. 175-176.

The *water rushes down* in a thin sheet of glass between the soft white mounds of the banks; it rushes below the knees, carrying the amputated feet forward like broken pedestals before an avalanche. Forward on their icy stumps they glide, their bat wings spread, their garments glued to their limbs. And always *the water mounting, higher, higher*, and the air growing colder, the snow *sparkling like powdered diamonds*. From the cypresses above a dull metallic green sweeps down, sweeps like a green shadow over the banks and stains the clear icy depths of the stream. The *woman* is seated like an angel on a river of ice, her wings spread, her hair flown back *in stiff glassy waves....*

Like a prodigal son I walk in golden leisure down the street of my *youth*. I am neither bewildered nor disappointed. From the perimeter of the six extremes *I have wandered back by devious routes to the hub where all is change and transformation*, a white lamb continually shedding its skin. When along the mountain ridges I *howled with pain*, when in the sweltering white valleys I was choked with alkili, when fording the sluggish streams my feet were splintered by rock and shell, when I licked the salty sweat of the lemon fields or lay in the burning kilns to be baked, *when was all this that I never forgot what is now no more*? (These last italics are Miller's; all the others are my own)

When down *this cold funereal street* they drove the hearse which I hailed with joy had I already shed my skin? I was the lamb and they *drove me out*. I was the lamb and they made of me a striped tiger. *In an open thicket I was born* with a mantle of soft white wool. *Only a little while* did I graze *in peace*, and then *a paw was laid upon me*. In the sultry flame of closing day I heard a breathing behind the shutters; past all the houses I wandered slowly, listening to *the thick flapping of the blood*. And then one night I *awoke* on a hard bench in the frozen garden of the South. Heard the mournful whistle of the train, saw the white sandy roads *gleaming* like skull tracks.[23]

Obviously, both the Rimbaud and Miller poems describe miniature birth myths. The flood can be likened to the bursting forth of the placenta's amniotic fluids, the release from the warmth and coziness of the womb is dramatized by the cold glitter of stones and ice in the alien outside world, the allusion to blood in both writers underscores the violence of the ejection, and the sense of mourning is the result of a transition (or transformation) to a workaday world where, as Rimbaud would put it, "La vraie vie est absente!" The painfulness experienced by both writers during this transition is comparable to the throes of the birth trauma, the primal "fall" from the heaven of "inner" to the hell of "outer." I would say that in view of the extent of Miller's ingenious mimicry of Rimbaud's style and substance, it

23 *Black Spring*, pp. 150-151.

was surely a rare understatement for him to maintain merely that in the author of *Illuminations* he saw himself "as in a mirror." There is conscious, albeit somewhat camouflaged, technical and ideological discipleship in evidence here. Both in terms of tone and of theme, the above passages were written by two writers who have a great deal in common.

Not surprisingly, Miller's most vivid rages (like Rimbaud's) are reserved for the City and for what is commonly called "civilization." Both men yearn for a return to paradise which is, by definition, "primitive" and "simple," and the greatest obstacle to the realization of this peaceable kingdom they dream of is the complex hell of the modern city. Rimbaud's knowledge of the urban desperations of Paris and London was intimate and is powerfully encapsulated in an "illumination" entitled "Ville":

Je suis un éphémère et point trop mécontent citoyen d'une métropole crue moderne parce que tout goût connu a été éludé dans les ameublements et l'extérieur des maisons aussi bien que dans le plan de la ville. Ici vous ne signaleriez les traces d'aucun monument de superstition. La morale et la langue sont réduites à leur plus simple expression, enfin! Ces millions de gens qui n'ont pas besoin de se connaître amènent si pareillement l'éducation, le métier et la vieillesse, que ce cours de vie doit être plusieurs fois moins long que ce qu'une statistique folle trouve pour les peuples du continent. Aussi comme, de ma fenêtre, je vois des spectres nouveaux roulant à travers l'épaisse et éternelle fumée de charbon – notre ombre des bois, notre nuit d'été! – des Erinnyes nouvelles, devant mon cottage qui est ma patrie et tout mon coeur puisque tout ici ressemble à ceci, – la Mort sans pleurs, notre active fille et servante, un Amour désespéré en un joli Crime piaulant dans la boue de la rue.[24]

It is easy to agree with Wallace Fowlie when he terms the cities of Rimbaud "the renewed expression of the age-long history of Babel"[25] (i.e., confusion, loss of community, despair). The characterization, however, could just as easily apply to Henry Miller's cities. Like Rimbaud's, Miller's cities are filled with benumbed "millions de gens qui n'ont pas besoin de se connaître":

When I think of this city where I was born and raised, this Manhattan that Whitman sang of, a blind, white rage licks my guts. New York! The white prisons, the sidewalks swarming with maggots, the bread lines, the opium joints that are built like palaces, the lepers, the thugs, and above all, the *ennui*, the

24 *Oeuvres*, p. 188.

monotony of faces, streets, legs, houses, skyscrapers, meals, posters, jobs, crimes, loves... A whole city erected over a hollow pit of nothingness. Meaningless. Absolutely meaningless. And Forty-Second Street! The top of the world, they call it. Where's the bottom then? You can walk along with your hand out and they'll put cinders in your cap. Rich or poor, they walk along with head thrown back and they almost break their necks looking up at their beautiful white prisons. They walk along like blind geese and the searchlights spray their empty faces with flecks of ecstasy.[26]

Citing the "classic flights" of such artists as Rimbaud, Melville, Gauguin, Jack London, and D.H. Lawrence from the hell of "civilization," Miller intones a long and all-too-familiar litany of particulars which he claims stem from "modern progress":

colonization, trade, free Bibles, war, disease, artificial limbs, factories, slaves, insanity, neuroses, psychoses, cancer, syphilis, tuberculosis, anemia, strikes, lockouts, starvation, nullity, vacuity, restlessness, striving, despair, ennui, suicide, bankruptcy, arteriosclerosis, megalomania, schizophrenia, hernia, cocaine, prussic acid, stink bombs, tear gas, mad dogs, auto-suggestion, auto-intoxication, psychotherapy, hydrotherapy, electric massages, vacuum cleaners, pemmican, grape nuts, hemorrhoids, gangrene. No desert isles. No paradise. Not even *relative* happiness. Men running away from themselves so frantically that they look for salvation under the ice floes or in tropical swamps, or else they climb the Himalayas or asphyxiate themselves in the stratosphere....[27]

Rimbaud, as usual, had said the same thing much more succinctly: "Ce ne peut-être que la fin du monde, en avançant."[28]

"Progress," even in the most dissimilar works of Rimbaud and Miller, tends to bring out the most ruthlessly demonic cravings for "the end of the world" because, as they define it, progress makes men strangers to each other. It hopelessly diminishes the possibilities of real community. When this diminution has reached its limits, as Rimbaud says in one of his most poignantly ambiguous lines in *Illuminations*, the humanizing factors which are usually available to us in *exploration, gratitude*, and *recognition* (the three different meanings which the French word "reconnaisance" can have) are destroyed in a single stroke: "Pour l'étranger de notre temps la reconnaisance est

25 *Rimbaud*, p. 197.
26 *Cancer*, p. 72.
27 *Black Spring*, p. 40.
28 *Oeuvres*, p. 178.

impossible."[29] What most persuasively reveals the affinity between the hell-as-city of Arthur Rimbaud and that of Henry Miller is the absolute absence of any kind of coordination *for human ends* in these places:

I. (Rimbaud)	II. (Miller)
Quelques divans de velours rouge: on sert des boissons polaires dont le prix varie de huit cents à mille roupies. A l'idée de chercher des théâtres sur ce circus, je me réponds que les boutiques doivent contenir des drames assez sombres? Je pense qu'il y a une police; mais la loi doit être tellement étrange, que je renonce à me faire une idée des aventuriers d'ici.[30]	New York is cold, glittering, malign. The buildings dominate. There is a sort of atomic frenzy to the activity going on; the more furious the pace, the more diminished the spirit. A constant ferment, but it might just as well be going on in a test-tube. Nobody knows what it's all about. Nobody directs the energy.[31]

The Colossus of Maroussi is Miller's account of his rediscovery of paradise in Greece and, as such, it is almost totally free of the uninhibited "demonic" furies of his earlier books. Like Rimbaud's *Illuminations*, it seldom recalls the "season in hell" which had preceded it and which had been recorded with roars of anguish in earlier books; it is intended to be a panegyric and not a "carnet de damné."[32] But even the light-filled *Colossus* is not entirely free of the rumblings of "hell" both behind and in the distance. Miller's awareness of the terrors of modern warfare, cited in connection with the motif of murder in Chapter One, provides an ominous counterpoint to the prevailing sense of ecstasy in *Colossus* and serves to remind the comfortably dozing demon in him that no reconciliation is really

29 *Ibid.*, p. 191.
30 *Ibid.*, p. 192.
31 *Cancer*, p. 72.
32 Arthur Rimbaud, *Oeuvres*, p. 219. Although it was believed for many years that Rimbaud's *Une saison en enfer* was his final work and "farewell to literature," such respected Rimbaud scholars as Wallace Fowlie and M.-A. Ruff, following in the footsteps of Bouillane de Lacoste, now believe that important segments of *Illuminations* were composed after *Une saison en enfer*. Indeed M.-A. Ruff goes so far as to characterize *Illuminations* as "la manifestation dernière, la plus riche et la plus éclatante de son génie" (cf. Fowlie's *Rimbaud*, p. 48 and pp. 79-80, and Ruff's *Rimbaud*, pp. 198, 206, 211-212, and 238-239).

possible with the madness of "civilization." This fundamental antagonism is reawakened when Miller visits Eleusis, where he realizes that "there is no salvation in becoming adapted to a world which is crazy.... Eleusis is still intact and it is we who are broken, dispersed, crumbling to dust. Eleusis lives, lives eternally in the midst of a dying world."[33]

Later on Miller visits the palace of Minos at Knossos and, after describing one of the most paradisaical moments of illumination in *Colossus*, he tells of waiting for the bus in a little village in which it seemed "as though the secret of life had been lost."[34] While there, "a group of louts" produce a Greek newspaper and one of them reads the war headlines aloud while another translates for Miller. This is followed by some bloody-minded histrionics in which the super-patriotic translator proclaims his zest for the war and threatens to "kill everybody – German, Italian, Russian, Turk, French. Greek no 'fraid."[35] Miller is immediately prompted to reflect, in a manner that recalls the *Tropic* books, on "the stormy sea of civilization" and all its

> derelicts exploited by the octopus whose tentacles stretch from London, Paris, Berlin, Tokio, New York, Chicago to the icy tips of Iceland and the wild reaches of Patagonia. The evidences of this so-called civilization are strewn and dumped higgledy-piggledy wherever the long, slimy tentacles reach out. Nobody is being civilized, nothing is being altered in any real sense. Some are using knives and forks who formerly ate with their fingers; some have electric lights in their hovels instead of the kerosene lamp or the wax taper; some have Sears-Roebuck catalogues and a Holy Bible on the shelf where once a rifle or musket lay; some have gleaming automatic revolvers instead of clubs; some have straw hats which they don't need; some have Jesus Christ and don't know what to do with Him. But all of them, from the top to the bottom, are restless, dissatisfied, envious, and sick at heart. All of them suffer from cancer and leprosy, in their souls.[36]

This section concludes with a tirade that begins "The aeroplane brings death; the radio brings death; the machine gun brings death, etc., etc., etc.," and ends "wherever we cast our shadow, wherever we breathe, we poison and destroy. Hooray! shouted the Greek. I too yell Hooray! Hooray for civilization! *Hooray! We will kill you all,*

33 *Colossus*, pp. 45-46.
34 *Ibid.*, p. 122.
35 *Ibid.*, p. 125.
36 *Ibid.*, p. 127.

everybody, everywhere. Hooray for Death! Hooray! Hooray!"[37]

There is a demonic verve in this nihilistic outburst that strongly recalls one of Rimbaud's responses to the insanity of war, a fierce poem called "Démocratie" which ends:

> "Aux pays poivrés et détrempés! – au service des plus
> monstrueuses exploitations industrielles et militaires.
>
> "Au revoir ici, n'importe où. Conscrits du bon vouloir
> nous aurons la philosophie féroce; ignorants pour la science,
> roués pour le confort; la crevaison pour le monde qui va.
> C'est la vraie marche. En avant, route![38]

Like Rimbaud before him, Miller obligingly apes the homicidal fury of the war-enthusiasts and goons whom he is ridiculing with such heavy-handed sarcasm. Like Rimbaud, his rhetoric is excessive almost to the verge of hysteria. Rimbaud is a "mirror" to Henry Miller in more ways than one, however. It's instructive to remember while reading the "barbarious passacaglia" in *Colossus* – with its marvelously incorruptible and unbamboozled cast of Negro jazz musicians headed by Count Basie, "last direct lineal descendant of the great and only Rimbaud" – that the name which Rimbaud had originally chosen for his *Saison en enfer* was *Livre Nègre*! Unlike the uninhibited anarchic life of the Black music-makers praised by Miller in

37 *Ibid.*, p. 128.

38 *Oeuvres*, p. 204. Many admirers of Rimbaud's poetry are often shocked to discover that the poet resorted, in the closing years of his life, to gun-running on behalf of unscrupulous desert kings and brigands and even profiteered, to all appearances, from the African slave-trade. This is "demonism" with a vengeance. One is reminded, however, of the words spoken by another Orphic figure, the German poet Goethe, to his biographer and friend, Eckermann: "I have never heard of a crime, no matter how vile, that I might not have committed myself." There is a similar life-giving candor pervading much of Henry Miller's allusions to certain "demonic" episodes in his own life. Towards the close of *Cancer*, for instance, he unhesitatingly pockets money meant for the pregnant and abandoned girl-friend of the panic-stricken Fillmore, squanders much of it foolishly, then brings the account to a close with a description of the "golden peace" which his irresponsible act produced in him. But Miller's capacity for blithe demonism extends to more than petty thefts. In *Capricorn* (pp. 125-126), he tells how he and a group of his boyhood friends "killed one

this pivotal section of *Colossus*, the life of "civilized" man

> has become an eternal Hell for the simple reason that he has lost all hope of attaining Paradise. He does not even believe in a Paradise of his own creation. By his own thought processes he condemns himself – to the deep Freudian hell of wish fulfillment.[39]

What Miller proposes instead is what *The Colossus of Maroussi* is really about: a return to the "angelic" condition from which both he and Rimbaud, rightly or wrongly, believe humankind has fallen. Miller's most explicit statement of this aim occurs in *Tropic of Capricorn:*

> I want to become more and more childish and to pass beyond childhood in the opposite direction. I want to go exactly contrary to the normal line of development, pass into a supra-infantile realm of being which will be absolutely crazy and chaotic but not crazy and chaotic as the world about me. I have been an adult and a father and a responsible member of society. I have earned my daily bread. I have adapted myself to a world which never was mine. I want to break through this enlarged world and stand again on the frontier of an unknown world which will throw this pale, unilateral world into shadow. I want to pass beyond the responsibility of fatherhood to the irresponsibility of the anarchic man who cannot be coerced nor wheedled nor cajoled nor bribed nor traduced. I want to take as my guide Oberon the nightrider who, under the spread of his black wings, eliminates both the beauty and the horror of the past; I want to flee toward a perpetual dawn....[40]

"Dawn" ("aube") is one of the most pregnant words in Rimbaud's lexicon of magical words. I intend to give a good deal of attention to it in "The Poet as Alchemist." It's no exaggeration to equate it, in the Rimbaldian cosmos, with Paradise – the Golden Age, *in illo tempore.*

---

of the rival gang" in a rock fight, then casually went home to Aunt Caroline, who "gave us our usual two big slices of sour rye with fresh butter and a little sugar over it and we sat there at the kitchen table listening to her with an angelic smile." This is understandable perhaps on the part of small children, but there is a segment in *Cosmological Eye* in which Miller the grown man writes of "one of the strangest days I ever spent at the ocean" on a beach in New Haven, Connecticut, when he suddenly and inexplicably felt "that I could commit the most dastardly crime with a clear conscience. A crime without reason. Yes, it was that that I felt strongly: to kill some innocent person without reason (cf. *Cosmological Eye*, p. 221)."

39 *Assassins*, p. 85.

40 *Capricorn*, p. 145.

3. *The Poet as Angel*

> *"That first ship to leave the earth, and possibly never return – what I would not give to know the titles of the books it will contain! Methinks the books have not been written which will offer mental, moral, and spiritual sustenance to these daring pioneers. The great possibility, as I see it, is that these men may not care to read at all, not even in the toilet: they may be content to tune in on the angels, to listen to the voices of the dear departed, to cock their ears to catch the ceaseless celestial song."*
>
> Henry Miller in *The Books in My Life*

Before embarking on my analysis of the elusive and variegated role of the theme of angelism in Henry Miller's *The Colossus of Maroussi*, I believe a bit of attention to the etymology of the word "angel" would be useful to the reader. "Angel" is derived, ultimately, from the Hebrew by way of the Ancient Greek word *ángelos*, meaning, quite simply, a "messenger." Since a messenger must usually traverse distances to deliver his message, the additional meaning of "traveler," fleet of foot, soon came to attach to the word. Eventually, "angel" came to mean solely a "*spiritual* messenger" who bears messages from God to mortals, as in the Old and New Testaments. In fact, the Judeo-Christian iconography of angels, abetted by the great painters of the Western European tradition, has so conditioned us to regarding these beings as pious-looking, long-robed, winged creatures who run God's errands that it comes as a mild shock to a new reader of Sophokles' *Oedipus the King* in Greek to see the comic messenger in that play referred to as an *ángelos*!

But it is a fact that in its original connotation the word "angel" could be applied to any person whose function it was to bear a message from one person to another. It is of some interest in the present study that the poet Rilke has given revitalized currency to this more general concept of "angel" in his magnificent *Duino Elegies* by deliberately widening the range of meaning of the word to include any presence, animate or inanimate, which has the power to impart strength or wisdom through its irresistible magnetism. Following in Rilke's footsteps, the contemporary American poet and Rilke translator, A. Poulin, Jr., has even assigned the name and function of "angel" – in a poem called "Angelic Orders," whose very name he appropriated from Rilke's First Elegy (cf. Poulin's *In Advent*, pp. 73-78) – to such objects as doors, rocking chairs, flags, and refrigerators, all of which he feels are endowed with the uncanny *mana* necessary to transmit "messages" to him.

The uniquely obsessive drive to restore humanity to its pristine "angelic" state which is discernible in the literary *Weltanschauung* of Arthur Rimbaud and Henry Miller derives, in the final analysis, from their enthusiasm for Swedenborg. In Miller's case, the French novelist Balzac appears to have been one of the important transmitters of the doctrine. In the essay "Balzac and His Double," Miller calls the Swedenborgist theory of the angels "the highest expression of the duality" which Balzac "sensed in his own nature and which he transmuted through art." He goes on to quote Balzac on the angel as

> an individual in whom *the inner being conquers the external being.* If a man desires to earn his call to be an angel, as soon as his mind reveals to him his twofold existence, he must strive to foster the delicate angelic essence *that exists within him.* If, for lack of a lucid apprehension of his destiny, he allows bodily action to predominate, instead of confirming his intellectual being, all his powers will be absorbed in the use of his external senses, and the angel will slowly perish by the materialization of both natures.... In the contrary case, if he nourishes his inner being with the aliment needful to it, the soul trimphs over matter and strives to get free...[T]h- wide distance between a man whose torpid intelligence condemns him to evident stupidity, and the one who, by the exercise of his inner life, has acquired the gift of some power, allows us to suppose that there is as great a difference *between men of genius and other beings* as there is between the blind and those who see (Italics mine).[41]

Later in the essay, Miller approvingly cites Balzac's Swedenborgian notion that "the earth is the nursery ground for heaven. The angels are not angels by original nature; they are transformed into angels by

41 *Wisdom*, pp. 225-226.

an intimate union with God which God never refuses, the very essence of God being never negative....”[42] Miller's personal conclusion, like that of Balzac, is that the angel's “intimate union with God” can only be achieved “through Desire.”[43] This becomes one of the crucial themes of Miller's work in general and of the *Colossus* in particular. I'll return to it later in this section.

In Rimbaud, the most explicit formulation of Swedenborg's concept of the “duality” which the angel must overcome in order to give full expression to his angelism (“the inner being conquers the external being”) can be found in the famous *Lettre du Voyant* of May 15, 1871, to his friend Paul Demeny:

Car JE est un autre. Si le cuivre s'éveille clairon, il n'y a rien de sa faute. Cela m'est évident: j'assiste à l'éclosion de ma pensée: je la regarde, je l'écoute: je lance un coup d'archet: la symphonie fait son remuement dans les profondeurs, ou vient d'un bond sur la scène.... L'intelligence universelle a toujours jeté ses idées naturellement; les hommes ramassaient une partie de ces fruits du cerveau: on agissait pas, on en écrivait des livres: telle allait la marche, l'homme ne se travaillant pas, *n'étant pas encore éveillé, ou pas encore dans la plénitude du grand songe*.... La première étude de l'homme qui veut être poète est sa propre connaissance, entière; il cherche son âme, il l'inspecte, il la tente, l'apprend. *Dès qu'il la sait, il doit la cultiver!*[44]

The fateful urgency to summon into existence this deeper “JE” (“I”) had also been experienced, in a way that is eerily reminiscent of Rimbaud's famous letter, by Henry Miller. In “The Brooklyn Bridge,” written not long prior to his departure for Greece, Miller tells about the agonized period of self-searching that immediately preceded the discovery of his own voice as a writer. The following passage gives with unerring accuracy a Swedenborgian conquest of the “external being” by the “inner being”:

I found myself of a sudden in the body of a man bearing my name in this God-forsaken spot on the Pacific Coast, and as I walked aimlessly from one end of the city to the other I had the very distinct sensation of *not belonging to this body* which I had been made to inhabit. It was decidedly not my body. It had been loaned to me, perhaps, out of mercy, but it was not me. It was not terror so much as desolation that I knew. I who was suffering – where was I in this

42 *Ibid.*, p. 236.
43 *Ibid.*, p. 248.
44 *Oeuvres*, p. 270.

world at that moment? There I was conveniently *incarcerated in a body* which was walking through a strange city for reasons I knew not. This lasted a whole afternoon. It was perhaps the brief period when, according to the astrologers, insanity menaced me [Rimbaud records identically the same kind of experience of near-madness on the first page of *Une saison en enfer*: "Et j'ai joué de bons tours à la folie. Et le printemps m'a apporté l'affreux rire de l'idiot."]. There was no struggle, no great anguish; I was simply stricken desolate. In fact *"I" was absent during the time*. The "I" was simply a dim, approximate awareness of an ego, a consciousness temporarily held in leash during a crucial planetary conjunction in which *my proper destiny was being worked out for me*. It was the skeleton of an ego, the congealed cloud spirit of the self.

Not long after that I awoke one night, got dressed automatically, went down to the telegraph office and *sent myself a telegram to come home*. The next day I was on the train bound for New York, and when I arrived home the telegram was waiting for me (Italics mine throughout).[45]

The brilliant Rimbaud biographer and scholar, Wallace Fowlie, seems to me to have provided the definitive analysis of Rimbaud's exercises in the conscious cultivation of the angelic in his own nature. Fowlie contends that "the poet's mission and the angel's have so intimate a resemblance that they often appear identical: that of putting men in some kind of relationship with a limitless world."[46] According to Fowlie, Rimbaud's nostalgia for a reality higher and more satisfying than quotidian reality was so fervid that it impelled him to risk everything, even madness and self-destruction, to attain it. Earlier, I quoted Katsimbalis' enthusiastic praise of the Greek poet/critic, Pericles Yannopoulos, who was as "mad" as Icarus in his dizzying flights of genius, and I compared Rimbaud with Yannopoulos. Icarus is clearly one of the typical metamorphoses of the Rimbaldian angel.

Poetry, as Wallace Fowlie suggests, is perhaps the most uniquely powerful *askesis* man has at his disposal to attempt to change his earth-clinging being into an angelic being. "The great ambition of the lyric poet," he writes in his *Rimbaud*, "is to pass beyond or obliterate all the obstacles which might impair his principal ambition: the song

45 *Cosmological Eye*, pp. 349-350. It's of some interest that Miller should speak here of being "incarcerated in a body" in the course of this account of his weird, near-schizoid experience. The Orphics, it will be recalled, also spoke of man's incarnated condition as a kind of imprisonment. Their famous dictum, *Soma-sema*, means literally "The body's a prison."
46 *Rimbaud*, p. 249.

of the world's original purity."[47] It is the self-same ambition which Rimbaud succeeds in realizing in the beautiful poem "Aube" in *Illuminations* when, after a long and ardent chase after "la déesse," he finally subdues her and exclaims: "J'ai embrassé l'aube d'été." It is also the ambition Henry Miller realizes at Phaestos when, after his long and "circumlocuitous voyage," he finally conquers his "external being" and reaches "the perpetual dawn of man's awakening."[48]

It is noteworthy that Fowlie's description of Rimbaud's program of self-transformation bears an extremely close resemblance to Henry Miller's account of Balzac's blueprint for achieving a state of angelism in one's human nature, quoted earlier:

> Rimbaud tried to make of poetry a magic means of seizing and articulating what is ineffable, and therefore to make of the poet a kind of medium as receptive to poetic speech *as an angel's will is receptive to God's*. He tried to make of the poetic word an *instrument of discovery*, a new language which is not so much an expression in the usual sense as it is *a sign of his spirit*. His temperament unquestionably had traces of auto-divinization. *Car JE est un autre* might well mean that he is a potential god. *Mage ou ange*? he queries. His tremendous *effort to establish a relationship between the lowest and the highest in him*, by means of his celebrated derangement (*dérèglement*), is another version of the Apollonian-Dionysian union, a will to escape from his purely human condition (Italics mine).[49]

But when Fowlie describes the specific aims of Rimbaud's program, it is almost as if he were giving us a synopsis of Henry Miller's magian book, *The Colossus of Maroussi:*

> Rimbaud's mythology seeks to create a very concrete angelic love and poetry in which *the concepts of freedom and revolution* will liberate the human spirit. When he considers his past, he beholds a series of metamorphoses, a spirit *seeking an emancipation from some form of enslavement* or limitation. When he considers his future, he sees the emancipated spirit *in a recovered state of innocency and limpidness* (Italics added).[50]

It is not difficult to recall numerous passages from the *Colossus*, many of them already quoted at length, in which the central themes of "freedom" and "revolution" are invoked by Miller and the backward-

47 *Ibid.*, p. 239.
48 *Colossus*, p. 159.
49 *Rimbaud*, p. 257.
50 *Ibid.*, p. 254.

and-forward vistas describing identically the same "enslavement" (past) and "limpidness" (future) occur.

The resemblances between Rimbaud's literary uses of the doctrine of angelism in *Illuminations* and Miller's *The Colossus of Maroussi* are not only implicit and on the surface, but deep-rooted and at times quite explicit. All three parts of the *Colossus* adapt, both thematically and structurally, the theory of the angel which Miller had acquainted himself with in Balzac and Rimbaud. Part One, as I have pointed out earlier, opens and closes with three emblematic "angels" whose function, on the Swedenborgean level, is to lure Miller into "the country of enchantment which the poets have staked out and which they alone may lay claim to."[51] Betty Ryan, Lawrence Durrell, and Rainer Maria Rilke at the outset and the "two men and a woman" at the close of this chapter are "angels" in the strictest sense, i.e., the numinous quality of their being transmits messages to Miller whose effect, ultimately, will be to permit him to achieve a "relationship with a limitless world," as Wallace Fowlie defines the angel's and poet's mission on earth. And it would certainly be redundant to point out that the great talkers who fill the rest of *Colossus* – Katsimbalis, Aram Hourabedian, Seferis – all occupy privileged places in Miller's angelic orders; they all bear eloquent messages from "the country of enchantment."

In Part Two of *Colossus*, Miller becomes much more explicit about communicating his views on angelism. During the airplane trip to Crete, he wistfully muses that "Man is made to walk the earth and sail the seas; the conquest of the air is reserved for a later stage of his evolution, when he will have sprouted real wings and assumed the form of the angel which he is in essence."[52] A little later, in the Negro jazz cadenza, he says that Epaminondas (who is "for war and civilization" and brings on "the white plague which ended in the

51 *Colossus*, p. 4. Miller shows a similar awareness of the etymology of "angel" in a short essay on the painter Max Ernst, "one of the few poets among the painters of our time," published only a few months after the appearance of *The Colossus of Maroussi*. In the essay, entitled "Another Bright Messenger," Miller writes of Ernst as a member of the "angelic hosts," a being who "can pick his way among the galaxies" and "the arcane realms where creation never ceases." Cf. *Of-By-and-About Henry Miller* (Yonkers, New York, 1947), pp. 32-34.

52 *Colossus*, pp. 112-113.

basement of Clytemnestra's palace where the cesspool now stands") made "even the angels weep"[53]; the Duke of Ellington's favorite mood is "indigo which is that of the angels when all the world is sound asleep."[54] At Phaestos, Miller experiences a desire to "take a running leap and vault into the blue...to float in the air like an angel."[55] Moments later, this nicely frivolous image crystallizes into a much more doctrinaire pronouncement:

> From this sublime, serene height it has all the appearance of the Garden of Eden. At the very gates of Paradise the descendants of Zeus halted here on their way to eternity to cast a last look earthward and saw with the eyes of innocents that the earth is indeed what they had always dreamed it to be: a place of beauty and joy and peace. In his heart man is angelic; in his heart man is united with the whole world.[56]

It's in Part Three, though, that Miller's art is most in evidence in the manner in which he addresses himself to the subject of angels. Early in this chapter, the colossal statue of "Antinous, last of the gods" which he visits at Thebes prompts Miller to a meditation on "this enigmatic figure of the last god on earth who flung himself into the Nile." He identifies the mysterious Antinous with Balzac's Séraphita and then terms the statue "this most wonderful idealization in stone of the eternal duality of man." In this context, Miller speaks of the angel as a being in whom "the sexes fuse into the sublime spiritual being which man essentially is."[57]

The remarkable "illumination" which I quoted in its entirety in Chapter Two in which Miller describes the Corinthian flautist's haunting Christmas Eve solo ("a duet in which the other instrument is silent") occurs less than twenty pages after the description of the statue of Antinous. This luminous prose poem strikes me as a superb variation on the Antinous/duality theme found so often in Rimbaud. The setting is superlatively handled. It is Christmas Eve, an appropriate moment for angels to be delivering messages. Corinth is particularly bleak and Miller's need for communion is heightened by the words he uses to situate the action: "a lonely house lit up by a smoky kerosene

53 *Ibid.*, p. 138.
54 *Ibid.*, p. 140.
55 *Ibid.*, p. 159.
56 *Ibid.*, p. 162.
57 *Ibid.*, p. 196.

lamp." The flautist's "fierce, sad, obsessive" music to which "there promises to be no end" is interrupted by the arrival of a telegraph messenger – the word "angel," it will be recalled, means "messenger" – who reminds Miller of another messenger whom he had once come upon on a winter night "walking the streets of New York in a daze with a fistful of undelivered messages." The messenger, as I indicated earlier, is a composer whose career ends "at Bellevue where he was pronounced insane."[58] He is yet another example among many – Orpheus, Icarus, Dante, Oberon the nightrider, Rimbaud, Dostoevsky, Yannopoulos – whose doubleness causes them to "fall" while attempting to attain great heights.

Miller has devoted numerous pages of *Tropic of Capricorn* to the harrowing experiences of the invisible telegraph messenger/angels whom he encountered as employment manager of the "Cosmococcic Telegraph Company of North America." Much of the pathos of their lives, as Miller describes them, was the result of the failure of their barren mass-society environment to "see" them as human beings and to respond to them as message-bearers worth cherishing. In the rambling "Letter to Pierre Lesdain" in *The Books in My Life* in which he dwells on his years as employment manager for Western Union (where he was "*the supreme cosmodemoniacal messenger* – God's own"), Miller disgresses at length on the "failures" of Whitman and Dostoevsky in their materialistic nineteenth-century societies. Dostoevsky, he writes,

> thought no more of "reward" than Whitman, but his dignity as a human being was ever deprived him. In another sense, of course, it could be said that this very fact made it easier for him to act the "ministering angel." It nullified all thought of *being* an angel. He could see himself as a victim and a sufferer because in fact he was one.[59]

There is a very exact correlation between this passage and the more minutely dramatized lives of the messengers in *Capricorn*. The difference between being and *not* being an angel, Miller implies, is the

58 *Ibid.*, pp. 213-215.

59 *Books*, pp. 242-244. Miller is clearly aware of the connection between the words "angel" and "messenger" since in the same context in which he describes the Western Union messenger, he launches into a brief discussion of Swedenborg's " 'solitary' angels" and the contemporary phenomenon of the "angel-worm," as he calls the incipient specimen. (Cf. also *Books*, pp. 246-247).

difference between the victim and the non-victim. As long as one continues to "*see* himself as a victim," one is imperiled. But if one cultivates a powerful enough "Desire" for angelhood, the chances of attaining what Swedenborg had called "intimate union with God" remain a real possibility. "Desire" is the Rimbaud factor.

The poet Rimbaud had fully understood this in his charming cameo of wish-fulfillment, "Royauté." The young man and young woman in this poem are magically transformed into royalty "toute une matinée" and "toute l'après-midi" because they had found what Rimbaud elsewhere[60] calls "la formule":

> Un beau matin, chez un peuple fort doux, un homme et une femme superbes criaient sur la place publique: "Mes amis, je veux qu'elle soit reine!" "Je veux être reine!" Elle riait et tremblait. Il parlait aux amis de révélation, d'épreuve terminée. Ils se pâmaient l'un contre l'autre.
>
> En effet ils furent rois toute une matinée, où les tentures carminées se relevèrent sur les maisons, et toute l'après-midi, où ils s'avancèrent du côté des jardins des palmes.[61]

Rimbaud could not have been more explicit: " 'Mes amis, je *veux* qu'elle soit reine!' 'Je *veux* être reine!' " (Italics mine). Twice in *Colossus*, in both instances in connection with the act of breaking through to angelhood, Miller speaks of the primacy of "desire." "Nothing can bring about a new and better world but our desire for it... [*G*]*enius* is the norm, not mediocrity,"[62] he writes in Part One. And at the close of Part Three, he reiterates the idea: "To *desire* is to become that which one essentially is."[63] We have seen earlier that it is Miller's belief that what man "essentially" is is "angelic."

It's no accident for a Rimbaldian writer like Henry Miller to equate angelhood with genius; his master Rimbaud had done the very same thing. The poem "Génie," which Wallace Fowlie singles out among the poems in *Illuminations* as the "autobiography of the angel-man,"[64] is one of the most stunning examples in all literature of what I earlier referred to as "illuminisme révolutionnaire," in

60 *Oeuvres*, p. 190.
61 *Ibid.*, p. 183.
62 *Colossus*, p. 83.
63 *Ibid.*, p. 237.
64 *Rimbaud*, p. 237.

Auguste Viatte's phrase. The brilliantly charismatic apparition whom Rimbaud conjures up in this poem bears a suspicious resemblance to the Armenian soothsayer's projection of Henry Miller as a man who "would bring great joy to the world, to everybody in the world." The imagery of the poem abounds in locutions that could be called Millerian: "le délice surhumain," "jouissance de notre santé," "élan de nos facultés," "affection égoiste," "gaietés des hommes." Most important, there's the implication that this radiant messenger of Rimbaud's is the harbinger of universal joy *by his very existence* and by mankind's eager acceptance of him: "c'est fait, lui étant, et étant aimé."[65] When the French critic Jean-Pierre Richard calls "Génie" the poem by Rimbaud "qui nous donne l'idée la plus exacte peut-être du bonheur poétique rimbaldien...et précisément le poème où Rimbaud solitaire rêve au miracle d'un *Génie* qui réunirait êtres et objets séparés, et qui rétablirait entre eux un courant tout humain, une nappe horizontale de solidarité,"[66] one is unavoidably reminded of Henry Miller sending out a benediction at Phaestos which "included everybody and everything on this earth." It is at that point in *Colossus* that Miller says: "We have nothing to solve: it has all been solved for us. We have but to melt, to dissolve, to swim in the solution. We are soluble fish and the world is an aquarium,"[67] a beautifully pun-filled complex of images that might very possibly owe something to Rimbaud's poem, "Bottom," with its magnificent line: "Tout se fit ombre et aquarium ardent."[68] "Bottom" also happens to concern itself with a search for the "solution" to the problem of identity and with a "grand caractère" who finds reality "trop épineuse" and mysteriously dissolves into a stream for others to swim and delight in. And there is the implication, both in the Miller and Rimbaud statements, that such marvelous metamorphoses can occur only if one is willing to surrender totally to a sort of vertigo of willlessness – which alone will take us to the very "bottom" of our imaginative potential.

Wallace Stevens calls the imagination "the necessary angel" and suggests that the poet's function *vis-à-vis* other people is "to make his imagination theirs and...he fulfills himself only as he sees his imagina-

65 Rimbaud, *Oeuvres*, pp. 205-206.

66 Jean-Pierre Richard, *Poésie et profondeur* (Paris: Editions du Seuil, 1955), p. 249.

67 *Colossus*, pp. 162-163.

68 *Oeuvres*, p. 202.

tion become the light in the minds of others. His role, in short, is to help people to live their lives."[69] When the imagination becomes "the reigning prince," Stevens suggests,

> the study of the imagination and the study of reality come to appear to be purified, aggrandized, fateful. How much stature, even vatic stature, this conception gives the poet! He need not exercise this dignity in vatic works. How much authenticity, even orphic authenticity, it gives to the painter! He need not display this authenticity in orphic works. It should be enough for him that that to which he has given his life should be so enriched by such an access of value. Poet and painter alike live and work in the midst of a generation that is experiencing essential poverty in spite of fortune.[70]

Henry Miller is no less aware than Wallace Stevens that "the necessary angel" of the imagination has the power to banish what Stevens calls our "essential poverty." Here is the way Miller puts it in his critical study of Rimbaud:

> At the periphery the world is dying away; at the center it glows like a live coal. In the great solar heart of the universe the golden birds are gathered in unison. There it is forever dawn, forever peace, harmony and communion. Man does not *look to the sun* in vain; he demands light and warmth not for the corpse which he will one day discard but for his inner being. His greatest desire is to burn with esctasy, to commerge his little flame with the central fire of the universe. If he accords the angels wings so that they may come to him with messages of peace, harmony and radiance from worlds beyond, it is only to nourish his own *dreams of flight*, to sustain his own belief that he will one day reach beyond himself, and on *wings of gold* (Italics mine).[71]

This richly cryptic passage happens, coincidentally, to make allusion to all three of the Rimbaldian roles which Miller himself learned to adopt in order to achieve the sense of "dawn" which his angelism demands: the roles of Dromomaniac, Alchemist, and *Voyant* – "dreams of flight," "wings of gold," and "look to the sun." I will now take up each in turn: the compulsion to movement, the transmutation of base matter into "gold," and the phenomenon of voyance.

69 *Necessary Angel*, p. 29.
70 *Ibid.*, p. 171.
71 *Assassins*, pp. 74-75.

4. The Poet as Dromomaniac

> *"One should walk, as the men of old walked, and allow one's whole being to become flooded with light. This is not a Christian highway: it was made by the feet of devout pagans on their way to initiation at Eleusis. There is no suffering, no martyrdom, no flagellation of the flesh connected with this processional artery. Everything here speaks now, as it did centuries ago, of illumination, of blinding, joyous illumination."*
>
> Henry Miller in *The Colossus of Maroussi*

Perhaps the most conspicuous thematic similarity between Rimbaud's *Illuminations* and Miller's *The Colossus of Maroussi* is the *joy in motion* which both writers so consistently exhibit – the compulsive drive to move beyond the limits of the commonplace into terrains which are distant, irresistible, exhilarating, life-expanding. Both books could be called transcripts of flights from the quotidian, but they were composed by a pair of writers who suffered from a wanderlust so transcendent that one is tempted to characterize it as demented.

The French scholar, Jacques Plessen, has in fact referred to Rimbaud's numerous and ultimately self-destructive fugues as having "quelque chose de pathologique." Plessen himself calls Rimbaud "ce phénomène ambulant" and cites, among other psychiatric studies a 1928 *thèse de médecine* by Dr. J.-L. Delattre entitled *Le déséquilibre mental d'Arthur Rimbaud* in which Delattre diagnoses Rimbaud's tireless mania for walking as "paranoia ambulatoire."[72] Nor have French literary critics been less fascinated by Rimbaud's extraordinary lust for walking and movement in general. Professor F. Ruchon writes that Rimbaud's unique description of Nature owes everything

72 Jacques Plessens, *Promenade et poésie* (The Hague: Mouton & Co., 1967), p. 8.

to the fact that "il ne la décrit pas statiquement, ne la voit pas étant immobile et assis, mais l'a animée et surprise, vagabond et errant, au cours de ses pérégrinations, a vécu tout près d'elle, couché le long des routes, sur les talus, et à l'orée des bois: il la suggère avec une curieuse abondance de verbes et d'expressions de mouvement."[73] Albert Thibaudet goes so far as to say that Rimbaud was a hobo ("un chemineau"), a type for whom life consisted essentially in wandering "indéfiniment à pied sur les grandes routes." Thibaudet calls *Illuminations* "précisément le livre de la route: c'est de la littérature décentrée, exaspérée par l'optique de la marche et par une tête surchauffée de chemineau." He goes on to argue that one has little difficulty in reading a book like *Illuminations* once one has come to appreciate the Rimbaldian *parti pris* of the hobo, "l'homme des routes."[74]

But Jacques Plessens' analysis is much more illuminating in that it points perceptively to the central role played by Rimbaud's difficult mother in the dynamics of the poet's dromomania:

> En ce qui concerne également l'expérience ambulatoire (qui, comme il a été suggéré, et pour Rimbaud en quelque sorte homologue de l'expérience poétique), ce qui compte, c'est sa signification indivise, *où le corporel et le spirituel se penètrent*. La première chose à noter c'est que, dans cet exercise, l'homme vit pleinement l' "éloignement de tout ce qui lui fait sentir sa dépendance," pour employer une expression de Rousseau. Ceci est très net dans le cas de Rimbaud, pour qui la promenade a souvent pris la forme d'une véritable fugue. Dans *Ma Bohème*, par exemple, nous voyons Petit Poucet tenter, dans la joie, de s'émanciper. Les relations entre Rimbaud et sa mère ont été déjà suffisamment mises en lumière, et souvent de façon pertinente (dans l'intention *d'expliquer ses fugues*, son homosexualité, son échec, etc.), pour que l'on n'ait plus besoin ici de faire une psychanalyse selon le modèle classsique. N'oublions donc pas que très tôt la promenade a constitué pour Rimbaud *une occasion de vivre la dialectique de la liberté et de la dépendance*, qui n'est autre que la dialectique de la *route* et de la *maison*, du mouvement et du repos (Italics mine).[75]

As I now intend to illustrate with pertinent passages from their works, both Rimbaud's and Miller's dromomania have a positive and negative side, the result of either a strong craving *for* or revulsion *against* unusually severe mother-figures. The flight from the mother as "witch" produces a euphoric sense of well-being commingled with guilt in both

73 Cited in *Ibid*., p. 9.
74 Cited in *Ibid*., p. 9.
75 *Ibid*., p. 25.

writers, whereas the return to the mother as all-powerful earth-goddess produces both dread and a retrieval of a lost sense of security. This may recall Freud's "Oedipus complex," in a general way, but it is potentially a different method of discussing the poets' ambulatory responses of attraction and revulsion to the themes of Heaven and Hell, of *palingénesis* and *katábasis*, which we examined earlier. The problem of Rimbaud's and Miller's compulsive walking sprees is not a simple problem, and I intend to make every effort to resist the temptation to simplify it.

If Henry Miller's dromomaniacal obsession can often achieve a sort of blissful poetic appeasement in *Colossus* (largely because he has managed to find a happy equilibrium in Greece), the earlier *Tropic* trilogy seldom evinces such tranquility. It is much more directly concerned with the darker aspects of his lust for walking and the monsters that still pursue him on his walks. In fact, the anxieties which impel dromomaniacs to flights of escape seem to be all-pervasive in the earlier books. In *Tropic of Cancer*, a narrative account of the artist's frenzied flight from the nightmares of "the world," Miller writes of

> the flight which the poet makes over the face of the earth and then, as if he had been ordained to re-enact a lost drama, the heroic descent to the very bowels of the earth, the dark and fearsome sojourn in the belly of the whale, the bloody struggle to liberate himself, to emerge clean of the past, a bright, gory sun-god cast upon an alien shore. It was no mystery to me any longer why he [Strindberg] and others (Dante, Rabelais, Van Gogh, etc., etc.) had made their pilgrimage to Paris. I understood then why it is that Paris attracts the tortured, the hallucinated, the great maniacs of love. I understood why it is that here, at the very hub of the wheel, one can embrace the most fantastic, the most impossible theories, without finding them in the least strange; it is here that one reads again the books of his youth and the enigmas take on new meanings, one for every white hair. One walks the streets knowing that he is mad, possessed, because it is only too obvious that these cold, indifferent faces are the visages of one's keepers. Here all boundaries fade away and the world reveals itself for the mad slaughter-house that it is. The treadmill stretches away to infinitude, the hatches are closed down tight, logic runs rampant, with bloody cleaver flashing. The air is chill and stagnant, the language apocalyptic. Not an exit sign anywhere; no issue save death. A blind alley at the end of which is a scaffold.[76]

76 *Cancer*, pp. 178-179.

Tropic of Capricorn, in which "the street" is perhaps the most compelling single symbol, virtually opens with Miller's "definition" of this term as he came to understand it in America:

> I can think of no street in America, or of people inhabiting such a street, capable of leading one on toward the discovery of the self. I have walked the streets in many countries of the world but nowhere have I felt so degraded and humiliated as in America. I think of all the streets of America combined as forming a huge cesspool, a cesspool of the spirit in which everything is sucked down and drained away to everlasting shit.... The whole continent is a nightmare producing the greatest misery of the greatest number. I was one, a single entity in the midst of the greatest jamboree of wealth and happiness (statistical wealth, statistical happiness) but I never met a man who was truly wealthy or truly happy. At least I knew that I was unhappy, unwealthy, out of whack and out of step. That was my only solace, my only joy.[77]

But it's to *Black Spring* that we must turn for Miller's most explicit statement of the dromomaniac's *credo*, especially to the pertinent essays "A Saturday Afternoon," "The Tailor Shop," and "Walking Up and Down in China." In "A Saturday Afternoon," Miller is prompted by a reference to Robinson Crusoe's withdrawal from "civilized" life (which he has read in Larousse) to a diatribe against "our marvelous Faustian culture":

> Henceforward everyone is running away from himself to find an imaginary desert isle, to live out this dream of Robinson Crusoe. Follow the classic flights, of Melville, Rimbaud, Gauguin, Jack London, Henry James, D.H. Lawrence . . . thousands of them. None of them found happiness. Rimbaud found cancer, Gauguin found syphilis. Lawrence found the white plague. The plague – that's it! Be it cancer, syphilis, tuberculosis, or what not. *The Plague*! The plague of modern progress: colonization, free Bibles, war, disease, artificial limbs, factories, slaves, insanity, neuroses, psychoses, cancer, syphilis, tuberculosis, anemia, strikes, lockouts, starvation, nullity, vacuity, restlessness, striving, despair, ennui, suicide, bankruptcy, arterio-sclerosis, megalomania, schizophrenia, hernia, cocaine, prussic acid, stink bombs, tear gas, mad dogs, auto-suggestion, auto-intoxication, psychotherapy, hydrotherapy, electric massages, vacuum cleaners, pemmican, grape nuts, hemorrhoids, gangrene. No desert isles. No paradise. Not even *relative* happiness. Men running away from themselves so frantically that they look for salvation under the ice floes or in tropical swamps, or else they climb the Himalayas or asphyxiate themselves in the stratosphere....

77 *Capricorn*, p. 12.

What fascinated the men of the eighteenth century was the vision of the end. They had enough. They wanted to retrace their steps, climb back into the womb again.[78]

The effects of the "white plague," which Rimbaud and many others had tried to evade with pathetic unsuccess in the nineteenth century, have by Miller's time reached even the Bowery in New York, as the following passage from "The Tailor Shop" indicates:

Walking along the Bowery. . .and a beautiful snot-green pasture it is at this hour. Pimps, cooks, cokies, panhandlers, beggars, touts, gunmen, chinks, wops, drunken micks. All gaga for a bit of food and a place to flop. *Walking and walking and walking*. Twenty-one I am, white, born and bred in New York, muscular physique, sound intelligence, good breeder, no bad habits, etc. Chalk it up on the board. Selling out at par. Committed no crime, except to be born here.

In the past every member of our family did something with his hands. I'm the first idle son of a bitch with a glib tongue and a bad heart.[79]

The sense of guilt which often characterizes the dromomaniac's desire to "get away from it all" is very much in evidence here. One is reminded of the famous letter to his teacher, Georges Izambard, which Rimbaud wrote – brimming over with thoughts of escaping from the familial tyranny imposed by his highly respectable mother – and signed with the words: "Ce 'sans-coeur' de A. Rimbaud."[80] Dromomaniacs are often given to traveling light (no baggage, no "principles") and Henry Miller was quick to recognize himself in this sardonic sobriquet of Rimbaud's:

What a jolt I got when I read that Rimbaud, as a young man, used to sign his letter – "that heartless wretch, Rimbaud." Heartless was an adjective I was fond of hearing applied to myself. I had no principles, no loyalty, no code whatsoever; when it suited me, I could be thoroughly unscrupulous, with friend and foe alike.[81]

Dromomaniacs, it would seem, must be prepared – whether they hail from Charleville or Yorkville – to jettison whatever threatens to

78 *Black Spring*, p. 40.
79 *Ibid.*, pp. 110-111.
80 *Oeuvres*, p. 265.
81 *Assassins*, p. 15.

burden their restless souls from taking their feverish walks, including their own lives and well-being. Rimbaud walked thousands of miles over the face of Europe and Africa; in the end he died a horrible death after the amputation of a right leg afflicted with carcinoma, a disease that was surely not helped by the long trek he undertook in Harrar despite an infected knee swollen to several times its normal size.

"Walking Up and Down in China," a basic document to anyone interested in understanding the pleasures and jeopardies of dromomania, catalogues some eighty cities through which Henry Miller feverishly walked in his lifetime – from Quebec, Chula Vista, and Brownsville to Mobile, Widdecombe-in-the-Moor and Louveciennes.[82] Along with Walt Whitman's "Song of the Open Road," Francis Parkman's *The Oregon Trail*, and Jack Kerouac's *On the Road*, I regard this strangely oneiric prose poem as one of the great celebrations of the joys of movement in American literature. But more important than that, I believe the essay gives an uncanny portrayal of the forces that drive dromomaniacs down their double-jointed itineraries to and fro:

> Whenever I come to La Fourche I see endless roads radiating from my feet and out of my own shoes there step forth the countless egos which inhabit my world of being. Arm in arm I accompany them over the paths which once I trod alone; what I call the grand obsessional walks of my life and death. I talk to these self-made companions much as I would talk to myself had I been so unfortunate as to live and die once and thus be alone forever. *Now I am never alone. At the very worst I am with God*!
>
> There is something about the little stretch from the Place Clichy to La Fourche which causes all the grand obsessional walks to bloom at once. It's like moving from one solstice to another. Supposing I have just left the Café Wepler and that I have a book under my arm, a book on Style and Will. Perhaps when I was reading this book I didn't comprehend more than a phrase or two. Perhaps I wasn't at the Café Wepler at all, but hearing the music I left my body and flew away. *And where am I then*? Why, I am out for an obsessional walk, a short walk of fifty years or so accomplished in the turning of a page.
>
> It's when I'm leaving the Café Wepler that I hear a strange, swishing noise. No need to look behind – I know it's my body rushing to join me (Miller's italics).[83]

82 *Black Spring*, p. 175.
83 *Ibid.*, p. 162.

What makes "Walking Up and Down in China" particularly useful as a source of information on the subject of dromomania is that in this sketch Miller conclusively depicts both the positive and negative polarities of his (and Rimbaud's) problem. Here is Miller's image for the "fall" into time:

> I am in communication with the whole earth. Here I am in the womb of time and nothing will jolt me out of my stillness. One more wanderer who has found the flame of his restlessness.
> Here I sit in the open street composing my song. It's the song I heard as a child, the song which I lost in the new world and which I would never have recovered had I not fallen like a twig into the ocean of time.[84]

And here, towards the close of the essay, is the way he presents the corollary to this "fall," the "ascent" into eternity:

> When I walk down the street with a rapt air does any frog know *what* street I'm walking down? Does he know that I am walking inside the great Chinese wall? Nothing is registered in my face – neither suffering, nor joy, nor hope, nor despair. I walk the streets with the face of a coolie. I have seen the land ravaged, homes devastated, families uptorn. Each city I walked through has killed me – so vast the misery, so endless the unremitting toil. From one city to another I walk, leaving behind me a grand procession of dead and clanking selves. *But I myself go on and on and on*. And all the while I hear the musicians tuning up... (Miller's italics).[85]

Rimbaud's search for a substitue "paradise" to replace the warmth of the womb from which he had been expelled, as a prologue to the many unhappy fugues from the loved/hated mother's narrowly provincial Charleville, closely parallels Henry Miller's search. In one of his earliest rhymed poems, the well-known "Sensation" written when he was only sixteen, Rimbaud brings together the intensely suggestive triad of images which will serve to triangulate the flight of the dromomaniac in his later *Illuminations* as well as in Henry Miller's "Walking Up and Down in China": *dream, open road, woman*. The poem brims over with the extreme euphoria which the conjunction of these three images produced in Rimbaud and Miller:

84 *Ibid*., p. 167.
85 *Ibid*., pp. 177-178.

> Par les soirs bleus d'été, j'irai *dans les sentiers*,
> Picoté par les blés, fouler l'herbe menue:
> *Rêveur*, j'en sentirai la fraîcheur *à mes pieds*.
> Je laisserai le vent baigner ma tête nue.
>
> Je ne parlerai pas, je ne penserai rien:
> Mais l'amour infini me montera dans l'âme,
> Et j'irai *loin, bien loin*, comme un bohémien,
> Par la Nature, – heureux *comme avec une femme*.
> (Italics my own)[86]

Typically in both Rimbaud and Miller, the open road has an oneiric and promissory aspect. And what it very often promises is an extreme state of joyousness "comme avec une femme."

But the compulsive appeal of the road, in the two writers, is manifestly the result of a bitter maladaptation between son and mother which inspires in both sons a deep loathing for the locales where their mothers gave them birth. Miller describes the feeling thus in *The Time of the Assassins:*

> Like Madame Rimbaud, my mother was the Northern type, cold, critical, proud, unforgiving, and puritanical. My father was of the South, of Bavarian parents, while Rimbaud's father was Burgundian. There was a continual strife and clash between mother and father, with the usual repercussions upon the offspring. The rebellious nature, so difficult to overcome, here finds its matrix.... Like Rimbaud, I hated the place I was born in. I will hate it till my dying day. My earliest impulse is to break loose from the home, from the city I detest, from the country and its citizens with whom I feel nothing in common.[87]

The conclusion of the first section of Rimbaud's *Illuminations*, "Après le déluge" (an account of the birth trauma, with its attendant feelings of anxiety and desolation), ably dramatizes Rimbaud's profound resentment at the mother-figure for withholding from him the secrets of that uterine bliss of which he has now been permanently deprived: "Car depuis qu'ils se sont dissipés, – oh! les pierres précieuses s'enfouissant, et les fleurs ouvertes! – c'est un ennui! et la Reine, la Sorcière qui allume sa braise dans le pot de terre, ne voudra jamais nous raconter ce qu'elle sait, et que nous ignorons."[88] And

86 *Oeuvres*, p. 41.
87 *Assassins*, p. 12.
88 *Oeuvres*, p. 176.

"Enfance," the poem which immediately follows this in the traditional sequence of *Illuminations*, records a series of ineffectual attempts to find "ce... que nous ignorons" in hectic flights "elsewhere," either "sur des plages nommées par des vagues sans vaisseaux de noms férocement grecs, slaves, celtiques" or in places where "il n'y a rien à voir" and where "quand l'on a faim et soif, quelqu'un...vous chasse."[89]

Though Rimbaud is clearly committed to the enticements of his dromomaniacal quest *ahead*, it is extremely poignant for the reader of the following passage to observe that what actually beckons the poet most insistently lies *behind:*

Je suis le piéton de la grand'route par les bois nains; la rumeur des écluses couvre mes pas. Je vois longtemps la mélancolique lessive d'or du couchant.

Je serais bien l'enfant abandonné sur la jetée partie à la haute mer, le petit valet suivant l'allée dont le front touche le ciel.

Les sentiers sont âpres. Les monticules se couvrent de genêts. L'air est immobile. Que les oiseaux et les sources sont loins! Ce ne peut-être que la fin du monde, en avançant.[90]

There's an extremely penetrating exegesis of this moment of discouragement, positing the poet's sense of futility on the mother's unfeeling harshness and rejection of him, in Henry Miller's *The Time of the Assassins:*

What a mother! The very incarnation of stupidity, bigotry, pride and stubbornness. Whenever the harassed genius threatened to accommodate himself to his hell, whenever his tormented spirit flagged, she was there to jab him with the pitchfork or pour a bit of burning oil on his wounds. It was she who thrust him out into the world, she who denied him, betrayed him, persecuted him. She even robbed him of that privilege which every Frenchman craves – the pleasure of having a good funeral.

The body finally delivered up to the worms, Rimbaud returns to the dark kingdom, there to search for his true mother. In life he knew only this witch, this harridan from whose loins he sprang like the missing wheel of a clock. His revolt from her tyranny and stupidity converted him into a solitary....

89 *Ibid.*, pp. 176-177.
90 *Ibid.*, pp. 177-178.

> Incapable of adapting or of integrating, he seeks endlessly – only to discover that it is *not* here, *not* there, *not* this, *not* that. He learns the not-ness of everything. His defiance remains the one positive thing in the void of negation in which he flounders. But defiance is unfruitful; it saps all inner strength.
>
> This negation begins and ends with the creature world, with those experiences *sans suite* which teach nothing. No matter how vast his experience of life, it never goes deep enough for him to give it meaning. The rudder is gone, and the anchor too. He is condemned to drift. And so the vessel which goes aground on every shoal and reef, which submits helplessly to the buffetings of every storm, must go to pieces finally, become mere flotsam and jetsam.[91]

Earlier in *Assassins*, in fact, Miller writes that his own experiences had been identical with Rimbaud's in this respect. As a youngster, he was possessed by a "demon of revolt" which his mother had "implanted" in him, Miller maintains:

> At twenty-one I broke away, but not for long. Again, like Rimbaud, the opening flights were always disastrous. I was always returning home, either voluntarily or involuntarily, and always in a state of desperation. There seemed no egress, no way of achieving liberation.... As a youngster I was often referred to as "an angel." But the demon of revolt had taken possession of me at a very early age. It was my mother who implanted it in me. It was against her, against all that she represented, that I directed my uncontrollable energy.[92]

There is an excellent analysis of this syndrome in Karl Stern's *The Flight from Woman*. Stern writes that the type of *poète damné* who both flees and seeks his redemption through woman is marked by "a sense of *loss of roots*" (all italics Stern's). Stern singles out Faust, Don Juan, Ahasverus, and the Flying Dutchman as having a common "*homelessness*" and an "inability to find peace." According to Stern, the personal malaise of this Faustian type – and we know from the personal testimony of both Rimbaud and Miller that Goethe's *Faust* exercised a profound fascination on them – "takes the form of *perpetual craving and insatiability*."[93]

These characteristics are precisely the ones that Rimbaud's and

91 *Assassins*, pp. 139-141.

92 *Ibid.*, pp. 14-16.

93 Karl Stern, *The Flight from Woman* (New York: Farrar, Straus and Giroux, 1965), pp. 230-231. For evidence of the interest of Rimbaud and Miller in the *Faust* of Goethe, cf. Pierre Arnoult; *Rimbaud* (Paris: Editions Albin Michel, 1955), p. 256, and Henry Miller, *The Time of the Assassins*, p. 13.

Miller's dromomania earnestly seek to satisfy. Miller describes Rimbaud's intemperate walking binges in *Assassins* and then goes on to speak of his own

> thousands and thousands of miles on an empty stomach. Always looking for a few pennies, for a crust of bread, for a job, for a place to flop. Always looking for a friendly face! At times, even though I was hungry, I would take to the road, hail a passing car and let the driver deposit me where he liked, just to get a change of scene. I know thousands of restaurants in New York, not from visiting them as a patron but from standing outside and gazing wistfully at the diners seated at the tables inside. I can still recall the odor of certain stands on street corners where hot dogs were being served. I can still see the white-robed chefs in the windows flipping waffles or flapjacks into the pan. Sometimes I think I was born hungry. And with the hunger is associated the walking, the tramping, the searching, the feverish, aimless to and fro.[94]

In Rimbaud's *Illuminations*, this voraciousness takes the form of an insatiable appetite for exotic cities which are laid out like a delicious banquet for the poet to gorge himself on in the magnificent "Promontoire,"[95] a poem which amply compensates Rimbaud for the deprivations suffered earlier in *Illuminations* at the hands of a female authority-figure who is clearly a projection of the stern mother from whom he recoils:

> Se peut-il qu'Elle me fasse pardonner les ambitions continuellement écrasées, – qu'une fin aisée répare les âges d'indigence, – qu'un jour de succès nous endorme sur la honte de notre inhabileté fatale?
>
> (O palmes! diamant! – Amour! force! – plus haut que toutes joies et gloires! – de toutes façons, partout, – Démon, dieu, – jeunesse de cet être-ci: moi!)
>
> Que les accidents de féerie scientifique et des mouvements de fraternité sociale soient chéris comme restitution progressive de *la franchise première*?...
>
> Mais la Vampire qui nous rend gentils commande que nous nous amusions *avec ce qu'elle nous laisse*, ou qu'autrement nous soyons plus drôles.
>
> Rouler aux *blessures*, par l'air lassant et la mer; aux *supplices*, par le silence des eaux et de l'air meurtriers: aux *tortures qui rient*, dans leur silence atrocement houleux (All italics mine).[96]

94 *Assassins*, p. 22.
95 *Oeuvres*, p. 199.
96 *Ibid.*, pp. 196-197. The title of this nightmarish poem is "Angoisse."

Clearly, the "angoisse" of the dromomaniac cannot be appeased merely with "ce qu'elle nous laisse." As Eva Kushner has aptly put it, many a contemporary writer has failed to find in religious dogma or politics the means of lulling his restlessness and anxieties. Most writers prefer to affront the causes of their anguish by themselves. They assume an attitude of *defiance* towards these problems, as Professor Kushner argues, because they have discovered,

> comme Orphée, quelque monde secret. Le mythe d'Orphée est en effet, reconnaissons-le d'emblée, le mythe de l'évasion. Mais c'est là une tendance trop décriée qu'il faudrait réhabiliter. L'évasion n'est pas toujours une fuite hors du réel, comme celle qu'entraînent certaines névroses. Elle peut être aussi un retrait temporaire, une halte propice à l'approfondissement, après quoi un affrontement plus efficace avec le réel devient possible. C'est ainsi que le mythe d'Orphée fut pour plusieurs...auteurs...un symbole de leur propre effort pour transcender et embellir une réalité décevante. Ils ont vu en Orphée la beauté en lutte contre la laideur du monde: la poésie transfigurant une vie quotidienne trop prosaique; ou encore, la verité venant transpercer le mensonge des apparances. On voit alors que ce n'est pas vraiment l'évasion en elle-même que désire l'admirateur moderne d'Orphée, mais l'Ailleur: Dieu, la beauté, ou l'appel de quelque extraordinaire amour paraissent émouvoir puissamment sa sensibilité privilégiée.[97]

Henry Miller would find it easy to agree. In *The Time of the Assassins*, he anticipates Kushner's conclusions when he writes:

> The world which Rimbaud sought as a youth was an impossible world. He made it full, rich, vibrant, mysterious – to compensate for the lack of these qualities in the world he was born into. The impossible world is a world which even the gods never inhabited; it is the Land of Nod which the infant seeks when he has been denied the breast. (It is here the zebus dream probably, and all those other animals which dot the shores of the Dead Sea.)[98]

97 *Le mythe d'Orphée*, pp. 13-14. It should be pointed out that Professor J.B. Bury, in his definitive *A History of Greece*, contends that the Orphic religion is "based on three institutions: the worship of Dionysos, the mysteries connected with the gods of the underworld, and *the itinerant prophets*" (italics mine). Cf. Bury, *A History of Greece*, 3rd ed., (London: Macmillan & Co., 1963), p. 312.
98 *Assassins*, p. 141.

At this point in the career of the two writers, there is an enormous divergence of the ways. "La vraie vie est absente. Nous ne sommes pas au monde," Rimbaud had said in *Une saison en enfer.*[99] The "vrai royaume des enfants de Cham" which the poet had exuberantly hoped to enter proved to be a hell-on-earth when Rimbaud actually went to Africa as a trader, after having irrevocably turned his back on poetry. There was to be no actual "Land of Nod" for him. But such a place did materialize for Henry Miller. And that was Greece – at least the vision of that country which Miller reconstructs for his readers in the pages of *The Colossus of Maroussi*. While the French poet was able to attain the paradisaical only in his wish-fulfilling verbal constructs, Miller claims to have found it in a "real" place.

"No man could have chosen a more circumlocuitous voyage than mine. Over thirty years I had wandered, as if in a labyrinth,"[100] writes Henry Miller from "the strangely silent amphitheatre" at Epidaurus. The passage recalls another, earlier in *Colossus*, wherein Miller describes Katsimbalis' peculiar "mania for Haussmannizing the big cities of the world,"[101] i.e., redesigning them according to his heart's desire, then wandering out of his self-created labyrinth like a dream-crazy dromomaniac still bent on discovering the "Land of Nod":

> While working on Constantinople, for example, he would be seized by a desire to alter Shanghai. By day he would be rebuilding Constantinople and in his sleep he would be remodeling Shanghai. It was confusing, to say the least. Having reconstructed one city he would go on to another and then another. There was no let up to it. The walls were papered with the plans for these new cities. Knowing most of these cities by heart he would often revisit them in his dreams; and since he had altered them throughout, even to such a detail as changing the names of the streets, the result was that he would pass sleepless nights trying to extricate himself and, on awakening, had difficulty recovering his own identity.[102]

The image of the ego-seeking, ego*centric* Katsimbalis bears a subtle resemblance to Miller's fine description of "the Katsimbalistic monologue" and the way this monologue evokes both the art of walking

99 *Oeuvres*, p. 229.
100 *Colossus*, p. 79.
101 *Ibid.*, p. 58.
102 *Ibid.*, pp. 58-59.

and the more difficult art of "discovering" which, strictly speaking, is its aim:

As he talked I was taking in for the first time with my own eyes the true splendor of the Attic landscape, observing with a growing exhilaration that here and there over the bare brown sward, amidst anomalous and eccentric growths, men and women, single, solitary figures, were strolling about in the clear fading light, and for some reason they appeared to me as being very Greek, *walking as no other people walk, making clearcut patterns in their ethereal meandering*, patterns such as I had seen earlier in the day on the vases in the museum. There are so many ways of walking about and the best, in my opinion, is the Greek way, because *it is aimless, anarchic, thoroughly and discordantly human*. And this walking about on the brown sward amidst the eccentric, inelegant trees, the thick foliage flying like hair stiff-brushed in the well of the distant mountains, *blended strangely with the Katsimbalistic monologue which I heard, digested and silently communicated* to the Asiatic loungers below who were fading softly now in the dimming light.... He went on and on and on, unhurried, unruffled, inexhaustible, inextinguishable, *a voice that had taken form and shape and substance*, a figure that had *outgrown its human frame*, a silhouette whose reverberations rumbled in the depths of the distant mountain sides (Italics mine).[103]

The conclusion is inescapable that both the walking and talking which Miller artfully links together in this passage are, in their "anarchic" and "discordantly human" way, fundamentally strategies of self-discovery or self-definition. This "ethereal meandering," as Miller pointedly calls it, has the intrinsic power to produce "clearcut patterns" such as he had seen on the vases in the museum (works of art): both walking and talking, if they are practiced with sufficient art, can help their practitioners take "form and shape and susbstance."

Writing of such favorite travelers "in quest of reality" as Jason, Theseus, Robinson Crusoe, Gulliver, and Lewis Carrolls' Alice in *The Books in My Life*, Miller contends that

all these....spellbinders were also "spacebinders." Even some of the historical figures seem to possess the faculty of *dominating time and space*. All were sustained and fortified by miraculous powers which they either wrested from the gods or developed through the cultivation of native ingenuity, cunning or faith. The moral underlying most of these stories is that *man is really free*, that he only begins to use his God-given powers *when the belief that he possesses them becomes unshakable*. Ingenuity and cunning appear again and again as basic qualities of the intellect. Perhaps it is only one little trick which the hero

103 *Ibid.*, pp. 39-40.

is given to know, but it more than suffices for all he does not know, never will know, never need know [cf. Rimbaud's "ce qu'elle sait, et ce que nous ignorons" in "Après le déluge"]. The meaning is obvious. *To jump clear of the clockwork we must employ whatever means are in our possession.* It is not enough to believe or to know: *we must act* (Italics added).[104]

Miller tells us that it's in Greece that he finally learned how to achieve the coordination between "vision and action."[105] There is a passage in *Colossus* which projects this achievement with a genuinely Rimbaldian plenitude:

One is impelled to keep walking, to move on towards the mirage which is ever retreating. When one comes to the edge, to the great wall of mountains, the light becomes even more intoxicating; one feels as if he could bound up the side of the mountain in a few giant strides, and then – why then, if one did get to the top, one would race like mad along the smooth spine and jump clear into the sky, one clear headlong flight into the blue and Amen forever.[106]

The dromomaniac has finally found both "le lieu et la formule" which his mentor, Arthur Rimbaud, had sought so ardently in his own endeavor to become "fils du soleil:"[107] he is "free." It is a moment in Miller whose magic is worthy of the vibrantly beautiful "alchemical" transfiguration in Rimbaud's *Illuminations:*

J'ai tendu des cordes de clocher à clocher; des guirlandes de fenêtre à fenêtre; des chaînes d'or d'étoile à étoile, et je danse.[108]

104 *Books*, p. 167.
105 *Colossus*, p. 237.
106 *Ibid.*, p. 44.
107 *Oeuvres*, p. 190.
108 *Ibid.*, p. 186.

5. *The Poet as Alchemist*

"The attempt to become a god is the Great Work of magic and alchemy. The belief that man can attain the divine while still in the body, with the parallel between this process and the transmutation of base metals to gold, was grafted on to the metalworking techniques of the ancient world by Gnostic Graeco-Egyptian alchemists. One of them, Zosimos of Panopolis in Egypt, writing about A.D. 300, describes a dream in which he saw a priest sacrificing at a dome-shaped altar at the top of fifteen steps. He heard the voice of the priest saying, 'I have accomplished the action of descending fifteen steps towards the darkness, and the action of ascending the steps towards the light. The sacrifice renews me, rejecting the dense nature of the body. Thus consecrated by necessity, I become a spirit.' "

Richard Cavendish in *The Black Arts*

The significant image of "stars of gold" quoted at the close of the previous section occurs in a group of short prose poems in Rimbaud's *Illuminations* bearing the title "Phrases." It is a telling instance of Rimbaud's actual practice of his famous theory of "l'alchimie du verbe," in which the dross of mere words ("phrases") is transmuted by the poet's art into the purest gold of poetic metaphor. Rimbaud had elaborated this theory at some length in the section entitled "Délires II" in *Une saison en enfer*. The poet as alchemist, he tells us, believes "à tous les enchantements."[109] He invents the color of

109 *Oeuvres*, p. 232.

the vowels, regulates the form and movement of every consonant, and "avec des *rhythmes instinctifs*," prides himself "*d'inventer un verbe poétique* accessible, un jour ou l'autre, *à tous les sens*" (italics mine).[110] This, of course, is one of the classic statements of the poetic technique of synesthesia.

But Rimbaud's theory goes much deeper. What truly differentiates Rimbaud's poetic techniques from that of the common practitioner of synesthesia is that Rimbaud is prepared to run the risk of *assigning arbitrary meanings to words* in his desire to create bizarre and mysterious effects. The confusion of the senses and the deliberate refusal to accept commonplace lexical connotations of words are intricately and inextricably bound together in Rimbaud's audacious "alchimie du verbe":

> Je m'habituai à l'hallucination simple: je voyais très franchement une mosquée à la place d'une usine, une école de tambours faite par des anges, des calèches sur les routes du ciel, un salon au fond d'un lac: les monstres, les mystères; un titre de vaudeville dressait des épouvantes devant moi.
>
> Puis j'expliquai mes sophismes magiques avec l'hallucinations des mots!
>
> Je finis par trouver sacré le désordre de mon esprit. J'étais oisif, en proie à une lourde fièvre: j'enviais la félicité des bêtes, – les chenilles, qui représentent l'innocence des limbes, les taupes, le sommeil de la virginité![111]

In addition, Rimbaud's theory goes to the dangerous extreme of questioning the very grounds of Being as most people conceive of it. The awful limits to which he is prepared to press his determination (articulated earlier in the *voyant* letter of May 15, 1871, to Paul Demeny) to cultivate "un long, immense et raisonné *dérèglement* de *tous les sens*" (Rimbaud's italics) is dramatically attested in the following excerpt from *Une saison en enfer:*

> A chaque être, plusieurs *autres* vies me semblaient dues. Ce monsieur ne sait ce qu'il fait: il est un ange. Cette famille est une nichée de chiens. Devant plusieurs hommes, je causai tout haut avec un moment d'une de leurs autres vies. – Ainsi, j'ai aimé un porc.

110 *Ibid.*, p. 233.
111 *Ibid.*, p. 234.

Aucun des sophismes de la folie, – la folie qu'on enferme, – n'a été oublié par moi: je pourrais les redire tous, je tiens le système.

Ma santé fut menacée. La terreur venait. Je tombais dans des sommeils de plusieurs jours, et, levé, je continuais les rêves les plus tristes. J'étais mûr pour le trépas, et par une route de dangers ma faiblesse me menait aux confins du monde et de la Cimmérie, patrie de l'ombre et des tourbillons.[112]

It should be pointed out that the passage referring to the derangement of the senses, quoted above from the letter to Rimbaud's friend, is immediately followed by Rimbaud's claim that the poet "épuise en lui tous les poisons, pour n'en garder que *les quintessences*,"[113] a term which Rimbaud undoubtedly appropriated from one of the numerous books on the lore of alchemy which he is known to have read before formulating his theory.[114]

Wallace Fowlie has made some very pertinent observations on the way Rimbaud delights in almost perversely creating intractably difficult structures of words, the hocus-pocus formulas which the poet intends as mere *means* to transmute the base matter of the quotidian into the gold of the alchemist:

The supreme language that Rimbaud has in mind is not the means of knowing, but of forgetting ordinary language, a means of losing one's self and discovering one's monstrous nature.... Rimbaud believes that poetic language contains all sensations: perfumes, sounds, colors. Words are magical recipes and self-contained myths. They possess a unique kind of truthfulness, not to be confused or contaminated with historical truth. The new method of attaining poetic truth is lofty and perilous. It demands the destruction of order, convention, patterns, rules.... The enterprise has a superhuman aspect, in seeking to reach visions that existed before the poet himself did, in reaching to his race memory. Such poetry is an *ascesis*, a power that will convert man into a real poet, a stealer of fire.[115]

Fowlie believes that each "illumination" is designed to give way "in an all-engulfing, mysterious chaos to the next world," which will be clearly perceptible for a short moment as if it were a finished picture.

112 *Ibid.*, p. 237.
113 *Ibid.*, p. 270.
114 For an account of the extensive reading Rimbaud did in hermetic and alchemical lore, cf. esp. Enid Starkie, *Arthur Rimbaud*, pp. 159-178 and *passim*, and Pierre Debray, *Rimbaud, le magician désabusé* (Paris: Julliard, 1949), *passim*.
115 *Rimbaud*, p. 99.

This, according to Fowlie, is "the child's world of order that is really disorder," a world which is "a continually emerging chaos where only the poet's mind can rescue what seems to be reality before it sinks back into the void out of which it first arose." It is a world which enacts "telescopings of fields and city buildings, the deliverance of words from their usual utilitarian meanings, the creation of monsters which can leap through the air and dance as do the very words which designate them." Such illuminations "glow with the essential words of speech, with the dizzying juxtaposition of sentences and impredictable metaphors. All is vision in these tales" which, according to Fowlie, "defy coherent exegesis."[116]

This is reminiscent of the age-old hermeticism of the alchemical tradition, deliberately built-in "complexities" designed to safeguard the mysteries from unwarranted intrusions by non-adepts. C.G. Jung has written of his own initial exasperations when he undertook the extensive probings of alchemical texts that ultimately led to the writing of his pivotal *Psychology and Alchemy*. Jung often felt the texts were "blatant nonsense" despite the fact that, here and there, he encountered "a few sentences which I thought I could understand." Finally, he realized that the alchemists were "talking in symbols – those old acquaintances of mine." In the final analysis, Jung regards

> my work on alchemy as a sign of my inner relationship to Goethe. Goethe's secret was that he was in the grip of that process of archetypal transformation which has gone on through the centuries. He regarded his *Faust* as an *opus magnum* or *divinum*. He called it his "main business," and his whole life was enacted within the framework of this drama. Thus, what was alive and active within him was a living substance, a suprapersonal process, the great dream of the *mundus archetypus* (archetypal world).[117]

The historian of the occult, Richard Cavendish, writes that alchemists

> wrapped their processes in veils of mystery which frequently confused other alchemists, and which make much of their art still impenetrable, because the processes were mystical as well as chemical.... The Stone did not only turn metals to gold. It was also the spiritual transformation of man from a state of earthly impurity to one of heavenly perfection. Some alchemists never went

116 *Ibid.*, pp. 124-125.
117 *Memories*, pp. 204-206.

near a laboratory and scorned the attempt to make gold as mere money-grubbing, but many of those who laboured hopefully over furnaces and stills believed that the Stone could be made only by one who had achieved a profound understanding of the inner mysteries of the universe. These mysteries could not be stated in plain language, even if the risk of revealing them to the unworthy was discounted. They could only be conveyed through symbolism and allegory, and the full richness of their significance could only be grasped through mystical experience.[118]

Jung provides a plausible explanation of this type of "hermeticism" in the behavior of the Pueblo Indians of the American West, whom he visited in the 1920's. These Indians proved "absolutely inaccessible" in matters of religion. In fact, Jung found them so "close-mouthed" that after a while he

abandoned as hopeless any attempt at direct questioning. Never before had I run into such an atmosphere of secrecy; the religions of civilized nations today are all accessible; their sacraments have long ago ceased to be mysteries. Here, however, the air was filled with a secret known to all the communicants, but to which whites could gain no access. This strange situation gave me an inkling of Eleusis, whose secret was known to one nation and yet never betrayed. I understood what Pausanias or Herodotus felt when he wrote: "I am not permitted to name the name of that god." This was not, I felt, mystification, but a vital mystery whose betrayal might bring about the downfall of the community as well as of the individual. Preservation of the secret gives the Pueblo Indian pride and the power to resist the dominant whites. It gives him cohesion and unity; and I feel sure that the Pueblos as an individual community will continue to exist as long as their mysteries are not desecrated.[119]

The value of abracadabra, mystical lore, magical phrases and incantations is, it would seem, to lead their users into a deeper communion with their own deep psychic reserves. If they are pronounced with due reverence and "purity of heart," they can reveal to those who make use of them a clearer sense not of objective truth but of subjective identity. The purpose of magic – and of "magical" poetry like Rilke's and Rimbaud's – lies in pure process; it is a consecration.

No poem in Rimbaud's *Illuminations* more triumphantly eludes the

118 Richard Cavendish, *The Black Arts* (New York: Capricorn Books, 1968), p. 145.

119 *Memories*, pp. 249-250. Rimbaud felt the same jealous need to guard his "mysteries" when, at the end of the especially enigmatic poem "Parade," he boasted sassily: "J'ai seul la clef de cette parade sauvage (Cf. Arthur Rimbaud, *Oeuvres*, p. 180)."

"desecration" of exegetical analysis than the totally enigmatic "Dévotion." It is the outstanding example both of Rimbaud's abiding love of untranslatability and of his magically arbitrary use of language. It is also a strange kind of "ritual":

A ma soeur Louise Vanaen de Voringhem: – Sa cornette bleue tournée à la mer du Nord. – Pour les naufrages.

A ma soeur Léonie Aubois d'Ashby. Baou! – l'herbe d'été bourdonnante et puante. – Pour la fièvre des mères et des enfants.

A Lulu, – démon – qui a conservé un goût pour les oratoires du temps des Amies et de son éducation incomplète. Pour les hommes. – A madame...

A l'adolescent que je fus. A ce saint vieillard, ermitage ou mission.

A l'esprit des pauvres. Et à un très haut clergé.

Aussi bien à tout culte en telle place de culte mémoriale et parmi tels événements qu'il faille se rendre, suivant les aspirations du moment ou bien notre propre vice sérieux.

Ce soir, à Cicerto des hautes glaces, grasse comme le poisson, et enluminée comme les dix mois de la nuit rouge – (son coeur ambre et spunk), – pour ma seule prière muette commes ces régions de nuit et précédant des bravoures plus violentes que ce chaos polaire.

A tout prix et avec tous les airs, même dans les voyages métaphysiques. Mais plus *alors.*[120]

No one has succeeded yet in identifying the women with the wonderfully exotic names in this poem. None of Rimbaud's ingenious commentators has succeeded in justifying or explaining the odd epithets or the activities he assigns to these characters, real or imaginary, within the closed universe of this puzzling poem. Nevertheless, the compelling power of the poem's radically impenetrable *mysterium* is such that it prompted the French poet, André Breton, to erect an altar to one of the "plus mystérieuses passantes qui traversent les *Illuminations*, Léonie Aubois d'Ashby" at the *Exposition Internationale du Surréalisme* in 1947.[121] And there are countless other ex-

120 *Oeuvres*, p. 203.

121 M.-A. Ruff, *Rimbaud* (Paris: Connaissance des Lettres – Hatier, 1968), p. 230.

amples of this sort of "hallucination des mots," on a less enigmatic level, throughout the *Illuminations*: the mysteriously gratuitous "Splendide-Hôtel" in "Après le déluge," the baffling *Prince* and *Génie* in "Conte" ("Le Prince était le Génie. Le Génie était le Prince."), the magnificently misleading use of the word "canon" in "Being Beauteous," the superbly arbitrary use of place-names in "Promontoire," the outright charades in "Bottom" and "H," and the lovely geographical and psychological reinvention of the "myth" of Helen of Troy in "Fairy."[122]

In one of his best-known early poems, "Ma bohème," Rimbaud succeeded in creating for himself an exuberantly versatile *persona* of Tom Thumb which, though it antedates the more sophisticated alchemist's crucible of poetic theory of later years, serves Rimbaud as an admirable medium for executing his incomparable magic tricks. The lyric is worth quoting in its entirety for the nimble suddenness with which, at the close, the future Orphic/alchemist suddenly metamorphoses his vagabond's shoestrings into the strings of a lyre:

> Je m'en allais, les poings dans mes poches crévées;
> Mon paletot aussi devenait idéal;
> J'allais sous le ciel, Muse! et j'étais ton féal;
> Oh! là! là! que d'amours splendides j'ai *rêvées*!
>
> Mon unique culotte avait un large trou.
> – *Petit Poucet rêveur*, j'égrenais dans ma course
> *Des rimes.* Mon *auberge* était à la Grande-Ourse.
> – Mes étoiles au ciel avaient un doux frou-frou.
>
> Et je les écoutais, assis au bord des routes.
> Ces bons soirs de septembre où je sentais des gouttes
> De rosée à mon front, comme un vin de vigueur;
>
> Ou, rimant au milieu des *ombres fantastiques*,
> Comme des *lyres*, je tirais les élastiques
> De mes souliers blessés, un pied près de mon coeur!
> (Italics mine)[123]

I'm convinced that the following passage in Henry Miller's *Black Spring* – partly because it has numerous internal similarities, partly because it immediately introduces a distinctly Rimbaldian digression on "l'hallucination des mots" which, in Miller's case, is triggered by

122 Cf. Arthur Rimbaud, *Oeuvres*, pp. 175, 178-179, 181, 199, 202, 204.
123 *Ibid.*, p. 69.

the word "Valparaiso" – may well have been inspired by the memorable Rimbaud poem:

> And so, when I stand at the *bar* of Little *Tom Thumb* and see these *men with three-quarter faces* coming up through the trapdoors of hell with pulleys and braces, dragging locomotives and *pianos* and cuspidors, I say to myself: "Grand! Grand! All this bric-a-brac, all this machinery coming to me *on a silver platter.* It's grand! It's marvelous! It's a *poem* created *while I was asleep* (Italics added)."[124]

The "Valparaiso" *obbligato* which immediately follows this comes close to being, in my opinion, Henry Miller's definitive statement on the subject of the "alchemy of the word." It closes, not inappropriately, with three terms very dear to alchemists: the earth, the egg, and the honeycomb – all three frequently used by alchemists to symbolize the transmutation of base substances into "gold":

> Valparaiso, when I say it, means something totally different from anything it ever meant before. It may mean an English cunt with all her front teeth gone and the bartender standing in the middle of the street searching for customers. It may mean an angel in a silk shirt running his lacy fingers over a black harp. It may mean an odalisque with a mosquito netting around her ass. It may mean any of these things, or none, but whatever it may mean you can be sure it will be something different, something new [an echo of Rimbaud's *voyant* letter to Paul Demeny, perhaps? "En attendant, demandons au *poète* du *nouveau...*"]. Valparaiso is always five minutes before the end, a little this side of Peru, or maybe three inches nearer. It's the accidental square inch that you do with fever because you've got a hot pad under your ass and the Holy Ghost in your bowels – orthopedic mistakes included. It means "to piss warm and drink cold," as Trimalchio says, "because our mother the earth is in the middle, made round like an egg, and has all good things in herself, like a honeycomb."[125]

If anything is clear, so far, regarding Rimbaud's and Miller's adeptness at practicing the murky art of "l'hallucination des mots," it's that their most artful effects are achieved by the manipulation of a number of favorite symbols. *Illuminations* and *Colossus* can be regarded as mystic configurations – the Greek word *mystikós* means "secret" – of shifting symbols, book-shaped kaleidoscopes in which a relatively small number of concrete particulars assume a protean range of sug-

124 *Black Spring*, p. 26.
125 *Ibid.*, pp. 26-27.

gestive patterns for the eye of the reader to behold and delight in. The most potent and most recurrent of these symbols in both books seem to me to be *blood* and *fire, water* and *wine*, the colors *green* and *blue*, and the highly emblematic figure of the *queen*. Before commenting on the manner in which their common use in the medium of the "prose poems" of their respective creators contributes to their specifically "elusive" effects, I will devote a few pages to establishing parallels between Rimbaud's and Miller's "alchemical" handling of these few critical symbols. I will then close with some attention to their quintessential illuminist's symbol: *gold*, the concretized form of the "light" of the sun and spirit. The symbols I have identified occur in numerous combinations and permutations in the two texts; I will merely draw attention to examples that strike me as bespeaking a decisive literary consanguinity between Rimbaud and Miller.

Blood and fire. Rimbaud pointedly identifies blood with birth at the outset of *Illuminations*. In "Après le déluge," we find a curiously vertiginous flow of blood associated with the trauma that follows birth: "Le sang coula, chez Barbe-Bleue, – aux abattoirs, – dans les cirques, où le sceau de Dieu blêmit les fenêtres. Le sang et le lait coulèrent."[126] Similarly at the opening of *The Colossus of Maroussi*, Henry Miller associates the birth of the Greek genius with "seas of blood" which he can still feel, saturating a narrow pass in Corfu which he is forced to traverse "into the clear, bright work-a-day world" of the little mountain village beyond:

> Going through the pass, which demands a sort of swastika manoeuvering in order to debouch free and clear on the high plateau, I had the impression of wading through phantom *seas of blood*; the earth was not parched and convulsed in the usual Greek way but bleached and twisted as must have been the mangled, death-stilled limbs of the slain who were left to rot and give their blood here in the merciless sun to the roots of the wild olives which cling to the steep mountain slope with vulturous claws.... All Greece is diademed with such antinomian spots; it is perhaps the explanation for the fact that Greece has emancipated itself as a country, a nation, a people, in order to continue as the luminous carrefour of a changing humanity.[127]

Cirlot speaks of blood as "a perfect symbol of sacrifice" and cites an Arabic saying ("Blood has flowed, the danger is past.") as expressing

126 *Oeuvres*, p. 175.
127 *Colossus*, pp. 21-22.

"succinctly the central idea of all sacrifice: that the offering appeases the powers and wards off the most severe chastisements which might still befall."[128] This is entirely in keeping with the propitiatory function of blood as used in the passages by Rimbaud and Miller which I have cited, but both passages also reveal a lingering "horror of spilt blood" which is associated with "the rule of Orpheus."[129] This is another way in which both poets see eye-to-eye in their use of blood-symbolism.

I've pointed out earlier how C.G. Jung and Henry Miller, in dreams which I quoted in the section entitled "*Orpheus Descending: the Katábasis Theme*," both link the symbolism of blood and fire with the death and rebirth of the hero. Jung's dream involves a "glowing red crystal" and a thick spurt of blood, whereas Miller's involves "being gently...rocked by the omnipotent Zeus in a burning cradle" and then being "gently dumped into a sea of blood." Miller might have found in Rimbaud's *Illuminations* the same association of blood with fire in a "mauvais rêve" which climaxes in an equally frightful moment of self-exaltation: "Les yeux flambent, le sang change, les os s'élargissent, les larmes et des filets rouges ruisselent."[130] But the same combination of blood ("viande saignante") and fire ("les deux à la pluie du vent de diaments jetée par le coeur terrestre éternellement carbonisé") could even more directly have precipiated a dream such as Miller records. Rimbaud even ascribes his mingled imagery of blood and fire to "vieilles fanfares d'héroisme."[131]

Fire alone figures much more prominently in Rimbaud. Guy Michaud ventures to assert that Rimbaud seems to have been born "sous le signe du feu. Le feu qui embrasse, mais aussi le feu qui dévore et qui consume. Il s'est dressé contre la civilisation occidentale moderne, mais il en a hérité la précipitation et l'instabilité tourmentée."[132] Rimbaud himself says, in his *voyant* letter to Paul Demeny, that the poet "est vraiment voleur de feu."[133] The fire-imagery in Rimbaud's writings, both major and minor, might easily provide

128 *Dictionary*, p. 28.
129 E.R. Dodds, *The Greeks and the Irrational* (Berkeley & Los Angeles: University of California Press, 1963), p. 154.
130 *Oeuvres*, p. 180.
131 *Ibid.*, p. 198.
132 *Message poétique*, p. 127.
133 *Oeuvres*, p. 271.

enough materials for a separate book. But there are two powerful passages dealing with fire in terms of *knowledge* and *daring* which must be cited even in a cursory tabulation of symbols such as this one. These passages might easily have provided Henry Miller with suggestive hints which his own alchemist's crucible could later have melted down and rendered differently. The first is an allusion to "la Sorcière qui allume sa braise dans le pot de terre" and who "ne voudra jamais nous raconter ce qu'elle sait, et que nous ignorons" at the close of "Après le déluge."[134] The second is the very beautiful single sentence in "Phrases" which reads (the sentence being a self-sufficient entity within the group): "Pendant que les fonds publics s'écoulent en fêtes de fraternité, il sonne une cloche de feu rose dans les nuages." [135] How easy it is to see in the first a possible model for Miller's description of the wizard's knowledge of Katsimbalis in such a passage as: "By what miracle is the *hot magma of earth* transformed into that which we call *speech*? If out of *clay* such an abstract medium as *words* can be shaped what is to hinder us from leaving our bodies at will and taking up our abode on other planets...? Why should we stop at *words*, or at planets, or at *divinity* (Emphases added)?"[136] And is it too far-fetched to see in the second a model for the "buccaneering spirits" of Hydra, those antitheses to the Chamber of Commerce spirit of "fêtes de fraternité?" Miller's words about them certainly echo the atmospherics of Rimbaud's other-wordly "phrase" very closely: "To recount the exploits of the men of Hydra would be to write a book about a race of madmen; it would mean writing the word DARING across the firmament in letters of fire."[137] At the very least, both Rimbaud and Miller consistently display that curious concern with the "mastery of fire" which Mircea Eliade has investigated among shamans who

> are thought to have passed beyond the human condition and to partake of the condition of *spirits*; just like spirits, they become invisible, they fly in the air, they mount up to Heaven, go down to Hell and, finally, they enjoy incombustibility. The mastery of fire expresses in sensory terms a *transcendence of the human condition*; here again, the shaman is demonstrating that he is raised to

134 *Ibid.*, p. 176.
135 *Ibid.*, p. 186.
136 *Colossus*, p. 73.
137 *Ibid.*, p. 55.

a *spiritual condition*, that he has become – or can become...a spirit (Eliade's italics).[138]

Water and wine. Miller states in *Colossus* that the first Greek word he learned was the word for water: *neró* – "and a beautiful word it is." He was struck by the ubiquity of the glass of water all over Athens:

The glass of water. . . everywhere I saw the glass of water. It became obsessional. I began to think of water as a new thing, a new vital element of life. Earth, air, fire, water [the alchemists' traditional four elements]. Right now water had become the cardinal element. Seeing lovers sitting there in the dark drinking water, sitting there in peace and quiet and talking in low tones, gave me a wonderful feeling about the Greek character. The dust, the heat, the poverty, the bareness, the containedness of the people, and the water everywhere in little tumblers standing between the quiet, peaceful couples, gave me the feeling that there was something holy about the place, something nourishing and sustaining. I walked about enchanted on this first night in the Zapion.[139]

Water, of course, is a basic life-symbol. Cirlot writes that it symbolizes "the universal congress of potentialities, the *fons et origo*, which precedes all form and all creation. Immersion in water signifies a return to the preformal state, with a sense of death and annihilation on the one hand, but of rebirth and regeneration on the other, since immersion intensifies the life-force." He goes on to speak of water in terms of "the idea of the irreversible flow along a given path," and quotes from *La tradizione ermetica* of Evola: "Without divine water, nothing exists, according to Zosimus. On the other hand, among the symbols of the female principle are included those which figure as origins of the waters (mother, life), such as: Mother Earth, Mother of the Waters, Stone, Cave, House of the Mother, Night, House of Depth, House of Force, House of Wisdom...."[140] Rimbaud is clearly thinking of water as signifying "a return to the preformal state" in his great metamorphosis-poem, "Barbare," when he writes: "O Douceurs, ô monde, ô musique! Et là, les formes, les sueurs, les chevelures et les yeux, flottant. Et les larmes blanches, bouillantes, – ô douceurs! – et la voix féminine arrivée au fond des volcans et des grottes arctiques."[141] He merely elaborates on this wonderfully fluid imagery in

138 *Myths, Dreams, and Mysteries*, p. 70.
139 *Colossus*, p. 12.
140 *Dictionary*, p. 345 & p. 347.
141 *Oeuvres*, p. 198.

the more richly suggestive poem, "Bottom" (originally entitled "Métamorphose"), in which the central figure appears first as a "gros oiseau gris-bleu," then a "gros ours aux gencives violettes" who dissolves into tears. Then everything "se fit ombre et aquarium ardent" and the poet dissolves into a donkey-like stream that goes meandering down the fields for "Sabines of the suburbs" to come and bathe in![142] I've already related this Rimbaud poem to Miller's "We have but to melt, to dissolve, to swim in the solution. We are soluble fish and the world is an aquarium," which is immediately followed in *Colossus* by Miller's eloquent description of the *mavrodaphne* wine to which he was treated by Kyrios Alexandros.

It is a fitting transition. It is also fitting for the beverage of Dionysos, wine, to figure symbolically in the writings of two such Orphics as Rimbaud and Miller. Part One of *Colossus*, in fact, opens with Miller's conversation with Betty Ryan "over a glass of white wine"[143] and closes, when the "wine has come," with a toast to Lawrence Durrell. It's entirely redundant, I hope, for me to quote Cirlot to the effect that wine is an "ambivalent symbol like the god Dionysos himself. On the one hand wine, and red wine in particular, symbolizes blood and sacrifice; on the other, it signifies youth and eternal life, like that divine intoxication of the soul hymned by Greek and Persian poets which enables men to partake...of the mode of being attributed to the gods."[144]

There is a trifling detail in *Colossus* which, I believe, establishes a possible link of consanguinity (not to call it something much less "legitimate") between Rimbaud and Henry Miller. It is Miller's use of the exotic and picturesque epithet "winey"[145] to describe the air in Phaestos. The word is rather uncommon in English and there's at least a strong probability that Miller is pilfering it outright from Rimbaud's strikingly similar use of it in "ciel vineux" in *Illuminations,*[146] where the context uncannily matches the moment of "terrific synchronization of dream and reality" to which Miller transfers it in his own book. But this is not necessarily the only "steal" in *Colossus*. The Milleresque battle-cry "Genius is the norm," given without benefit of

142 *Ibid.*, p. 202.
143 *Colossus*, p. 3.
144 *Dictionary*, p. 354.
145 *Colossus*, p. 188.
146 *Oeuvres*, p. 197.

personal attribution or quotation marks on page 83 of *Colossus*, derives, according to Miller's own testimony elsewhere, from a "blind professor in Passy."[147] One is tempted, only half playfully, to call it a case of old wine in new bottles.

Green and blue. Wallace Fowlie asserts, quite rightly I think, that green and blue are Arthur Rimbaud's favorite colors.[148] It is easy to make too much of something as uncertain as an author's use of colors. In *The Orphic Vision*, Gwendolyn Bays devotes several pages to an attempt to prove that Rimbaud – who had prided himself on inventing "the colors of the vowels" – had consciously followed the spectrum of the alchemists' colors, from the black of corruption to the blue which immediately precedes the transmutation into gold, in his notorious sonnet, "Voyelles."[149] It is an extremely ingenious theory, but most Rimbaud scholars (including M.-A. Ruff, Wallace Fowlie, Enid Starkie, and Yves Bonnefoy) have either expressed skepticism or tended to disallow altogether the likelihood that Rimbaud ever applied such a theory as systematically as that. I agree. Personally, I will content myself with pointing out a couple of intriguing parallels between Rimbaud's and Miller's use of their two favorite colors in *Illuminations* and *Colossus*, in spite of genuine doubts which I entertain regarding the extent to which this was adopted with a measurable degree of conscious awareness.

Enid Starkie has suggested[150] that the "idole" in the first paragraph of Rimbaud's "Enfance" is really hashish. If so, it would make sense for Rimbaud to associate the colors green (which usually signifies "life" and "growth") and blue (often used to signify the "high" of the infinite, of ecstasy) with the "artificial paradises" which he creates in "Enfance": "son domaine [i.e., the domain of the "idole"], *azur* et *verdure* insolents, court sur des plages nommées par des vagues sans vaisseaux de noms férocement grecs, slaves, celtiques."[151] Miller similarly employs the Latinate term for green, "verdure," to refer to the life- and ecstasy-giving potential of his Greek "Paradise":

147 Cf. letter of December 11, 1939, in Henry Miller, *Letters to Anaïs Nin*, p. 190.
148 *Rimbaud*, p. 179.
149 *Orphic Vision*, pp. 229-235.
150 *Arthur Rimbaud*, pp. 235-237.
151 *Oeuvres*, p. 176.

Greece is now, bare and lean as a wolf though she be, the only Paradise in Europe. What a place it will be when it is restored to its pristine *verdure* exceeds the imagination of man today. Anything may happen when this focal spot blazes forth with new life. A revivified Greece can very conceivably alter the whole destiny of Europe.... A *verdant* Greece may give hope to a world now eaten away by the white-heart rot.[152]

At the close of Part One of *Colossus*, Miller deftly creates a veritable magnetic field of poetic reference by means of the repeated use of the color green: parrots, money, toads, and the Irish green of the field outside Agamemnon's inn.[153] And in Miller's "clear headlong flight into the *blue* and Amen forever," we recognize a verve which is kindred to Rimbaud, particularly when Rimbaud calls himself "le petit valet suivant l'allée dont le front touche le *ciel*"[154] or when he describes the lustrous blue reflections of the sky in this fashion: "La douceur fleurie des étoiles et du ciel et du reste descend en face du talus, comme un panier, – contre notre face, et fait l'abîme fleurant et *bleu* là-dessous."[155]

Queens. The remarkable queen-figures who flit through Rimbaud's *Illuminations* and Miller's *Colossus* pretty obviously owe their origins to Rimbaud's reading of the French occultist Eliphas Lévi, as Enid Starkie has suggested. Professor Starkie even quotes a tell-tale passage in Lévi which Rimbaud was to echo in his famous *voyant* letter of May 15, 1871: "Woman," says Lévi, "is the *queen* of harmony and that is why she must be at the head of the regenerating movement of the future. Woman is higher in the scale of love than man and when love comes to the fore then woman will be the *queen* of the universe."[156] The three key allusions to women-as-queens in *Illuminations* occur in the following: a.) in the very first poem, "Après le déluge," where the Queen/Sorceress/mother is shown to be the

152 *Colossus*, p. 48.
153 *Ibid.*, p. 87. The sequence is repeated in extended form on pp. 94-96.
154 *Oeuvres*, p. 178.
155 *Ibid.*, p. 193.
156 *Arthur Rimbaud*, p. 111. The actual words of Rimbaud's letter are: "Quand sera brisé l'infini servage de la femme, quant elle vivra pour elle et par elle, l'homme, – jusqu'ici abominable, – lui ayant donné son renvoi, elle sera poëte, elle aussi! La femme trouvera de l'inconnu! Ses mondes d'idées différeront-ils des nôtres? – Elle trouvera des choses étranges, insondables, repous-

numinous repository of all knowledge;[157] b.) in the impassioned outcry of the ardent young couple in the anecdotal poem, "Royauté": " 'Mes amis, je veux qu'elle soit *reine*!' 'Je veux être *reine*!' " Both youngsters desire to be transformed into "royalty," it should be noted, but it is the term "reine" to which Rimbaud gives the primacy of emphasis;[158] and c.) in the visionary last section of "Phrases," wherein Rimbaud summons up queenly apparitions in the gloom of his darkened and isolated room in order to clinch his mastery as a magus: "Avivant un agréable goût d'encre de Chine, une poudre noir pleut doucement sur ma veillée. – Je baisse les feux du lustre, je me jette sur le lit, et, tourné du côté de l'ombre, je vous vois, mes filles! mes *reines*!"[159]

Coincidentally or not, there are also three overt references to women-as-queens in *The Colossus of Maroussi*: a.) the reference to the poet Seferis' sister: "I shall remember his sister Jeanne too, and other Greek women whom I met, because of their *queenliness*. It is a quality we scarcely ever meet with in the modern woman."[160]; b.) the reference to Phaestos in Crete as "the abode of the queens": "I had another strong insistent intuition: that Phaestos was the female stronghold of the Minos family....[I]n that instant and forever afterwards, regardless of proofs, regardless of logic, Phaestos became the abode of the *queens*. Every step I took corroborated the feeling."[161]; and c.) the extension, two pages later, of woman's redeeming grace to man (close, in spirit, to Rimbaud's and Lévi's view that woman-as-queen must lead "the regenerating movement of the future"): "Phaestos contains all the elements of the heart; it is feminine through and through. Everything that man has achieved would be lost were it not for this final stage of contrition which is here incarnated in the abode of the heavenly *queens*."[162] Naturally, there are numerous other

santes, délicieuses; nous les prendrons, nous les comprendrons." These are extremely "advanced" views for a boy of 16 to be espousing in 1871. Considering the fact that Rimbaud's experiences with women had been in the main violently unpleasant up to that point in his life (especially those with his mother), his impressive feminism can only be the product of an idealistic boy's reading – most probably in Lévi, as Professor Starkie has suggested.

157 *Oeuvres*, p. 176.
158 *Ibid*., p. 183.
159 *Ibid*., p. 186.
160 *Colossus*, p. 48.
161 *Ibid*., p. 160.
162 *Ibid*., p. 162.

words and images shared fraternally by Rimbaud and Miller ("gold" and "light" will be taken up shortly). But the few singled out here should appear crucial and indicative enough to constitute what Ezra Pound calls "luminous details," derived from the common alembic of the alchemical/illuminist tradition to which both Rimbaud and Miller belong and from which they borrowed freely.

I referred in my *Prólogos* to Rimbaud's and Miller's partiality to the genre of the prose poem which outlines a journey of discovery, pointing out that this is a form that was pioneered by such French *Symbolistes* as Aloysius Bertrand and Charles Baudelaire. There can be no doubt that both Rimbaud and Miller have succeeded in deepening the sense of the mysterious and the unpredictable in their own work by using such a form as opposed to more conventional forms. The element of the magical which Jung associates with "process" is far better served by the liquid, malleable rhythms of the prose poem than, say, by the sonnet. In general, the literary mind can be divided into two different camps: the lovers of *process* and the lovers of the *finished product*. Temperamentally, the latter will prefer a neat epigram by La Rochefoucault or a couplet by Alexander Pope to the fluid, self-caressing, magical "trips" of Anaïs Nin's *Diary* or Blaise Cendrar's long, chaos-sustained narrative poems. The latter, however, are more efficacious as techniques for achieving "strangeness," the *Symboliste* hallmark, than the former. And Suzanne Bernard regards the evolution of such prose poetry at the hands of a Baudelaire and a Rimbaud as "l'instrument d'un lyrisme moderne":

> Né de la "fréquentation des villes énormes" et des élans romantiques vers l'infini, nous le verrons se multiplier et se diversifier à l'extrême à mesure que les poètes le plieront à leurs efforts pour traduire une réalité intérieure de plus en plus complexe, pour "trouver une langue" [Rimbaud's phrase] répondant à des aspirations jusqu'alors inconnues.[163]

She goes on to speak of Rimbaud's adaptation of the prose poem in *Illuminations* – which, as we have seen, is an indubitable model for Henry Miller – as enhanced by "metaphysical" elements which permit Rimbaud a freer hand at producing, out of the commonest substances of ordinary prose, both precious metals and life-enhancing elixirs. Rimbaud's aesthetic, she maintains,

163 Suzanne Bernard, *Le poème en prose de Baudelaire jusqu'à nos jours* (Paris: Librairie Nizet, 1959), p. 16.

tend à débarrasser l'esprit, aussi bien que l'art, "des limitations qu'imposaient le réel": la suppression des catégories (du temps et de l'espace), l'abolition des grands principes d'identité et de non-contradiction, l'anarchie qui ruine tous les rapports établis depuis toujours entre les choses, doivent sans doute nous permettre, une fois affranchis de la "réalité rugueuse" [Rimbaud's phrase] et pondéreuse, cet "élan insensé et infini aux splendeures invisibles" que Rimbaud n'a pas cessé de souhaiter; et plutôt qu'aux "sophismes magiques" de l'hallucination, ou aux charmes de la "vieillerie poétique," c'est maintenant aux prestiges d'une technique littéraire très nouvelle qu'il va demander le dépaysement nécessaire.[164]

I would go so far as to suggest that the peculiarly mystagogical dimensions which both Rimbaud and Miller have given to their prose poems in *Illuminations* and *Colossus* were absolutely indispensable to the creation of their latterday alchemists' *grimoires*, which, in a very fundamental sense, is what their best passages really are: extended magical formulas, of greater or lesser verbal density and obscurity, which can help direct the interested reader in his search for ways of transforming man into god, dross into gold. Miller states the case with characteristically Rimbaldian absoluteness in *The Time of the Assassins:*

I do not call poets those who make verses, rhymed or unrhymed. I call that man poet who is capable of profoundly altering the world. If there be such a poet living in our midst, let him declare himself. Let him raise his voice! But it would have to be a voice which can drown the roar of the bomb. He will have to use a language which melts men's hearts, which makes the blood bubble.[165]

The "poet" whom Miller is summoning will, in short, be a formidable "adept," a practitioner of pure "wizardry,"[166] as he puts it in *Colossus*.

It's obvious from a close scrutiny of *The Colossus of Maroussi* that Henry Miller, no less than Arthur Rimbaud, firmly believes in the literary possibilities of what Mircea Eliade termed "the soteriological function which is one of the main constituents of alchemy."[167] Not only is it possible to devise literary stratagems to transmute the dreck

164 *Ibid.*, p. 181.
165 *Assassins*, pp. 38-39.
166 *Colossus*, p. 72.
167 Mircea Eliade, *The Forge and the Crucible: The Origins and Structures of Alchemy* (New York and Evanston: Harper & Row, 1971), p. 11.

of human existence into fairer forms, but it's possible by means of this arcane process itself to find a way out, a sort of salvation (the Greek word *sotería* means "salvation"). As early as *Tropic of Cancer*, we find Miller suggesting as much – with buffoonish verve:

> When Rembrandt hit par he went below with the gold ingots and the pemmican and the portable beds. Gold is a night word belonging to the chthonian mind: it has dream in it and mythos. We are reverting to alchemy, to that fake Alexandrian wisdom which produced our inflated symbols. Real wisdom is being stored away in the sub-cellars by the misers of learning. The day is coming when they will be circling around in the middle air with magnetizers; to find a piece of ore you will have to go up ten thousand feet with a pair of instruments – in a cold latitude preferably – and establish telepathic communication with the bowels of the earth and the shades of the dead. No more Klondikes. No more bonanzas. You will have to learn to sing and caper a bit, to read the zodiac and study your entrails. All the gold that is being tucked away in the pockets of the earth will have to be re-mined; all this symbolism will have to be dragged out again from the bowels of man. But first the instruments must be perfected.[168]

I incline to the belief that the finest "instrument" Miller ever perfected for the purpose of establishing "telepathic communication with the bowels of the earth" is the *Symboliste* travelogue/prose poem, *The Colossus of Maroussi*.

Throughout *Colossus*, Miller's use of alchemical terminology is purposive and entirely in keeping with the aims of a writer who has begun his book by asking: "*When would life begin*?" I have already alluded to his reference to the four elements of Paracelsus: earth, air, fire, water. Early in the book, he speaks of being introduced to the Greek painter Ghika who gave him "a new Greece, the *quintessential* Greece which the artist had abstracted from the muck and confusion of time, of place, of history."[169] Shortly after this, he introduces Katsimbalis' account of his verbal alchemist's mania for transmuting the big cities of the world so as to "suit himself" with this pertinent simile: "A mist was coming up from the sea and all I could distinguish of him was the huge head which floated above me like *the auric egg* itself."[170] Juan Eduardo Cirlot ascribes to the alchemists the belief that the egg "was the container for matter *and for thought* (Italics

168 *Cancer*, pp. 236-237.
169 *Colossus*, p. 52.
170 *Ibid.*, p. 58.

mine)"[171] and Mircea Eliade cites "the alchemistic opinion which compares the growth of metals to the processes of animal embryology, whereby, like the chicken hatching out from the egg, any metal would ultimately become *gold* as a result of the slow maturation which goes on in the bowels of the earth."[172]

Gold, which the alchemists thought of as the occult (or "hidden") treasure as well as the finest concrete embodiment of supreme "illumination," also figures implicitly in the Keatsian metaphor which Miller employs to describe his experiences of discovery ("illumination") at Epidaurus: "Balboa standing upon the peak of Darien could not have known a greater wonder than I at this moment. There was nothing more to conquer: an ocean of peace lay before me."[173] And in the very next paragraph, Miller writes: "The wise man has no need to journey forth; it is the fool who seeks the pot of *gold* at the rainbow's end."[174] Also in Part One, there are several suggestive references to the gold from "the deep bowels of the earth" employed with such artistically and psychologically satisfying finesse by the Mycenaeans,[175] and to Argos, which Miller calls "a point of light shooting arrows of *gold* into the blue,"[176] not to mention a comic reference to a forbidding "pot of *gold*" at the bottom of the "slippery staircase" at the palace of Agamemnon, he of the golden mask.[177]

Part Two contains one of Miller's most elaborate experiments in Rimbaldian "alchimie du verbe": the virtuoso Negro jazz "cadenza" referred to earlier. It is Miller's *Livre Nègre*, inspired by Count Basie, "last and direct lineal descendant of the great and only Rimbaud." And not surprisingly in this glittering improvisation in which pure nonsense and comic willfulness are transmuted into a rhythmic diatribe of great mock-comic beauty, Miller loads every "riff" with ore. Gold-imagery abounds: from Louis the Armstrong's "golden torque" and joyfully sweating eyes (which "made two *golden* pools of joy one

171 *Dictionary*, p. 90.
172 *The Forge and the Crucible*, p. 51. Cf. also Eliade's reprint of an illustration of the "Philosopher's Egg under the test of fire" from the *Scrutinium Chymicum, Ibid.*, p. 76.
173 *Colossus*, pp. 79-80. The metaphor, of course, is taken from Keats' "realms of *gold*" sonnet, "On First Looking into Chapman's Homer."
174 *Ibid.*, p. 80.
175 *Ibid.*, p. 86 & p. 89.
176 *Ibid.*, p. 90.
177 *Ibid.*, p. 91.

of which he named the King of Thebes in honor of Oedipus, his nearest of kin, who had lived to meet the Sphinx") to "Lionel the *golden* boy" and "*golden*rods" and "yellow sassafras" and "*gold*en cockerells" all brought back to Agamemnon from the blood-soaked earth.[178] Miller stresses the sordidness and misery of the physical setting throughout the cadenza. There can be no gainsaying Louis the Armstrong's essentially "alchemistic" function in the poem. Not only does he appear in the role of artist-as-alchemist whose artistry turns muck into gold, but he succeeds in spreading joy and the "life more abundant" which, according to Rimbaud and Miller, is the alchemist's higher mission: "Louis soon found that the world was divided into black and white, very sharp and very bitterly. Louis *wanted to make everything golden*, not like coins or ikons but like ripe ears of corn, gold like the goldenrod, gold that everybody could look at and feel *and roll around in* (Italics added)."[179]

But it's at the close of Part Three of *Colossus*, in his light-filled litany of *voyant* images which I've quoted before and will return to in the next section, that Miller's artistry arrives at producing its noblest "gold as a result of the slow maturation which goes on in the bowels of the earth (Eliade)." It's significant that this powerful yantra of memories of Greece, capped off with an overt wish for "life more abundant" to "all men," should open and close with direct references to the earth:

> I see again the soft, low mounds in which the illustrious dead were hidden away; I see the violet light in which the stiff scrub, the worn rocks, the huge boulders of the dry river beds gleam like mica; I see the miniature islands floating above the surface of the sea, ringed with dazzling white bands; I see the eagles swooping out from the dizzy crags of inaccessible mountain tops, their sombre shadows slowly staining the bright carpet of earth below; I see the figures of solitary men trailing their flocks over the naked spine of the hills and the fleece of their beasts all golden fuzz as in the days of legend; I see the women gathered at the wells amidst the olive groves, their dress, their manners, their talk no different now than in Biblical times; I see the grand patriarchal figure of the priest, the perfect blend of male and female [the androgyne of alchemical tradition?], his countenance serene, frank, full of peace and dignity; I see the geometrical pattern of nature expounded by the earth itself in a silence which is deafening.

178 *Ibid.*, pp. 138, 139, 141, 142.
179 *Ibid.*, p. 139.

The Greek earth opens before me like the Book of *Revelation*. I never knew that the earth contains so much... (Italics mine).[180]

What Henry Miller once wrote about the French adventurer and poet, Blaise Cendrars, could just as easily have been written about himself:

To be sure, he possesses the art of distillation, but what he is vitally interested in is the alchemical nature of all relationships. This eternal quest of the transmutative enables him to reveal men to themselves and to the world; it causes him to extol men's virtues, to reconcile us with their faults and weaknesses, to increase our knowledge and respect for what is essentially human, to deepen our love and understanding of the world.[181]

180 *Ibid*., pp. 240-241.
181 *Books*, p. 61.

6. *The Poet as Voyant*

"Often when I attend the ritual procession on Good Friday, it is difficult for me to decide whether the god that is being buried is Christ or Adonis. Is it the climate? Is it the race? I can't tell. I believe it's really the light. There must be something about the light that makes us what we are. In Greece one is more friendly, more at one with the universe. I find this difficult to express. An idea becomes an object with surprising ease. It seems to become all but physically incarnated in the web of the sun."

George Seferis in *On the Greek Style*

The medieval philosopher Robert Grosseteste maintained that "just as physical light is the basis of all material forms, so the light of divine illumination is the foundation of our knowledge of intelligible things."[182] Obviously, what we refer to as "vision" is a twofold human activity. There is normal ocular perception with the eye (first sight) and supranormal or psychic perception (usually called "second sight"). The latter – the phenomenon of voyance – is manifestly what Arthur Rimbaud hankered after in his remarkable *voyant* letters to Georges Izambard and Paul Demeny, and what he actually practiced in *Illuminations*. It is also, I believe, what Henry Miller sought to perfect in himself and in his writings, most successfully in his illuminist travel book on Greece, *The Colossus of Maroussi*. The success of this attempt is writ large on almost every page of that book.

The revolutionary illuminists whom Rimbaud read believed that only by apprehending the supernal light which is circumambient

182 Julius R. Weinberg, *A Short History of Medieval Philosophy* (Princeton: Princeton University Press, 1964), p. 160.

among us in the universe would humanity succeed in changing life – that difficult aspiration so dear to Rimbaud's heart. Auguste Viatte cites illuminist/millenarian sources that bring to mind the programs of Arthur Rimbaud and Henry Miller:

Tous nous annonce une régénération universelle qui, en faisant le bonheur de tous, fera nécessairement la félicité de chacun. L'homme connaîtra sa veritable origine et le *bonheur qui lui est préparé*. Le Ciel ne changera pas, mais la pureté de nos âmes nous le fera trouver ce qu'il est. Tous les emblêmes, toutes les figures qui nous environnent, disparaîtront pour faire place à la vérité. *Sa lumière brille déjà à nos yeux*, ne la rejetons pas. Nous sommes arrivés au moment où nous avons plus qu'un espoir de la connaître, on ne nous dit pas: vous verrez la lumière; on nous dit: voilà la lumière; c'est en être bien près (Italics mine).[183]

This transcendent light which all the great illuminists have endeavored to put themselves in touch with is a topic of recurrent theoretical interest to Henry Miller, even before his trip to Greece.

In a pre-*Colossus* essay on the diary of Anaïs Nin, Miller had expressed thoughts on this subject which place him squarely in the illuminist tradition:

The totality of vision brings about a new kind of sympathy, a free, non-compulsive sort.... The eye too seems to close, content to let the body *feel* the presence of the world about, rather than pierce it with a devastating vision. It is no longer a world of black and white, of good and evil, of harmony and dissonance; no, now the world has at last become an orchestra in which there are innumerable instruments capable of rendering every tone and color, an orchestra in which even the most shattering dissonances are resolved into meaningful expression. It is the ultimate poetic world of *As Is*. The inquisition is over, the trial and torture finished.... This is the eternally abiding world which those in search of it never find. For with most of us we stand before the world as before a mirror; we never see our true selves because we can never come before the mirror unawares. We see ourselves as actors, but the spectacle for which we are rehearsing is never put on. To see the true spectacle, to finally participate in it, one must die before the mirror in a *blinding light of realization*. We must lose not only the mask and the costume but the flesh and bone which conceals the secret self. This we can only do *by illumination*, by voluntarily going down into death. For when this moment is attained we who imagined that we were sitting in the belly of the whale and doomed to nothingness suddenly discover that the whale was a projection of our own insufficiency. The whale remains, but the whale becomes the whole wide world, with stars and seasons, with banquets and

183 *Sources*, p. 233.

festivals, with everything that is wonderful to see and touch, and being that it is no longer a whale but something nameless because something that is inside as well as outside us.... One lives within the spirit of transformation and not in the act. The legend of the whale thus becomes the celebrated book of transformations *destined to cure the ills of the world*. Each man who climbs into the body of the whale and works therein his own resurrection is bringing about *the miraculous transfiguration of the world* which, because it is human, is none the less limitless. The whole process is a marvelous piece of dramatic symbolism whereby he who sat facing his doom *suddenly awakes and lives*, and through the mere act of declaration – the act of declaring his livingness – causes the whole world to become alive and endlessly alter its visage (Italics mine).[184]

In an earlier essay, Miller had written even more inspiringly of the accessibility of this "light" to all people and of the quality of the changes it empowered them to bring about in their lives:

Jupiter, according to astrologic lingo, is my benevolent planetary deity. What a remarkable face Jupiter bears! Never have I seen anything so radiant, so bursting with light, so fiery and so cold at the same time. Coming away from my friend's roof that night suddenly all the stars had moved in closer to me. And they have remained thus, some astronomical light leagues closer – and warmer, more radiant, more benevolent. When I look up at the stars now I am aware that they are all inhabited, every one of them, including the so-called dead planets such as our earth. The light which blazes forth from them is the eternal light, the fire of creation.... Since then I have crossed the Equator and made my peace with the Neptunian forces. The whole southern hemisphere lies exposed, waiting to be charted. Here entirely new configurations obtain. The past, *though invisible*, is not dead. The past trembles like a huge drop of water clinging to the rim of a cold goblet. I stand in the closest proximity to myself in the midst of an open field of light. I describe now only what is known to all men before me and after me standing in similar relationship to themselves.[185]

The strange passivity that attends the seer-experience seems to be common to both Rimbaud and Miller. In *Tropic of Capricorn*, Miller had written:

People often think of me as an adventurous fellow; nothing could be farther from the truth. My adventures are always adventitious, *always thrust on me, always endured rather than undertaken*. I am of the very essence of the proud,

184 *Cosmological Eye*, pp. 285-286.
185 *Ibid.*, pp. 355-356.

boastful Nordic people who have never had the least sense of adventure but who nevertheless have scoured the earth, turned it upside down, scattering relics and ruins everywhere (Italics mine).[186]

Rimbaud's ardent visionary creativeness manifests itself, according to Wallace Fowlie, in a similar state of passivity, in "total immobilization." In such a state, the poet "does not go to experiences;" rather they "offer themselves to him." Fowlie calls this "the inner vision of the voyant unfolding," an unpredictable state of being during which "stones can look at us and...a rabbit can say a prayer to the rainbow." Each *illumination* embodies

this power of the poet, his way of awakening everything that is habitually passive, of bestowing life on everything that habitually sleeps in the real world [cf. Miller's "(T)he whale becomes the whole wide world, with stars and seasons, with banquets and festivals, with everything that is wonderful to see and touch..."]. At the beginning of each prose poem, the curtain rises on a scene that is still and dormant. Then suddenly, with the magic lighting, the tableau comes alive, the vision takes on movement, and the action moves fast until the usual collapse comes at the end and the curtain is pulled down hurriedly [cf. Miller's "(T)he world has at last become an orchestra in which there are innumerable instruments capable of rendering every tone and color, an orchestra in which even the most shattering dissonances are resolved into meaningful expression. It is the ultimate poetic world of *As Is*."].[187]

There is a letter by Henry Miller to Anaïs Nin which further confirms Miller's understanding of the *consequences* the soul risked in embracing the light: the "death" of the everyday personality which is the necessary prelude to the "birth" of the *voyant*. It is dated January 12, 1940, just two weeks after Miller had left Greece and some time prior to his beginning work on *The Colossus of Maroussi:*

The last thing to disappear is the light, the light over the hills, that light which I never saw before, which I could not possibly imagine if I had not seen it with

186 *Capricorn*, p. 11. It's instructive to compare this passage with the following in Rimbaud's *Une saison en enfer*: "J'ai de mes ancêtres gaulois l'oeil bleu blanc, la cervelle étroite, et la maladresse dans la lutte.... Les Gaulois étaient les écorcheurs de bêtes, les brûleurs d'herbes les plus inepts de leur temps. D'eux, j'ai: l'idolâtrie et l'amour du sacrilège...surtout mensonge et paresse.... Ma race ne se souleva jamais que pour piller: tels les loups à la bête qu'ils n'ont pas tuée." (Cf. Rimbaud, *Oeuvres*, p. 220).
187 *Rimbaud*, pp. 177-178.

my own eyes. The incredible light of Attica! If I retain no more than the memory of this it will do. That light represents for me the consummation of my own desires and experiences. *I saw in it the flame of my own life consumed by the flame of the world. Everything seemed to burn to ash, and this ash itself was distilled and dispersed through the airs.* I don't see what more any country, any landscape, could offer than this experience. Not only does one feel integrated, harmonious, at one with all life, but – *one is silenced.* That is perhaps the highest experience I know of. It is a death, but a death which puts life to shame (First italics mine, second Miller's).[188]

One cannot but recall Rimbaud's *voyant* letter to Paul Demeny, at this point:

Ineffable torture où il a besoin de toute sa foi, de toute la force surhumaine, où il devient entre tous le grand malade, le grand criminel, le grand maudit, – et le suprême Savent! – Car il arrive à l'inconnu! Puisqu'il a cultivé son âme, déjà riche, plus qu'aucun! Il arrive à l'inconnu, et quant, affolé, il finirait par perdre l'intelligence de ses visions, il les a vues! Qu'il crève dans son bondissement par les choses inouîes et innommables: viendront d'autres horribles travailleurs; ils commenceront par les horizons où l'autre s'est affaisé![189]

Illuminist visions may come to the seer and be lost by him with equal unpredictability and with great risk to his personal well-being (I've already quoted both Rimbaud and Miller on episodes that led them both to the brink of "madness"), but, as Rimbaud poignantly observes, "*il les a vues*!" And one of the reasons he has "seen them" (i.e., the visions) is that he has dared make himself an extraordinary human being bent on achieving extraordinary things. His is a Promethean will power and, as Rimbaud points out in the letter to Demeny, he is "vraiment voleur de feu." E.R. Jaensch has pertinent

188 *Letters to Anaïs Nin*, pp. 193-194.
189 *Oeuvres*, pp. 270-271. Miller comments very perceptively on this passage in Rimbaud's letter in his study of Rimbaud, *The Time of the Assassins*: "Of what use is the poet unless he attains to a new vision of life, unless he is willing to sacrifice his life in attesting the truth and the splendor of his vision? It is the fashion to speak of these demonic beings, these visionaries, as Romantics, to stress their subjectivity and to regard them as breaks, interruptions, stopgaps in the great stream of tradition, as though they were madmen whirling about the pivot of self. Nothing could be more untrue. It is precisely these innovators who form the links in the great chain of creative literature. One must indeed begin at the horizons where they expire – "hold the gain," as Rimbaud puts it – and not sit down comfortably in the ruins and piece together a puzzle of shards." (Cf. Henry Miller, *Assassins*, p. 87).

things to say about the abnormality of what he calls "eidetic types" – i.e., people who "*see* something, although no object is actually present" and whose peculiar psychic endowments permit them to experience inordinately vivid mental images. Jaensch maintains that for the great majority of adults, an "unbridgeable gulf" exists between sensations and images. But it has "always been known," argues Jaensch, that this is not true "for a few individuals." Some people

> have peculiar "intermediate experiences" between sensations and images. From the description that such people have given of these experiences...we must conclude that their "experiences" are due to eidetic images. These phenomena, it is true, are rare among average adults. Their existence would, however, not have been doubted so often, and they would have been found to be fairly frequent even in adults, if those scientifically interested in such things had not always made their observations on people whose environment and interests were similar to their own, and therefore directed to abstract pursuits.... [S]ubjects should not always be taken from philosophical classrooms or psychological institutes, but occasionally from an academy of fine arts, or a group of people with artistic leanings and pursuits, to mention a group that is as widely different from the first as possible.[190]

Dr. Jaensch believes that the cultural spirit grows out of the spiritual life of such "different" individuals. Later in his book he cites the German poet Goethe – whom Henry Miller apostrophizes as "one of the best Virgo types the world has ever known"[191] – as a paramount example, an eidetic type who "experienced, in a purer and clearer form, what all or most of us feel in a confused way in the same circumstances in life."[192] It's interesting to note, while making this cultural-anthropological excursus, that both J.B. Bury and Äse Hultkranz consider the Orphic tradition (to which both Goethe and Miller clearly belong) to have been a tradition of seers and visionaries.[193]

The sheer frequency with which the word "light" appears in *The Colossus of Maroussi* would be enough to alert its readers to its extraordinary position in its author's thinking. I wouldn't necessarily want

190 E.R. Jaensch, *Eidetic Imagery* (New York: Harcourt, Brace & Co., 1930), p. 36.
191 *Colossus*, p. 106.
192 *Eidetic Imagery*, p. 36.
193 Cf. J.B. Bury, *A History of Greece*, p. 312, and Äke Hultkranz, *The North American Orpheus Tradition* (Stockholm: The Humanistic Foundation of Sweden, 1957), pp. 309-310.

to suggest that there is any conclusive heuristic significance to word-frequency counts in works of literary scholarship, but one cannot help but be impressed with the fact that the words "light," "eye" (or "eyes") and "sun" (or variants such as "sunlight," "solar," etc.) occur one hundred and eighty-four (184) times in *Colossus*. In addition, the word "illumination" occurs twenty-one (21) times. This is an extremely high frequency for a book that is only two hundred and forty-four pages long. The incidence of the illuminist triad of "light," "sun," and "eye" is particularly high (and quite conspicuous) in Part One, where these three key words occur ninety-two (92) times on a mere ninety-seven pages – an average of almost once per page![194]

But, ultimately, it is to the *quality* ascribed to the "light" throughout *Colossus* and not to the mere frequency with which Miller invokes it that we must turn our attention. In the opening paragraph of his book, Miller refers to Greece as "a world of *light* such as I had never dreamed of and never hoped to see."[195] One of his finest evocations of this "light" occurs in a description of a walk he takes along the Sacred Way at Eleusis "from Daphni to the sea." Miller would probably agree with his friend, the Nobel Prize poet George Seferis, that "the light cannot be explained; it can only be seen."[196] But the passage on the "light" of the Sacred Way, in its impressionistic fashion, establishes both a vital connection and a distinction between the light which is seen by the naked eye and that which is seen by the "soul":

Everything here speaks now, as it did centuries ago, of illumination, of blinding, joyous illumination. Light acquires a transcendental quality: it is *not the light of the Mediterranean alone, it is something more*, something unfathomable, something holy. Here the light *penetrates directly to the soul*, opens the doors and windows of the heart, makes one naked, exposed, *isolated in a metaphysical bliss* which makes everything *clear without being known*. No analysis can go on in this light: here the neurotic is either instantly healed or goes mad. The rocks themselves are quite mad: they have been lying for centuries exposed to this divine illumination: they lie very still and quiet, nestling amid dancing colored shrubs in a blood-stained soil, but they are mad, I say, and to touch them is *to risk losing one's grip* on everything which once seemed firm, solid and unshakeable (My italics).[197]

194 "C'est la vision des *nombres*!" one can hear Rimbaud guffawing sarcastically from a well-earned grave. Cf. *Une saison en enfer, Oeuvres*, p. 221.
195 *Colossus*, p. 4.
196 George Seferis, *On the Greek Style* (Boston: Little Brown & Co., 1966), p. 105.
197 *Colossus*, p. 45.

Miller is anything but a "deserter of the infinite" (in Ramon Fernandez' memorable phrase), but it is in keeping with his predilections as an alchemist of the word that he should know how to relate the "outer" light perceived by the eye – a "light" of secondary importance in the tradition of voyance – with the "inner" light of the psyche. He compares his own "illuminating voyage" from Poros to Tripolis to "the ascension of Séraphita, as it was glimpsed by her devout followers. It was a voyage into the light. The earth became illuminated by her own inner light."[198] Then, contrasting his own experiences with those of non-seers whose "inner eye...has now become a sickly gland," he gives us a vivid poetic picture of his encounters with the "light" at Corinth, at Arachova, at Leonidion:

> In each place I open a new vein of experience, a miner digging deeper into the earth approaching the heart of the star which is not yet extinguished. The light is no longer solar or lunar; it is the starry light of the planet to which man has given life. The earth is alive to its innermost depths; at the center it is a sun in the form of a man crucified. The sun bleeds on its cross in the hidden depths. The sun is man struggling to emerge towards another light. From light to light, from calvary to calvary. The earth song....[199]

The eidetic configuration made by the sun "in the form of a man crucified" and the extension of this trope to man's struggle "towards another light" is not, it goes without saying, something that every tourist to these spots in Greece would necessarily "see." But like the visions of the seer/poet Rimbaud, to whom he owes so much, one can say of Miller's visions, in view of the self-evident power of picturation with which he is able to transmit them to others: "*Il les a vues*!" And I would refer to such visual complexes – which are striking examples of the functioning of the eidetic or voyant sensibility – as a poetic eidolon. There are many others in *Colossus*.

The feeling of being "grateful for having eyes" persists at Phaestos, where Miller experiences what I regard as one of the most profoundly affective illuminations in the book. It's a small indication of his voyant's consistency that the word "eyes" appears six times during this five-page account of spiritual enlightenment. As in Rimbaud and their common Orphic ancestors, Miller's "light" leads via the eyes to

198 *Ibid*., pp. 56-57.
199 *Ibid*., p. 57.

inner awakening. This, after all, is the crucial meaning of *illumination*. The "light" not only radiates a greater glory *without* but leads to "life more abundant" within:

The rain has stopped, the clouds have broken; the vault of blue spreads out like a fan, the blue decomposing into that ultimate violet light which makes everything Greek seem holy, natural and familiar. In Greece one has the desire to bathe in the sky. You want to rid yourself of your clothes, take a running leap and vault into the blue. You want to float in the air like an angel or lie in the grass rigid and enjoy the cataleptic trance. Stone and sky, they marry here. It is the perpetual dawn of man's awakening.[200]

This is where "the descendants of Zeus halted" on their way to eternity and saw "with the *eyes* of innocents" that the earth "is indeed what they had always *dreamed* it to be: a place of beauty and joy and peace. In his heart...man is united with the whole world."[201] And considering the intensity of Miller's capacity to assimilate and transmit the "light" which has so bewitched him, it comes as somewhat less of a shock to the reader, later in *Colossus*, when Miller repeats Aram Hourabedian's somewhat hyperbolic prediction that he (Miller) would make a visit to the Orient from which "[he] would never return, neither would [he] die, but vanish in the light."[202] There has been sufficient forewarning built into the structure of the book.

Miller's awareness of himself as a *voyant* in the Rimbaud tradition can scarcely be doubted. Not only does he identify with Rimbaud's flair for dazzling visual phrase-making,[203] but he apotheosizes that quality in Rimbaud which he insists, with a democratic largesse, on also attributing to the rest of mankind – at least *in posse:*

Man was given a second sight that he might see through and beyond the world of phantasmagoria. The only effort demanded of him is that he open the eyes of his soul, that he gaze into the heart of reality and not flounder about in the realm of illusion and delusion.[204]

200 *Ibid.*, p. 159.
201 *Ibid.*, p. 162.
202 *Ibid.*, p. 203.
203 Cf. esp. *Assassins*, pp. 17-19.
204 *Ibid.*, p. 42. He makes clear his belief, later in *Assassins*, that unless all society learns to cultivate the seer-artist's vision, the very existence of the

In the development of this gift, Miller regards Rimbaud as a sort of absolute – as one "poised on the peak, a sort of *jeune Roi Soleil*."[205]

Miller had been conscious of his own peculiar endowments as a *voyant* even before undertaking the *Colossus* trip to Greece in 1939; the brilliant light of Greece merely provided him with the luminous images necessary to give that faculty its "objective correlative" and help crystalize its most convincing extended statement. Here is a lengthy analysis of the phenomenon of voyance given earlier by Miller in *The Cosmological Eye* in the course of commenting on the work of a kindred artist, Anaïs Nin:

The vision is first and foremost, always. And this vision is like the voice of conscience itself. It is a double vision, as we well know. One sees forwards and backwards with equal clarity. But *one does not see what is directly under the nose*; one does not see *the world which is immediately about.* [One is reminded here of Miller's sardonic comments on Rimbaud's "impracticality" and extreme lack of what is called "common sense" in many places in *The Time of the Assassins*.] This blindness to the everyday, to the normal and abnormal circumstances of life, is the distinguishing feature of the restless visionary. The eyes, which are unusually endowed, *have to be trained to see with normal vision.* Superficially this sort of individual seems to be concerned only with what is going on about him; the daily communion with the diary [the reference is to Anaïs Nin's *Diary* here] seems at first blush to be nothing more than a transcription of this normal, trivial, everyday life. And yet nothing can be further from the truth. The fact is that this extraordinary cataloguing of events, impressions, objects, ideas, etc. is only a keyboard exercise, as it were, *to attain the faculty of seeing what is so glibly recorded.* Actually, of course, few people in this world see what is going on about them. Nobody really sees *until he understands*, until he can create a pattern into which the helter-skelter of passing events fits and makes a significance. And for this sort of vision a personal death is required. One has to be able to see first with the eyes of a Martian, or a Neptunian. One has to have this extraordinary vision, this clairvoyance, to be able to take in the multiplicity of things with ordinary eyes. *Nobody sees with his eyes alone; we see with our souls* (Emphases added).[206]

---

artist is threatened: "The poet's passion is the result of his vision, of his ability to see life in its essence and its wholeness. Once this vision is shattered or deranged, passion dribbles away.... Despite all its powers, society cannot sustain the artist if it is impervious to the *vision* of the artist." (Cf. Henry Miller, *Assassins*, p. 131).

205 *Ibid.*, p. 149.

206 *Cosmological Eye*, pp. 281-282.

Both in eidetic and in strictly structural terms, *The Colossus of Maroussi* is Henry Miller's finest example of "a pattern into which the helter-skelter of passing events fits and makes a significance," as my first three chapters have partly made clear. But there's more.

To begin with, Part One of *Colossus* opens and closes with overt references to the ways of seeing. In the very first paragraph, Betty Ryan's lucid descriptions of her travels about the world make Miller *see* these travels vividly "because when she talked about her wanderings she seemed to paint them: everything she described remained in my head like finished canvases by a master."[207] And at the close, as we have seen earlier, Miller arrives, after multiple visitations and illuminations among the people and places of Greece, at "pure vision" and the wonderfully bedazzling eidolon of the "two men and a woman" with which the chapter comes to an artful close. It's in Part One that Miller makes the trip to the healing center at Epidaurus where, appropriately, the dirt that lingers in his eyes from the grubby *Tropic* experiences in Paris and New York will be washed clean and his remaining rags of prejudice stripped from him: "Everything here speaks now, as it did centuries ago, of *illumination*.... Here the *light* penetrates directly to the soul, *opens the doors and windows of the heart*, makes one *naked*, exposed, isolated in a metaphysical bliss which makes everything *clear*...." He rounds off Part One, though, with very pertinent reminders that too many people have yet to avail themselves of their birth-right: "In our world *the blind* lead *the blind* and the sick go to the sick to be cured. We are making constant progress, but it is a progress which leads to the operating table, to the poor house, to the insane asylum, to the trenches."[208] And later, speaking of the archeologists at Mycenea, he writes:

> Spades and shovels will uncover nothing of any import. The diggers are blind, feeling their way towards something they will never *see*. Everything that is unmasked crumbles at the touch. Worlds crumble too, in the same way. We can dig in eternally, like moles, but fear will be ever upon us, clawing us, raping us from the rear.[209]

207 *Colossus*, p. 3. In fact, the crucial closing word of this first paragraph is "see." The Greek world Betty Ryan shows Miller is "a world of light such as I had never *dreamed* of and never hoped to *see*."
208 *Colossus*, p. 77.
209 *Ibid*., p. 94.

Part Two virtually opens with the assertion that "seeing" is not the function of the eye alone. After looking at the stars through the telescope at the Athens observatory, Miller writes:

> I am not more convinced of the reality of a star *when I see it* through the telescope. It may be more brilliant, more wondrous, it may be a thousand times or a million times bigger than *when seen with the naked eye*, but it is not a whit more real. To say that this is *what a thing really looks like* just because one sees it larger and grander, seems to me quite fatuous. It is just as real to me *if I don't see it at all but merely imagine it to be there* (My emphases).[210]

He then immediately launches into what he calls an "emotional photograph" of the planet Saturn which, in its astute blending of melopoeic and phanopoeic effects, could qualify as an eidolon set to music. Yet another eidolon, shorter and much more severely controlled in order to give *visual* pleasure, occurs in Part Two in the marvelous montage that begins with the "woman with a vase on her shoulder descending a little bluff in bare feet."[211]

Finally, in Part Three (which I have called the *Paradiso* section of *Colossus*), Miller treats his readers to the most eye-opening illuminations of all: the extended eidolons describing Thebes – where "the air was winey; we seemed to be isolated in the midst of a great space which was dancing with a violet light; we were oriented towards another world"[212] – and Delphi – where "victory and defeat are meaningless in the light of the wheel which relentlessly revolves. We are moving into a new latitude of the soul, and a thousand years hence men will wonder at our blindness..."[213] But most important of all, in terms of sheer eidetic power, is Miller's climactic catalogue of images of Greece at the very close of Part Three. Here, in a grouping of crisply visualized and hard-edged visionary details that recall such Rimbaud *illuminations* as "Enfance" (especially sections III and IV), "Villes I," "Mystique," "Scènes," and the irresistible "Génie,"[214] Miller gives us what may well be the quintessential *voyant* moment in his entire *oeuvre*. Surely, one of the most seductive aspects of this

210 *Ibid.*, pp. 103-104.

211 *Ibid.*, p. 126. This is one of the most *exclusively* visual passages in the book, "pure vision."

212 *Ibid.*, p. 188.

213 *Ibid.*, p. 195.

214 Cf. *Oeuvres*, pp. 177-178, 189-190, 193, 199-200, and 205-206.

passage can be attributed to the specific attention Miller gives to the imagery of *seeing* and of *luminescence:*

> I *see* the violet *light* in which...the huge boulders...gleam like mica; I *see* the miniature islands...ringed with *dazzling* white bands;...I *see* the *figures* of solitary men...and the fleece of their beasts all *golden* fuzz...; etc., etc.[215]

In such an ably *finished* prose poem, we see with our own eyes the genesis of a paradise which is inhabitable by anyone because it has been adequately visualized by *some*one. The seer's gift is a gift outright of what already belongs to all of us. With images variously derived and variously ordered but rendered with a simultaneity of effect that shocks us into a recognition of our own limitless potential for suprasensible vision, Henry Miller has combined the act of seeing with the bodily eye with the act of seeing something which is not yet present to the eye. In the process, he has actualized within himself and through the well-wrought work of art which he offers us "the image's truth" of what we all desire. The seer is inseparable from what he sees. But more important, he is inseparable from those *for whom* he sees. We all truly see only as the seer sees.

215 *Colossus*, pp. 240-241.

CHAPTER FIVE

EPÍLOGOS

LES ANGES SONT BLANCS*

To Henry Miller

"Tout à coup Louis cessa de frotter ses jambes l'une contre l'autre et dit d'une voix lente: 'Les anges sont blancs.'"

BALZAC

Like a sailor in the masts he slipped over the tropic of Cancer and the tropic of Capricorn
and it was quite natural he couldn't stand before us at a man's height
but looked at the rest of us from the height of a glow-worm or from the height of a pine-tree
drawing his breath deeply in the dew of the stars or in the dust of the earth.
Naked women with bronze leaves from a Barbary fig tree were all around him
extinguished lamp posts airing the stained bandages of the great city
unattractive bodies that produced Centaurs and Amazons when their
hair touched the Milky Way.

And days have gone by since the first moment he greeted us taking his head off and placing it on the little iron table
while the face of Poland was changing shape like ink being drunk by blotting-paper
and we journeyed among the shores of islands bare like bones lying strange in the sand
and the whole sky was a huge pigeon's wing rhythmic with silence, empty and all white,
and dolphins beneath the colored water turned dark quickly like the movements of the soul
like movements of the imagination and the hands of men who grope and kill themselves in sleep
in the huge unbroken rind of sleep that wraps around us unseen, common to everyone, our common grave

---

*Translated into American by Eleni Fourtouni and Bertrand Mathieu from the volume entitled *Imerológico Katastrómatos* (*Logbook I*), 1940, by the Modern Greek poet George Seferis.

with brilliant and minute crystals crushed by the motion of reptiles.
And yet everything was white because the great sleep is white and the great death
calm serene isolated in an absolute silence.

And the cackling of the guinea-hen at dawn and the cock that crowed falling into a deep well
and the fire on the side of the mountain lifting up hands of smoke and autumn leaves
and the ship with its forked shoulder-blades more tender than the coming together of our first love,
were things isolated even more than the poem
which you abandoned when you fell heavily downward with its last word,
knowing nothing any more among the white eyeballs of the blind and the sheets
that you unfolded in fever to cover the daily processional
of creatures who don't bleed even when they scratch themselves with axes and nails;
they were things apart, things elsewhere, and the steps of whitewash
descended to the threshold of things past and found the silence and the door didn't open
and it was as if your friends, in terrific despair, knocked loudly and you were with them
but you heard nothing and the dumb dolphins dove up around you in the seaweed.

And again you fixed your eyes and that man with the teeth-marks of the tropics in his skin,
putting on his dark glasses as if he were going to work with a blow-torch,
said humbly, taking care, pausing at every word:
"The angels are white burning white and the eye that insists on confronting them shrivels
and there's no other way you've got to become like stone when you seek their company
and when you look for the miracle you've got to sow your blood to the eight points of the wind
because the miracle's nowhere except circulating in the veins of mankind."

George Seferis
Hydra-Athens, Nov. '39

APPENDIX

SOURCES OF SECTION EPIGRAPHS

CHAPTER 2

a. Friedrich Nietzsche, *Joyful Wisdom*. Trans. by Thomas Common (New York: Frederick Ungar, 1960), p. 221.
b. Henry Miller, *Tropic of Capricorn* (New York: Grove Press, 1961), p. 305.
c. F.O. Matthiessen, *American Renaissance* (London and New York: Oxford University Press, 1941), p. 641.
d. Henry Miller, *The Wisdom of the Heart* (New York: New Directions, 1941), p. 87.
e. Anaïs Nin, *The Diary of Anaïs Nin*, Vol. I, (New York: Harcourt, Brace & World, 1966), p. 36.
f. Henry Miller, *Tropic of Capricorn* (New York: Grove Press, 1961), pp. 230-231.

CHAPTER 3

a. Alfred Perlès, Henry Miller, & Lawrence Durrell, *Art and Outrage* (New York: E.P. Dutton, 1961), p. 19.
b. Wallace Stevens, *The Necessary Angel* (New York: Vintage Books, 1951), p. 61.
c. Wallace Stevens, *The Necessary Angel* (New York: Vintage Books, 1951), p. 61.
d. Lawrence Durrell, Alfred Perlès, & Henry Miller, *Art and Outrage* (New York: E.P. Dutton, 1961), p. 60.
e. Wallace Fowlie, *Mallarmé* (Chicago and London: University of Chicago Press, 1953), p. 233.
f. Anaïs Nin, *The Diary of Anaïs Nin*, Vol. I, (New York: Harcourt, Brace & World, 1961), p. 5.

CHAPTER 4

a. Henry Miller, *The Colossus of Maroussi* (San Francisco: Colt Press, 1941), p. 132.
b. C.G. Jung, *Man and His Symbols* (Garden City: Doubleday & Co., 1964), p. 23.
c. Henry Miller, *The Books in My Life* (New York: New Directions, 1952), p. 286.
d. Henry Miller, *The Colossus of Maroussi* (San Francisco: The Colt Press, 1941), p. 45.
e. Richard Cavendish, *The Black Arts* (New York: Capricorn Books, 1968), p. 154.
f. George Seferis, *On the Greek Style* (Boston: Little Brown & Co., 1966), p. 171.

SELECTED BIBLIOGRAPHY

Armstrong, John. *The Paradise Myth*. London: Oxford University Press, 1969.

Arnoult, Pierre. *Rimbaud*. Paris: Éditions Albin Michel, 1955.

Balakian, Anna. *The Symbolist Movement*. New York: Random House, 1967.

Balzac, Honoré de. Trans. by George Burnham Ives. *The Édition Définitive of the Comédie Humaine*. Philadelphia: George Barrie, 1899.

Barker, George. "*The Colossus of Maroussi*: A Review," *The Nation*, Vol. 154, 1942.

Bataille, Georges. *Death and Sensuality*. New York: Ballantine Books, 1969.

Baudelaire, Charles. *Oeuvres Complètes*. Paris: Éditions Gallimard, 1961.

Baxter, Annette Kar. *Henry Miller, Expatriate*. Pittsburgh: University of Pittsburg Press, 1961.

Bays, Gwendolyn. *The Orphic Vision: Seer Poets from Novalis to Rimbaud*. Lincoln: University of Nebraska Press, 1964.

Béguin, Albert. *L'âme romantique et le rêve*. Paris: José Corti, 1939.

Belmont, Georges. *Entretiens de Paris avec Georges Belmont*. Paris: Éditions Stock, 1970.

Bercovici, Konrad. *Savage Prodigal*. New York: The Beechhurst Press, 1948.

Bergin, Thomas G. *Dante*. Boston: Houghton Mifflin, 1965.

Bernard, Suzanne. *Le poème en prose de Baudelaire jusqu'à nos jours*. Paris: Librairie Nizet, 1959.

Bertocci, Angelo Philip. *From Symbolism to Baudelaire*. Carbondale: Southern Illinois University Press, 1964.

Bonnefoy, Yves. *Rimbaud par lui-même*. Paris: Éditions du seuil, 1967.

Bouillane de Lacoste, Henry de. *Rimbaud et le problème des Illuminations*. Paris: Mercure de France, 1948.

Bowra, C.M. *The Creative Experiment*. London: Macmillan, 1967.

————.*The Greek Experience*. New York: The New American Library, 1964.

————. *The Heritage of Symbolism*. New York: Schocken Books, 1961.

Briet, Suzanne. *Madame Rimbaud*. Paris: Minard, 1968.

Bucke, Richard Maurice. *Cosmic Consciousness*. New Hyde Park, New York: University Books, 1961.

Burnet, John. *Greek Philosophy*. New York: St. Martin's Press, 1968.

Bury, J.B. *A History of Greece*, 3rd ed. London: Macmillan, 1963.

Butler, E.M. *Rainer Maria Rilke*. New York: Macmillan, 1941.
———. *Ritual Magic*. Cambridge: The Cambridge University Press, 1949.
Campbell, Joseph. *The Hero with a Thousand Faces*. Princeton: Princeton University Press, 1949.
Caron, M. and S. Hutin. *The Alchemists*. New York: Grove Press, 1961.
Cassirer, Ernst. *Language and Myth*. New York: Dover Publications, 1946.
Cavendish, Richard. *The Black Arts*. New York: Capricorn Book, 1968.
Chadwick, N. Kershaw. *Poetry and Prophecy*. London: Cambridge University Press, 1942.
Chambers, Ross. *Gérard de Nerval et la poétique du voyage*. Paris: Librairie José Corti, 1969.
Chauvel, Jean. *L'aventure terrestre de Jean-Arthur Rimbaud*. Paris: Seghers, 1971.
Cirlot, Juan Eduardo. *A Dictionary of Symbols*. New York: Philosophical Library, 1962.
Cohn, Robert Greer. *The Poetry of Rimbaud*. Princeton: Princeton University Press, 1973.
Collingwood, R.G. *The Principles of Art*. London: Oxford University Press, 1938.
Cornell, Kenneth. *The Symbolist Movement*. New Haven: Yale University Press, 1951.
Debray, Pierre. *Rimbaud, le magician désabusé*. Paris: Julliard, 1949.
Dhôtel, André. *Rimbaud et la révolte moderne*. Paris: Gallimard, 1952.
Dick, Kenneth C. *Henry Miller: Colossus of One*. The Netherlands: Alberts-Sittard, 1967.
Dodds, E.R. *The Greeks and the Irrational*. Berkeley: University of California Press, 1963.
Durrell, Lawrence, Henry Miller, and Alfred Perlès. *Art and Outrage: A Correspondence About Henry Miller*. New York: E.P. Dutton, 1961.
Eliade, Mircea. *The Forge and the Crucible: The Origins and Structures of Alchemy*. New York and Evanston: Harper & Row, 1971.
———. *Images and Symbols: Studies in Religious Symbolism*. New York: Sheed and Ward, 1969.
———. *Mephistopheles and the Androgyne*. New York: Sheed and Ward, 1965.
———. *Myth and Reality*. New York: Harper & Row, 1963.
———. *The Myth of the Eternal Return*. Princeton: Princeton University Press, 1971.
———. *Myths, Dreams and Mysteries*. New York: Harper & Row, 1967.
———. *The Two and the One*. New York: Harper & Row, 1961.
Emerson, Ralph Waldo. *Essays of Ralph Waldo Emerson*. New York: The Book League of America, 1941.
Engleberg, Edward. *The Symbolist Poem*. New York: E.P. Dutton, 1967.
Êtiemble, R. *Le mythe de Rimbaud*. (3 vols.) I. *Genèse du mythe*, 1954. II. *Structure du mythe*, 1952. *L'année du centenaire*, 1961. Paris, Gallimard.
Faure, Elie. *The Dance Over Fire and Water*. New York: Harper & Brothers, 1926.

Feder, Lilian. *Ancient Myth in Modern Poetry*. Princeton: Princeton University Press, 1971.
Federmann, Reinhard. *The Royal Art of Alchemy*. Philadelphia: Chilton Book Co., 1969.
Feidelson, Charles, Jr. *Symbolism and American Literature*. Chicago: University of Chicago Press, 1959.
Fiedler, Leslie A. "*The Books in My Life*: A Review," in *Yale Review* XLII, Spring, 1953.
Fowlie, Wallace. *Mallarmé*. Chicago: University of Chicago Press, 1953.
———. *Rimbaud: A Critical Study*. Chicago: University of Chicago Press, 1965.
———. *"The Time of the Assassins: A Study of Rimbaud: A Review,"* in *New York Times Book Review*, March 1956.
Frohock, W.M. *Rimbaud's Poetic Practice*. Cambridge: Harvard University Press, 1963.
Fränger, Wilhelm. *The Millennium of Hieronymus Bosch*. Chicago: The University of Chicago Press, 1951.
Gascar, Pierre. *Rimbaud et la Commune*. Paris: Gallimard, 1971.
Gengoux, Jacques. *La pensée poétique de Rimbaud*. Paris: Nizet, 1950.
———. *Le Symbolisme de Mallarmé*. Paris: Nizet, 1950.
Gide, André. *Oeuvres complètes*. (Vol. I) Paris: NRF, Gallimard, 1932.
Gordon, William A. *The Mind and Art of Henry Miller*. Baton Rouge: Louisiana State University Press, 1967.
———. *Writer and Critic: A Correspondence with Henry Miller*. Baton Rouge: Louisiana State University Press, 1968.
Graves, Robert. *The Greek Myths*. 2 vols. Baltimore: Penguin Books, 1948.
———. *The White Goddess*. New York: Random House, 1958.
Guthrie, W.K.C. *The Greeks and their Gods*. Boston: Beacon Press, 1955.
———. *Orpheus and Greek Religion*. New York: W.W. Norton, 1966.
Hackett, C.A. *Rimbaud*. London: Bowes and Bowes, 1957.
Hanson, Elizabeth. *My Poor Arthur*. New York: Henry Holt, 1959.
Hare, Humphrey. *Sketch for a Portrait of Rimbaud*. London: Brendin Publishing Co., 1945.
Hassan, Ihab. *The Dismemberment of Orpheus*. New York: Oxford University Press, 1971.
———. *The Literature of Silence: Henry Miller and Samuel Beckett*. New York: Alfred A. Knopf, 1967.
Holthusen, Hans Egon. *Rainer Maria Rilke in Selbstzeugnissen und Bilddokumenten*. Hamburg, Germany: Rowohlt Verlag, 1958.
Hotson, Clarence Paul. *Emerson and Swedenborg*. Cambridge, Massachusetts: The Harvard University Press, 1929.
Hultkranz, Ake. *The North American Orpheus Tradition*. Stockholm: The Humanistic Foundation of Sweden, 1957.
Jaensch, E.R. *Eidetic Imagery*. New York: Harcourt, Brace & Co., 1930.
Johansen, Sven. *Le Symbolisme*. Copenhagen: Einar Munksgaard, 1945.
Jung, Carl Gustav. *Aion: Researches into the Phenomenology of the Self*, Vol.

9, Part II, of *The Collected Works of C.G. Jung*. New York: Bollingen Series XX, 1959.

Jung, Carl Gustav. *Archetypes and the Collective Unconscious*, Vol. 9, Part I, of *The Collected Works of C.G. Jung*. New York: Bollingen Series XX, 1959.

———. *Memories, Dreams, Reflections*. New York: Pantheon Books, 1963.

———. *Mysterium Coniunctionis*, Vol. 14 of *The Collected Works of C.G. Jung*. New York: Bollingen Series XX, 1963.

———. *Psychology and Alchemy*, Vol. 12 of *The Collected Works of C.G. Jung*. New York: Bollingen Series XX, 1963.

———. *Symbols of Transformation*, Vol. 5 of *The Collected Works of C.G. Jung*. New York: Bollingen Series XX, 1956.

Kahler, Erich. *The Disintegration of Form*. New York: George Braziller, 1968.

Kenner, Hugh. *The Pound Era*. Berkeley: University of California Press, 1971.

Kugel, James L. *The Techniques of Strangeness in Symbolist Poetry*. New Haven: Yale University Press, 1971.

Kushner, Eva. *Le mythe d'Orphée dans la littérature française contemporaine*. Paris: A.G. Nizet, 1961.

Labrunie (de Nerval), Gérard. *Les illuminés*. Paris: Nouvel Office d'Édition, 1964.

Lawler, James R. *The Language of French Symbolism*. Princeton: Princeton University Press, 1969.

Lévi, Eliphas. *The History of Magic*. Los Angeles: Border Publishing Co., 1963.

———. *Transcendental Magic: Its Doctrine and Ritual*. New York: Samuel Weiser, 1972.

Linforth, Ivan M. *The Arts of Orpheus*. Berkeley: University of California Press, 1941.

Luckiesh, Matthew. *Color and Colors*. New York: D. Van Nostrand Co., 1938.

Ludwig, Arnold M. *The Importance of Lying*. Springfield, Illinois: Charles C. Thomas, 1965.

McCartney, James. *Yoga: The Key to Life*. New York: E.P. Dutton, 1969.

Mallarmé, Stéphane. *Oeuvres Complètes*. Paris: Éditions Gallimard, 1945.

Martino, Pierre. *Parnasse et symbolisme*. Paris: Armand Colin, 1970.

Matarasso, Henri and Pierre Petitfils. *Vie d'Arthur Rimbaud*. Paris: Librairie Hachette, 1962.

Mathieu, Bertrand. *A Season in Hell*. A complete new American version of Rimbaud's *Une saison en enfer*. San Francisco: *City Lights Anthology*, Summer 1974.

———. *Illuminations*. A complete new American translation of Rimbaud's *Illuminations*, in *The American Poetry Review*, Vol. 2, No. 4, July/August, 1973.

———. "*In Advent* by A. Poulin, Jr.,: A Review," in *Concerning Poetry*, Vol. V, No. 2, Fall 1972.

———. "I've killed," A translation into American of Blaise Cendrars' "J'ai tué," in *Chicago Review*, Winter 1974.

———. "Seven Paragraphs on Rimbaud and *Illuminations*," in *The American Poetry Review*, Vol. II, No. 4, July/August 1974.

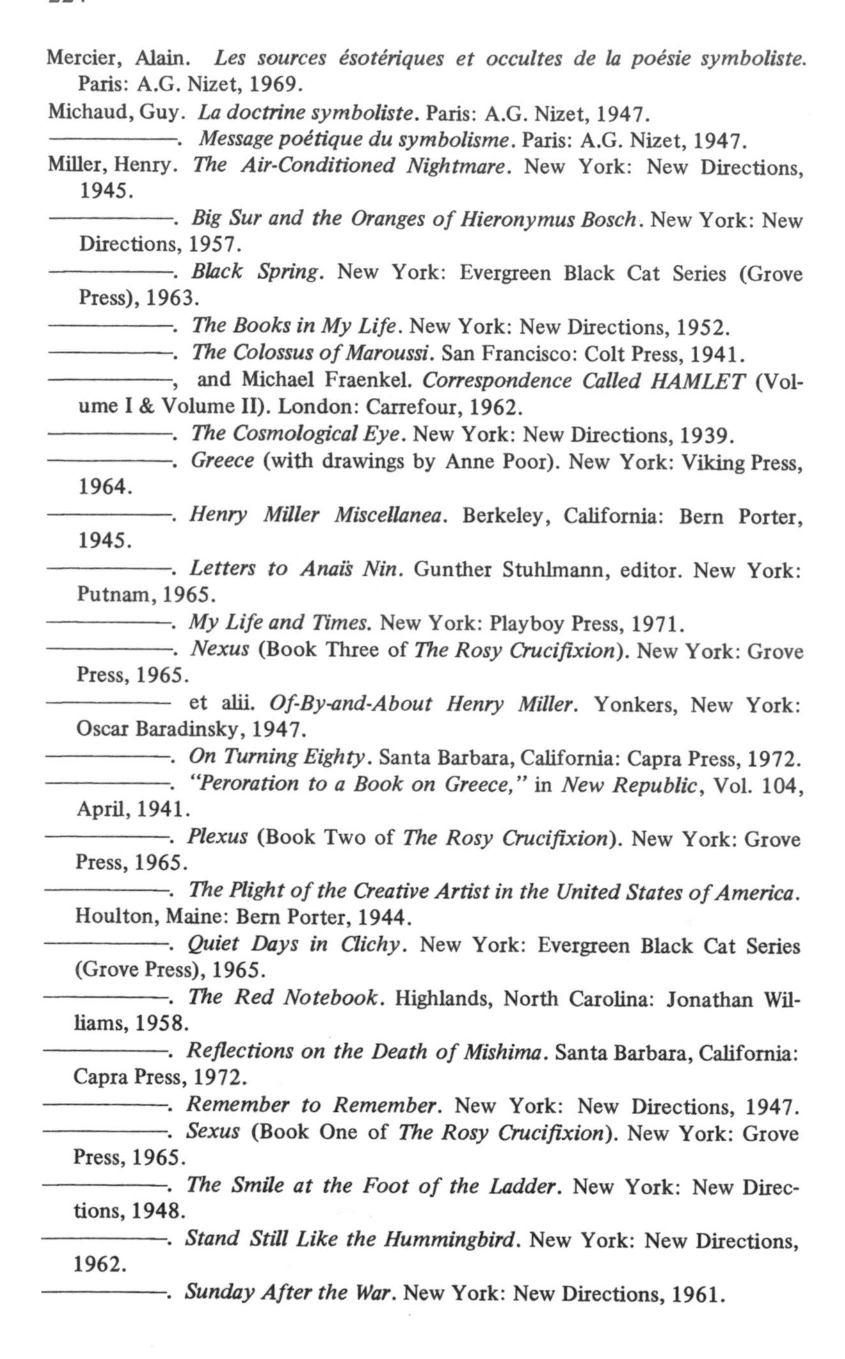

Mercier, Alain. *Les sources ésotériques et occultes de la poésie symboliste.* Paris: A.G. Nizet, 1969.

Michaud, Guy. *La doctrine symboliste.* Paris: A.G. Nizet, 1947.

———. *Message poétique du symbolisme.* Paris: A.G. Nizet, 1947.

Miller, Henry. *The Air-Conditioned Nightmare.* New York: New Directions, 1945.

———. *Big Sur and the Oranges of Hieronymus Bosch.* New York: New Directions, 1957.

———. *Black Spring.* New York: Evergreen Black Cat Series (Grove Press), 1963.

———. *The Books in My Life.* New York: New Directions, 1952.

———. *The Colossus of Maroussi.* San Francisco: Colt Press, 1941.

———, and Michael Fraenkel. *Correspondence Called HAMLET* (Volume I & Volume II). London: Carrefour, 1962.

———. *The Cosmological Eye.* New York: New Directions, 1939.

———. *Greece* (with drawings by Anne Poor). New York: Viking Press, 1964.

———. *Henry Miller Miscellanea.* Berkeley, California: Bern Porter, 1945.

———. *Letters to Anaïs Nin.* Gunther Stuhlmann, editor. New York: Putnam, 1965.

———. *My Life and Times.* New York: Playboy Press, 1971.

———. *Nexus* (Book Three of *The Rosy Crucifixion*). New York: Grove Press, 1965.

——— et alii. *Of-By-and-About Henry Miller.* Yonkers, New York: Oscar Baradinsky, 1947.

———. *On Turning Eighty.* Santa Barbara, California: Capra Press, 1972.

———. *"Peroration to a Book on Greece,"* in *New Republic*, Vol. 104, April, 1941.

———. *Plexus* (Book Two of *The Rosy Crucifixion*). New York: Grove Press, 1965.

———. *The Plight of the Creative Artist in the United States of America.* Houlton, Maine: Bern Porter, 1944.

———. *Quiet Days in Clichy.* New York: Evergreen Black Cat Series (Grove Press), 1965.

———. *The Red Notebook.* Highlands, North Carolina: Jonathan Williams, 1958.

———. *Reflections on the Death of Mishima.* Santa Barbara, California: Capra Press, 1972.

———. *Remember to Remember.* New York: New Directions, 1947.

———. *Sexus* (Book One of *The Rosy Crucifixion*). New York: Grove Press, 1965.

———. *The Smile at the Foot of the Ladder.* New York: New Directions, 1948.

———. *Stand Still Like the Hummingbird.* New York: New Directions, 1962.

———. *Sunday After the War.* New York: New Directions, 1961.

Miller, Henry. *The Time of the Assassins*. New York: New Directions, 1956.
—————. *Tropic of Cancer*. Paris: Obelisk Press, 1934.
—————. *Tropic of Capricorn*. New York: Evergreen Black Cat Series (Grove Press), 1962.
—————. *Watercolors, Drawings, and His Essay, "The Angel is My Watermark."* New York: Abrams, 1962.
—————. *The Waters Reglitterized*. San Jose, California: John Kidis, 1950.
—————. *The Wisdom of the Heart*. New York: New Directions, 1941.
—————. *The World of Sex*. New York: Evergreen Black Cat Series (Grove Press), 1965.
Millett, Kate. *Sexual Politics*. Boston: Atlantic, Little-Brown & Co., 1971.
Moore, Thomas H. *Bibliography of Henry Miller*. London: Neville Spearman, 1955.
—————, editor. *Henry Miller on Writing*. New York: New Directions, 1964.
Mylonas, George E. *Eleusis and the Eleusian Mysteries*. Princeton: Princeton University Press, 1961.
Nelson, Jane A. *Form and Image in the Fiction of Henry Miller*. Detroit: Wayne State University Press, 1970.
Neumann, Erich. *The Great Mother: An Analysis of the Archetype*. Princeton: Princeton University Press, 1955.
Nietzsche, Friedrich. *Philosophy in the Tragic Age of Greece*. Chicago: Henry Regnery Co., 1962.
—————. *The Portable Nietzsche*. Walter Kaufman, editor. New York: The Viking Press, 1954.
Nin, Anaïs. *The Diary of Anaïs Nin: 1931-1934*, Vol. 1. New York: Harcourt, Brace & World, 1967.
—————. *The Diary of Anaïs Nin: 1934-1939*, Vol. 2. New York: Harcourt, Brace & World, 1967.
—————. *The Diary of Anaïs Nin: 1939-1944*, Vol. 3. New York: Harcourt, Brace & World, 1969.
Peters, H.F. *Rainer Maria Rilke: Masks and the Man*. Seattle, Washington: The University of Washington Press, 1960.
Plessen, Jacques. *Promenade et poésie*. The Hague: Mouton & Co., 1967.
Poirier, Richard. *The Performing Self*. New York: Oxford University Press, 1971.
Porter, Bern, editor. *The Happy Rock*. Berkeley, California: Packard Press, 1945.
—————. *Henry Miller Miscellanea*. Berkeley, California: Bern Porter, 1945.
Poulin, A., Jr. *In Advent*. New York: E.P. Dutton, 1972.
Praz, Mario. *The Romantic Agony*. Cleveland: The World Publishing Co., 1963.
Prevelákis, Pandelís. "Prospéro le jeune," in *Synthèses*, February/March 1967.
Raine, Kathleen. *Blake and Tradition* (2 Volumes). Princeton: Princeton University Press, 1968.
Raymond, Marcel. *De Baudelaire au surréalisme*. Paris: Corréa, 1933.

Read, John. *Prelude to Chemistry: An Outline of Alchemy*. Cambridge, Massachusetts: The M.I.T. Press, 1966.

Regardie, Israel. *My Rosicrucian Adventure*. St. Paul, Minnesota: Llewwellyn Publications, 1971.

Reinach, Salomon. *Orpheus*. New York: Horace Liveright, Inc., 1930.

Renken, Maxine. *A Bibliography of Henry Miller, 1945-1961*. Denver: Alan Swallow, 1962.

Rexroth, Kenneth. "The Neglected Henry Miller," in *The Nation*, Vol. 181, November 1955.

Richard, Jean-Pierre. *Poésie et profondeur*. Paris: Éditions du seuil, 1955.

Rickword, Edgell. *Rimbaud: The Boy and the Poet*. New York: Haskell House, 1971.

Riley, Esta Lou. *Henry Miller, An Informal Bibliography, 1924-1960*. Hays, Kansas: Fort Hays Kansas State College, 1961.

Rilke, Rainer Maria. *Duino Elegies*. Trans. by A. Poulin Jr. in *The American Poetry Review*, Vol. 2, No. 5, September/October, 1973.

———————. *Selected Works*. Trans. by J.B. Leishman. New York: New Directions, 1960.

———————. *Sonnets to Orpheus*. Trans. by C.F. McIntyre. Berkeley: University of California Press, 1971.

Rimbaud, Arthur. *Oeuvres complètes*. Paris: Librairie Gallimard, 1954.

Roppen, Georg and Richard Sommer. *Strangers and Pilgrims*. New York: Humanities Press, 1964.

Ruff, Marcel-A. *Rimbaud*. Paris: Hatier, 1968.

Sackville-West, Edward. *The Apology of Arthur Rimbaud: A Dialogue*. London: The Hogarth Press, 1927.

Sanford, Charles L. *The Quest for Paradise*. Urbana: University of Illinois Press, 1961.

Schmiele, Walter. *Henry Miller*. Hamburg, Germany: Rowohlt Verlag, 1966.

Schuré, Edouard. *From Sphinx to Christ: An Occult History*. Blauvelt, New York: Rudolf Steiner Publications, 1970.

———————. *Les grands initiés*. Paris: Perrin et cie., 1927.

———————. *The Mysteries of Ancient Greece: Orpheus/Plato*. Blauvelt, New York: Rudolf Steiner Publications, 1971.

Seferis, George. *Delphi*. Munich: Knorr & Kirth Verlag, 1963.

———————. *Complete Poems*. Trans. by Edmund Keeley and Philip Sherrard. Princeton: Princeton University Press, 1967.

———————. *On the Greek Style*. Boston: Little Brown & Co., 1966.

Senior, John. *The Way Down and Out: The Occult in Symbolist Literature*. Ithaca: Cornell University Press, 1959.

Sewell, Elizabeth. *The Human Metaphor*. South Bend, Ind.: University of Notre Dame Press, 1964.

———————. *The Orphic Voice*. New York: Harper and Row, 1971.

Shapiro, Karl. *In Defense of Ignorance*. New York: Random House, 1961.

Snyder, Robert. *This is Henry, Henry Miller from Brooklyn*. Los Angeles: Nash Publishing, 1974.

Starkie, Enid. *Arthur Rimbaud*. New York: New Directions, 1961.
——————— *Arthur Rimbaud: 1854-1954*. London: Oxford University Press, 1954.
Stern, Karl. *The Flight from Woman*. New York: Farrar, Strauss & Giroux, 1965.
Stevens, Wallace. *The Necessary Angel*. New York: Vintage Books, 1951.
———————. *Opus Posthumous*. New York: Alfred A. Knopf, 1957.
Strauss, Walter A. *Descent and Return: The Orphic Theme in Modern Literature*. Cambridge: Harvard University Press, 1971.
Stuhlmann, Gunther, editor. *Henry Miller: Letters to Anaïs Nin*. New York: Putnam, 1965.
Swedenborg, Emanuel. Trans. by Samuel Noble. *Heaven and Hell*. New York: E.P. Dutton, 1911.
Sweeney, James Johnson. *Vision and Image*. New York: Simon & Schuster, 1967.
Symons, Arthur. *The Symbolist Movement in Literature*. New York: E.P. Dutton, 1958.
Taupin, René. *L'influence du symbolisme français sur la poésie américaine*. Paris: Champion, 1929.
Temple, F.-J. *Henry Miller*. Paris: Éditions Universitaires, 1965.
Temple, Ruth Z. *Critic's Alchemy, A Study of the Introduction of French Symbolism into England*. New York: Twayne, 1953.
Thoreau, Henry David. *Walden, or Life in the Woods*. New York: Holt, Rinehart & Winston, 1948.
Toksvit, Signe. *Emanuel Swedenborg, Scientist and Mystic*. New Haven: Yale University Press, 1948.
Trahard, Pierre. *Le mystère poétique*. Paris: A.G. Nizet, 1969.
Ullman, James Ramsey. *The Day on Fire*: A Novel Suggested by the Life of Rimbaud. Cleveland: The World Publishing Co., 1958.
Underhill, Evelyn. *The Essentials of Mysticism*. New York: E.P. Dutton, 1960.
Venetikos, Alexandros. "Letter to Henry Miller from Phaestos," in *Wanderlust*, I, No. 4, January 1959.
Verlaine, Paul. *Oeuvres Complètes*. Paris: Éditions Gallimard, 1949.
Viatte, August. *Les sources occultes du romantisme: Illuminisme-Théosophie*. Paris: Librairie Ancienne Honoré Champion, 1928.
Villa, Georges. *Miller et l'amour: une étude*. Paris: Correa, 1947.
Waite, Arthur Edward. *Alchemists Through the Ages*. Blauvelt, New York: Rudolf Steiner Publications, 1970.
Ward, Theodora. *Men and Angels*. New York: The Viking Press, 1969.
Watmough, J.R. *Orphism*. London: Cambridge University Press, 1934.
Weinberg, Julius R. *A Short History of Medieval Philosophy*. Princeton: Princeton University Press, 1964.
Wickes, George. *Americans in Paris: 1906-1960*. New York: Doubleday & Co., 1969.
———————, interviewer, "Henry Miller," in *Writers at Work: The Paris Review Interviews, Second Series*. New York: The Viking Press, 1963.

—————. *Henry Miller*. Minneapolis: University of Minnesota Press, 1966.

—————, editor. *Henry Miller and the Critics*. Carbondale, Illinois: Southern Illinois University Press, 1963.

—————, editor. *Lawrence Durrell and Henry Miller: A Private Correspondence*. New York: E.P. Dutton, 1963.

Widmer, Kingsley, *Henry Miller*. New York: Twayne Publishers, 1963.

Williams, Thomas A. *Mallarmé and the Language of Mysticism*. Athens: University of Georgia Press, 1970.

Wilson, Edmund. *Axel's Castle*. New York: Charles Scribner's Sons, 1936.

Wood, Richard Clement, editor. *Collector's Quest: The Correspondence of Henry Miller and J. Rives Childs, 1947-1965*. Charlottesville, Virginia: The University Press of Virginia, 1968.

Zweig, Stefan. *Balzac*. New York: The Viking Press, 1946.

INDEX